After Revolution

After Revolution

MAPPING GENDER AND CULTURAL POLITICS IN NEOLIBERAL NICARAGUA

Florence E. Babb

 University of Texas Press, Austin

An earlier version of the material in chapter 2 appeared in *Identities* 4(1): 45–70, 1997. An earlier version of the material in chapter 3 appeared in *City and Society* 1/2: 27–48, 1999. A portion of chapter 5 appeared in *Latin American Perspectives* 23(1): 27–48, 1996. A portion of chapter 6 appeared in *The Third Wave of Modernization in Latin America*, edited by Lynne Phillips, Wilmington, Del.: Scholarly Resources, Inc., 1998. An earlier version of chapter 7 appeared in *Journal of Latin American Anthropology* 6(1): 60–93, 2001.

Library of Congress Cataloging-in-Publication Data

Babb, Florence E.
    After revolution : mapping gender and cultural politics in neoliberal Nicaragua / Florence E. Babb.
    p.   cm.
    Includes bibliographical references and index.
    ISBN 0-292-70899-8 (cloth : alk. paper)—ISBN 0-292-70900-5 (pbk. : alk. paper)
    1. Poor women—Nicaragua—Managua.   2. Nicaragua—Economic policy.   I. Title.

    HQ1490.M36 B33   2001
    305.5′69′09728513—dc21   2001027433

CONTENTS

ACKNOWLEDGMENTS

I MADE my first trip to Nicaragua in 1989 during the final year of the Sandinista government, then returned briefly a year later, soon after the historic electoral defeat of the revolutionary leadership and the installation of a new coalition government. My research in the country extended through the uncertain decade that followed, generously supported by Fulbright and Wenner-Gren awards, as well as a three-year Faculty Scholar award and other research grants from the University of Iowa This period of abrupt political economic transition was tumultuous but not entirely grim, as my study of cultural responses to the post-Sandinista era sets out to show.

Over the years, I was fortunate to have the kind cooperation of many individuals in Nicaragua and the United States. In my double affiliation as a Fulbright scholar with the Central American University (UCA) and the Central American Institute of Business Administration (INCAE), I was made welcome by Amalia Chamorro, Nelly Miranda, Marcos Membreño, and Leslie Hunter. I also benefited greatly from my association in Nicaragua with Paola Pérez Alemán, Rita Arauz, Amy Bank, Alejandro Bendaña, Luis Carvajal, Antonio Chávez, Ana Criquillon, Hazel Fonseca, Mary Bolt González, Nadine Jubb, Lillian Hall, Stefan Platteau, Rita Fletes, Monika Fredebrecht, Patricia Castellón, Damariz Ruiz, Enrique Ulloa Barrera, and María Elena Palma, among others in a long list of researchers, activists, and working people.

U.S.-based scholars who read part or all of my manuscript at various stages and offered critical suggestions include Les Field, Karen Kampwirth, Frances Rothstein, Rosario Montoya, Tom Walker, Rose Spalding, Elsa Chaney, Stephen Tulley, Paula Ford, Elise LoBue, Jon Wolseth, Alyssa Cymene Howe, Julie Anderson, Mary Weismantel, Lynn Stephen, Sheryl Lutjens, Nina Glick Schiller, Karen Tranberg Hansen, Kim Marra, Sue Lafky, and Daniel Balderston. Others who have worked in Nicaragua were helpful in both intellectual and practical ways, including Ken Coleman,

Carmen Diana Deere, Laura Enríquez, Ann Ferguson, Roger Lancaster, Margaret Randall, T. M. Scruggs, and Richard Stahler-Sholk.

Living in Managua often presented challenges, and I have been grateful for the research assistance as well as the comforts provided me in various households and barrios of the city. Most especially, I have enjoyed the companionship and cuisine of Grant Gallup, whose Casa Ave María came to be my Nicaraguan home. Ana Patricia Moreno, a Nicaraguan graduate student at the University of Iowa, acted as a valued research assistant one summer in Managua and also transcribed a number of taped interviews back in the United States, as did another student, Consuelo Guayara. Two students from the Central American University, Alexandra Shutze and María del Socorro Miranda Blanco, also assisted in the study.

Colleagues and friends at the University of Iowa, some of whom I have already named, have urged me on to complete this work and provided the writing time I needed, for which I am grateful. I am also thankful to Will Thomson for designing the maps that appear in this book and to Joy Osborn Daniels for preparing the index. The fine editorial staff at the University of Texas Press, particularly Theresa May, Leslie Tingle, Sheila Berg, and Heidi Haeuser, helped this long-term project to become a book.

My son, Daniel Babb, shared with me some of the best and also the most difficult times during two summers in Managua, where he celebrated his sixth and seventh birthdays, and now he has grown up with this book. My *compañera* Victoria Rovine offered invaluable personal and intellectual support through the writing of this book, reading drafts even when her own book deadline was fast approaching, and she joined me during my most recent and gratifying trip to Nicaragua. I dedicate this work to Daniel and Vicki.

After Revolution

Chapter One

INTRODUCTION
Writing after Revolution

N ICARAGUA captured the world's imagination and received almost obsessive attention after the victory of the Sandinista revolution two
decades ago. This small Central American nation's success in ending a
forty-three-year dictatorship and its efforts to bring about a broad program
of social transformation that included agrarian reform, restructured urban
employment, and wide access to health care, education, and social services
were observed from afar with both admiration and consternation. In Nicaragua, opposition to the Somoza dictatorship was broad based, but lines
were drawn early on between supporters and critics of the revolutionary
government that came to power, even when it meant that family loyalties
were divided. Political differences, cutting across social class and gender
lines, were well established in the Sandinista decade of the 1980s, and they
have persisted, often taking new forms, in the market-driven neoliberal decade of the 1990s.

After Revolution focuses on the experiences of low-income residents of Managua, the capital city of Nicaragua, during a turbulent time when they were players on a local, national, and international stage. The process of social, political, and economic change undertaken in the country was dramatically altered by external interventions as well as by unresolved internal problems during the revolutionary period. This book considers the transition to the post-Sandinista 1990s, as elected governments have rolled back state-supported reforms and introduced measures that have favored the development of the market economy to the disadvantage of the working class, the poor, women, and other nonelite groups. Yet this decade has also seen the growth of civil society made up of grassroots, nongovernmental organizations (NGOs) and social movements constituted by the revolution's new social subjects. Often, the very groups disfavored by current policy have taken advantage of new openings for political mobilization.

Women and, more broadly, gender relations are central to the arguments advanced in this work. The changes brought about by the Nicaraguan revolution and its aftermath are shown to have clearly differentiated implications for women and men, due in no small measure to the continued responsibilities of women at home. Indeed, household duties have become more onerous as structural adjustment policies vital to the neoliberal development model have resulted in the reduction of state support for social services and of employment opportunities and wage levels. In the context of persistent gender inequality and growing social conservatism, working women are often encouraged by men and by the state, especially if they have young children, to give primary attention to family obligations. The contradictions this situation presents, both to the economic system that depends on women's participation and to women themselves, is apparent in the research offered here. Also apparent is the active manner in which some women and others in vulnerable positions are negotiating the terms of neoliberalism and making claims on new social spaces—in ways that are profoundly influenced by their personal and national histories.

There is much that is unique to Nicaragua, and there is also much in the experience of the country that resonates beyond its borders. I will have occasion to make comparisons with other postrevolutionary societies and with other nations that have followed the neoliberal development model. The situation of low-income women and all who are disenfranchised in the Nicaragua of the 1990s has much in common with that of subaltern groups in other areas where structural adjustment and conservative social agendas have been put in place. More positively, the recent course of events in Nicaragua has influenced and been influenced by the progressive cultural politics of other regions, in Latin America and elsewhere. Thus I expect that the implications of this study will embrace a far wider area than Managua or Nicaragua alone.

Some striking developments of the past ten years in Nicaragua bracket the period I examine and offer a brief glimpse of the project described here. Two quite different events that occurred in the early months of my research were to be watersheds in recent history. In March 1991, the government announced a "maxi-devaluation" of the currency designed to stabilize the grossly inflated economy, following the neoliberal program that for a decade had been producing harsh effects elsewhere in Latin America. That same month, the Festival of the 52 Percent celebrated International Women's Day by parting ways with the mass women's association of the Sandinista Party, bringing together a number of feminist groups and women's work cooperatives for several days of passionate cultural and political activity. In that context of abrupt economic adjustment and feminist rupture, I met a number of the women who were to be central to my project.

There are also startling juxtapositions as events ranging from the tragic to the absurd have marked the close of this neoliberal decade. In October 1998, Nicaragua and its neighbors were hit by the terrible devastation of Hurricane Mitch, whose effects will long be felt throughout the region. Nevertheless, a month later, public officials in Managua were celebrating the grand openings of a new commercial center catering to a small elite and a McDonald's restaurant, both hailed as welcome signs of modernity. Such disparate developments are common at the close of the twentieth century, and the irony is not lost on Nicaraguans, who are organizing to respond to the new conditions of struggle.

The present situation in Nicaragua must be understood in relation to the country's past, so let us turn to consider the historical setting for this period of contradictory developments and uneasy transitions from dictatorship to revolution to neoliberal market economy. What follows is a brief look at the broad sweep of Nicaraguan history, highlighting some recent developments that are taken up in later chapters.

The Historical View

Although it is only about the size of my home state of Iowa, Nicaragua is culturally and geographically diverse.[1] Known as the "land of lakes and volcanoes," this tropical country forms part of the Central American Isthmus, bordered to the north by Honduras and to the south by Costa Rica. Along the southern boundary, the San Juan River connects the Caribbean with Lake Nicaragua, leaving just ten miles of land to extend from the Atlantic to the Pacific, a characteristic that made Nicaragua an early contender for a canal, before U.S. and other interests focused on Panama. Nicaragua and the region had long been a location of wider geopolitical interest and continued to be for some years.

The Pacific area of western Nicaragua, which was colonized by the Spanish, is the most heavily populated, and its residents are generally referred to as mestizos, or Spanish speakers of mixed European and Indian descent. Although use of this term suggests a unified national identity, it masks the cultural and ethnic differences among the urban and rural people who live in this region that spans coastal regions, mountains, and cities in the interior. Researchers have brought attention to the myth of "Nicaragua mestiza," demonstrating that indigenous peoples, cultures, and communities continue to have a significant presence in the Pacific area as well as in the Atlantic Coast region. Diversity is more apparent on the broad but less populated Atlantic (or Caribbean) Coast, which came under British rule. The African diaspora brought about by slavery in the Caribbean resulted in an English-speaking African-Nicaraguan "Creole" people concentrated particularly in the area around Bluefields. Culturally and linguistically diverse indigenous groups along this coast and north to the Honduran border include the Miskito, whose conflict with the Sandinistas was much discussed in Western media.[2] Although the region attained some independence under the terms of the Constitution and the Autonomy Law of 1987, it continues to suffer from political marginalization at the national level.

The city of Managua, located in the Pacific region between Lake Managua and Lake Nicaragua, now dominates the country, but this is a fairly recent phenomenon. The nearby colonial cities of León and Granada were founded in 1524, soon after the Spanish arrival in what is now Nicaragua, and remained part of the Viceroyalty of New Spain (Mexico) until Central American independence was declared in 1821. Nicaragua declared its in-

Map 1. Nicaragua.

United States

Mexico

Cuba

area of detail

Ecuador

Colombia

HONDURAS

✪ Tegucigalpa

Coco River

Puerto
Cabezas ●

Atlantic Ocean

● Jinotega

Estelí ●

● Matagalpa

León
●

NICARAGUA

Lake Managua

Managua ✪

Bluefields ●

Masaya

Granada ●

Lake Nicaragua

Rivas
●

● San Carlos

Pacific Ocean

San Juan R.

N

COSTA RICA

✪ San José

0   25   50   75   100

MILES

dependence in 1838 and left the Central American Federation. The two cities vied for power in the nineteenth century during a prolonged period of contention between the Liberals, identified with León and its merchants and professionals, and the Conservatives, identified with Granada and its landed aristocracy and rural workers. Managua was declared a city and six years later, in 1852, the capital of Nicaragua in an effort to quell the rivalry and contribute to national unity. Nevertheless, the Liberals invited the American adventurer William Walker to join their forces against the Conservatives. He defeated both sides and declared himself president of Nicaragua, ruling from 1856 to 1857 before he was routed by allied Central American forces.

In 1893, the Liberals came to power and introduced reforms under the government of José Santos Zelaya, but U.S. intervention again changed the course of Nicaraguan history as a Conservative government was installed. The Liberals, under Benjamín Zeledón, led a rebellion that was subdued when the U.S. Marines landed at Corinto in 1912. The Marines remained in Nicaragua (except for a brief departure) until 1933, by which time they had organized and trained the National Guard. During the period of American occupation, a civil war again pitted Liberals against Conservatives. In 1927, all but one general, the Liberal Augusto César Sandino, agreed to an armistice. Sandino demanded the Marines' withdrawal, and when that did not occur, he led troops to the mountains to prepare for guerrilla war. The effort became broader and embraced an anti-imperialist politics, winning the support of international observers. Inspired by various leftist intellectual and activist currents, Sandino and his army fought the Marines and the National Guard until the United States withdrew from the country. Sandino negotiated a peace settlement with President Juan B. Sacasa, but in February 1934 the head of the National Guard, Anastasio Somoza, had Sandino assassinated and many of his supporters massacred.

The Somoza family regime (1936–79) began when Anastasio Somoza García (later succeeded by two sons, Luis and Anastasio Somoza Debayle) overthrew his uncle, Juan B. Sacasa. Corrupt and prone to using force, the Somozas and the National Guard grew wealthy and powerful at the country's expense and were widely feared and hated. In 1961, inspired by Sandino and by the Cuban revolution two years before, the Sandinista National Liberation Front (FSLN) was founded to oppose the oppressive regime. Under its banner, a popular movement of students, workers, and peasants emerged to protest the poverty and injustices experienced by the vast majority in the country. Following a devastating earthquake in 1972 that destroyed much of Managua, the cruel mismanagement of aid turned even more Nicaraguans against the Somoza government. Members of the middle and upper classes joined the urban and rural working class and the poor in seeking an end to the dictatorship. Overcoming internal differences in political orientation, the FSLN led the popular resistance to a general insurrection that culminated in victory in July 1979. A national directorate of nine men headed by Daniel Ortega took control of the government two days after the last Somoza dictator fled the country; women were active in the revolutionary struggle, but no woman held a seat on the FSLN's directorate while the party was in power.

The decade of revolutionary government (1979–90) began with the exuberance of its youthful leadership, a commitment to political economic transformation, and a passion for social justice — although class tensions arose early on when the Sandinistas' priority of redistributing resources in the interest of the poor majority threatened to undercut the privilege of the middle and upper classes. Agrarian reform, food price subsidies, housing, and universally available health care and education were areas that received the most attention. Sectoral organizations were established to oversee the implementation of Sandinista policy and vision at the neighborhood level, as well as among rural laborers, urban workers, artisans, youth, and women. While inspired by the example of socialist societies and desiring to bring about a thoroughgoing process of state-led change, the Sandinistas tolerated private enterprise in the new "mixed economy." Yet their reliance on popular, mass organizations to carry out the will of the government concealed a certain verticalism, a top-down administration that later received heavy criticism among the grassroots as well as within the FSLN.

Relations with the United States had an early and pronounced effect on Nicaraguan politics during the Sandinista decade. Whereas the Carter administration accepted the revolutionary government with cool resignation, the Reagan administration, which came on the scene eighteen months later, viewed the Sandinistas with alarm, as an extension of Soviet communism. Interventionist politics prevailed throughout the decade, as the United States trained and supported a Nicaraguan counterrevolutionary (Contra) army to wage war against its own government and cut off aid and trade relations with the country. The war and the economic embargo made

1. *Annual celebration, July 19, of the victory of the Sandinistas over the Somoza dictatorship (banner on the National Palace reads "Death to Somocismo").*

it increasingly difficult for the Sandinista government to pursue plans for innovative social programs; a less democratic stance was sometimes taken as defense was favored and other objectives were set aside.

Notwithstanding the great achievements of the Nicaraguan revolution, from the vantage point of the 1990s it is evident, for example, that local initiatives were often subordinated to party interests, feminist and gay organizing were suppressed, and major policy decisions such as the structural adjustment of 1988 were made without sufficient consultation. Analysts within and outside the Sandinista Party are still in disagreement over how far democratization might have been pursued under conditions of war and economic crisis — and what difference it might have made in the 1990 elections.

As it turned out, unlike 1984, when a democratic election supported the continued leadership of Daniel Ortega and the FSLN, 1990 saw the surprising election of Violeta Chamorro, representing the United National Opposition (UNO) coalition of fourteen parties. In hindsight, Nicaraguans' yearning for peace and economic security carried the vote, coupled with increasing criticism of the Sandinista government's management of the crisis. A gender gap in the vote, with more women favoring Chamorro, suggested that the revolutionary leadership had paid too little attention to the disproportionate effects of economic hardship and political turmoil on women.

Yet, despite President Chamorro's willingness to compromise with the FSLN, which continued to be the strongest political party in the country, her government introduced stabilization and adjustment measures mandated by the International Monetary Fund (IMF) that were crushing to the majority of Nicaraguans. The Contra war and economic embargo came to an end as expected, but U.S. aid was not as readily forthcoming as had been hoped. Moreover, cutting back the state sector and developing the market economy — hallmarks of neoliberalism — had a detrimental social impact on a broad base of the population. The devaluation of the currency brought soaring inflation under control, but unemployment reached alarming levels and the prices of newly available goods made them unattainable to all but the elite.

During the first half of the 1990s, the Sandinista Party regrouped and considered what role it would play once it was out of power and alternately acting to oppose or collaborate with the government. Recognizing the error of too much centralization, popular organizations such as the neighborhood Sandinista Defense Committees (CDSs) and the Nicaraguan Women's Association "Luisa Amanda Espinosa" (AMNLAE) had been granted somewhat greater autonomy even before the election. But within these groups there were demands for still greater independence that were unheeded by the party, leading some to form alternative associations. The tension in the FSLN over how much decision making to turn over to the grassroots continued until 1995, when the party split into two factions, the more orthodox FSLN and the newly formed Sandinista Renovationist Movement (MRS), which called for more democratization within the terms of the changed national situation.

The weakened Sandinista Party was unable to recapture the presidency in the 1996 elections, which brought Arnoldo Alemán to power. Formerly the mayor of Managua, this populist right-wing politician won the support of some Nicaraguans with his campaign to modernize and improve the city. Others were dismayed by his apparent lust for erasing evidence of the revolution and for carrying out, as president, a plan of further neoliberal development. During the final years of the twentieth century, Alemán's government continued to promote free enterprise in a competitive global context while his country suffered from still higher unemployment and underemployment, poor standards of health, and declining levels of education. He revealed the callous nature of his presidency most dramatically when he failed to act expeditiously in response to Hurricane Mitch. The response of many Nicaraguans has been to turn once again to popular and nongovernmental organizations, as civil society presents the best prospects for confronting the nation's need for economic and social justice.

This book's title, *After Revolution*, reflects its central focus on the years following the victory of the Nicaraguan revolution in 1979 and, particularly, following the Sandinista decade that ended with the elections of 1990. My research was carried out during the 1990s, a period of transition that saw the rolling back, or unmaking, of the revolution to a significant degree. Nevertheless, much of the revolution has endured and even deepened since the FSLN lost power, including forms of democratic participation and respect for political pluralism. Thus when I say *after* revolution, I do not intend to present the revolution as something static and now consigned to history but rather as something that has been in process and has undergone change — sometimes for better, other times for worse — and that continues to give shape to local and national politics. Without a doubt, there is much to regret in present-day Nicaragua, much that has been lost, but new political cultures are building on the past and enabling new generations to construct their own revolutionary visions for the future.

Reading the Revolution

Given the multitude of meanings attributed to Nicaragua in the country and in the world, past and present, it is useful to consider the ways in which the nation has figured as a contested site for a number of vexing political and cultural questions in a period of globalization. Depending on one's vantage point, Nicaragua has been the subject of longing or lament, hope or fear in a radical process of social transformation.[3] Judgments about the success or failure of the Nicaraguan revolution in overcoming past injustices and inefficiencies have often clashed, just as discussions of democratization and citizenship have frequently foundered on disagreements over how inclusive the political process has been. News of the Sandinista victory was celebrated by the Left in Latin America and throughout the world. Solidarity groups in the United States, as elsewhere, were quick to respond, and many individuals and brigades would travel to see the revolution and support it over the decade of transformation and, later, resistance. Academics as well as activists became part of the revolutionary project, many turning from other research agendas to do so. Writers, artists, economists, and engineers were among the diverse group that contributed time and energy to what they hoped would be a model of broad-based social change.

Many of those who traveled to Nicaragua during these remarkable years found that their lives were forever altered by their experiences in the country. The North American feminist writer and poet Adrienne Rich wrote a groundbreaking essay on the politics of location in 1984, a year after a trip to Nicaragua. There, she came to appreciate the way that "a place on a map is also a place in history" (1986: 212) and the importance of "recognizing our location, having to name the ground we're coming from" (219). In Nicaragua, she wrote, "I could feel what it means, dissident or not, to be part of that raised boot of power, the cold shadow we cast everywhere to the south" (220).[4]

Nicaragua was also the staging ground for an analysis of "women's interests" offered by the British socialist feminist Maxine Molyneux (1986), who developed her thesis of practical and strategic gender interests based on experiences in Nicaragua in the early 1980s. That framework, advanced to assess how well revolutionary societies have addressed women's concerns, has been much debated among scholars concerned more broadly about the situation of women. While some found her distinction between women's struggles over immediate, practical interests such as food, housing, and employment and longer-term strategic interests in transforming gender relations useful, others argued that the two are often intertwined, especially in third world societies. Here, however, it is most notable that Molyneux's experience led her to insights from "revolutions such as Nicaragua's which afford no simple conclusions because of the severe pressure they are under, the short span of the revolutionary governments, and the resulting unevenness of their records, especially in relation to women" (1986: 282–83).

The well-known feminist writer and poet Margaret Randall made her home in Nicaragua for several years in the 1980s after living for more than a decade in Cuba. As a North American–born activist, she devoted attention in both countries to the changing position of women in revolutionary

2. *Murals like these at a university in Managua (the* UNAN*), including the familiar portrait of the revolutionary Sandino, are now rare.*

society. Her conversations and interviews with Nicaraguan women led her to raise increasingly critical questions about the revolution's commitment to democratizing gender relations, although she remained a partisan, loyal to the principles of Sandinista politics (Randall 1981, 1992, 1994).

From another shore, the Indian writer Salman Rushdie traveled to Nicaragua for several weeks in 1986 and returned to London to write a memoir of his journey there. As he noted, he knew of the tendency of revolutions to "go wrong" and to start "with idealism and romance" and end "with betrayed expectations, broken hope" (1987: 12). Although he was in the country only a brief time, his encounter affected him deeply enough that in the end, he acknowledged with admiration, he had no choice but to write a book. He concluded, "I had left Nicaragua unfinished, so to speak, a country in which the ancient, opposing forces of creation and destruction were in violent collision. The fashionable pessimism of our age suggested that the destroyers would always, in the end, prove stronger than the creators, and indeed, those who would unmake the Nicaraguan revolution were men of awesome power" (168).

Like Rushdie, the Mexican writer and journalist Alma Guillermoprieto (1995) went to Nicaragua questioning how far the revolution had come in achieving democratization. Her visit coincided with the 1990 elections, when the population was struggling to make sense of the political upset. Noting the problems that the Sandinistas had faced as they sought to overcome the vast inequalities and lack of development under Somoza's government, she observed that the opposition's promise of peace and an end to the military draft, along with the likely end of the U.S. economic embargo, gave Violeta Chamorro the moral authority to capture the vote. Guillermoprieto's report of a demoralized nation seeking reconciliation despite fundamental differences suggests the powerful impression the place left on visitors.

The photojournalist Susan Meiselas (1981) left an unforgettable portrait of Nicaragua during the year preceding the Sandinista victory, 1978–79, and then returned to make a film as the country was in transition a decade later. Her political documentary, *Pictures from a Revolution* (1991), evokes the memories of those she photographed earlier, some heroic and others bitter but all reflecting on what the revolution was and what it might have become. As an internationalist who shared the hopes of the revolution, Meiselas commented ruefully on the meanings of the revolution in the aftermath of the 1990 elections: "a dream for some, . . . much more for Nicaraguans."

These are only a few of the many sympathetic accounts of the revolution that reached a wider public.[5] Nevertheless, the Western media were far less sympathetic in general and often gave a harshly critical view of the Sandinista government and of Nicaragua as a place that had gone out of control. In the United States in the 1980s, President Ronald Reagan's view that Nicaragua, in "our own backyard," presented a grave threat to national security dominated public discourse as shaped by the media.[6] Frequent distortions and fabrications served to underwrite the training and direction of the Contra forces and also the cutting off of loans to the rebel republic. Even in the post-Sandinista 1990s, conservative politicians in the United States have taken every opportunity to oppose aid to Nicaragua when they can show evidence of continued FSLN influence.[7] Thus it stands as a tribute to the Nicaraguan nation that broad-based international support for the revolution and its democratic ideals was so strong.

Arriving Late for the Revolution

My relationship to Nicaragua and my writing of this book reflect my desires, hopes, and preoccupations for a small country that courageously attempted to change the course of history. In July 1979, I was a graduate student writing a dissertation based on research in Peru, which faced economic crisis and was soon to be engulfed in political conflict amounting to civil war, and preparing to take my first teaching job. I shared the angst of many of my peers who sought to pursue their activist commitments as well as academic scholarship; as a member of Latin American solidarity groups, particularly Action for Women in Chile, I struggled to reconcile my anti-imperialist and feminist politics with my professional development.

I recall the summer evening in Buffalo, New York, when a friend and I sat talking outdoors at a café and learned of the Sandinista victory. After more than four decades of the Somoza dictatorship, backed by the United States, a popularly supported revolutionary movement had successfully seized power. I shared the euphoria of a generation that had come of age during the Vietnam War and longed for examples of people's triumphs of self-determination. Beginning at that time two decades ago, Nicaragua — like Cuba twenty years before — came to figure for many around the world as a beacon that other countries might follow.

My experience in Peru in 1977 had come at a time when that country's experiment in "revolution," ambivalent though it may have been under President Juan Velasco Alvarado (1968–75), had taken a rightward turn. During my return trips in the 1980s, I found increased tension as the military and the insurgent Shining Path faced off and violence in the Andes and in Lima escalated. Like a number of anthropologists working in Peru, I turned my attention elsewhere when it became too dangerous to continue my Andean research. Somewhat ironically, this provided the opportunity to visit Nicaragua, still regarded by many as a hotbed of political activity.

In retrospect, I have come to think of myself as a latecomer to revolutions. Having missed the radical reformist years of the early 1970s in Peru,

I studied the social impact of economic crisis there. I had had a similar interest in the Cuban revolution, the most far-reaching and enduring in the hemisphere, and as a new faculty member at Colgate University I arranged a study group to Cuba for winter 1980. Then the Mariel exodus forced cancellation of the trip and I did not visit the island until 1993, when it was in the throes of the "Special Period," a time of austerity during its worst postrevolutionary economic crisis. Again, I was too late to see the revolution in its heyday, but I surely was acquiring an appreciation of the similar struggles of Latin Americans who had achieved so much against the odds and who fought stubbornly against their losses.[8]

I made my first trip to Nicaragua in 1989, when it too was confronting economic hardship and political opposition. The Sandinistas were suffering from the effects of the U.S. embargo and the Contra war and had imposed structural adjustment measures, significantly downsizing and cutting back services provided by the state. Support for the revolutionary government appeared strong, nonetheless, and preparations for the 1990 presidential elections suggested an easy reelection for Daniel Ortega. What virtually everyone regarded as a difficult period for the Sandinista government turned out to be its final hour, however, as the UNO coalition's candidate, Violeta Chamorro, came to power.

By this time, I had been fortunate enough to receive funding for several years of continuing research in Nicaragua. I made trips there every year from 1989 through 1993, then returned in 1996, 1998, and 2000, staying for periods of a few weeks to several months, totaling more than a year, in Managua. My original proposal to study urban women workers in the second revolutionary decade had to be altered in light of the many reversals in the economy and society, and I shared the dismay of many Nicaraguans and their supporters during that time. But I also found that the historical experiences of women and men during the revolution had prepared them as social subjects who would confront the political and economic transition that was under way. From my research site in Managua, I have observed and documented cultural responses to neoliberalism, introduced by the UNO's more conciliatory government and then deepened by the right-wing government of Arnoldo Alemán's Liberal Alliance, which captured the 1996 election. Although international attention to Nicaragua has waned substantially since the Sandinistas lost power, it may be precisely *after* the revolution that the long struggle for democratization and economic justice will be waged. As this book shows, civil society and emergent social movements are offering an alternative to despair as a new political culture gains force in the country.

Writing after Revolution—Mapping This Book

My research in Managua began by considering the political economic transition in Nicaragua following the 1990 elections, particularly its effects on low-income women workers. I identified four urban cooperatives that I visited many times over the course of my study to see how women were faring in work settings that originated in the Sandinista period. In addition, I visited trade union organizations, government offices, and research centers in an effort to collect material that would allow me to make sense of the dramatic change in the country. I also developed a special relationship with one neighborhood, or barrio, where I have stayed in recent years and where I gathered ethnographic material and conducted interviews with residents, many of whom were participating in the informal (unregulated) economy.

While I continued in this general research direction, I also followed the social movements that were emergent in Nicaragua in the 1990s. The revitalized women's movement and the growing gay and lesbian movement were of special interest to me, although I was also impressed by the indigenous, environmental, and other movements that were gaining visibility. I came to realize that these movements were not unrelated to my research but indeed could be understood as a cultural response to neoliberalism and new terms of struggle in Nicaragua. In time, I was able to appreciate the opportunity that the movements offered civil society to define a "new way of doing politics" and to broaden the process of democratization that was begun under the Sandinistas.

In a number of ways, I came to consider my project a multi-sited ethnography.[9] First, I was interested in several vantage points from which we may view Nicaragua. I frequently had occasion to consider the ways that international attention to Nicaragua has framed our understanding of the country's experience. Not surprisingly, many of my initial impressions of Nicaragua came from the United States, from the media and from Left political organizations. I followed the competing discourses concerning Nicaragua at the national and international levels during the period of my research.

In part, this was facilitated by my double affiliation with two institutions during my early years in Nicaragua. Both the Central American University (UCA) and the Central American Institute of Business Administration (INCAE) lent support, giving me the opportunity to associate with a Jesuit, Sandinista-oriented university on the one hand and a neoliberal-oriented graduate school of management on the other.[10]

In addition, I maintained multiple sites of study in Managua. This city, with a population of more than one million, is a vast urban space that has grown even larger since it was devastated by an earthquake in 1972. I relied heavily on a series of cars and trucks in the course of my work to travel from one end of the city to the other as I visited cooperatives, research centers, ministries, women's centers, and people's homes. Over the years of my research, I lived in working-class and middle-class neighborhoods in several areas of the city, with a Miskito Indian family from the Atlantic Coast, with a professional woman and her children from a well-established Managua family, and with "internationalist" activists and researchers like myself. During the two summers that my son spent with me, I learned much about child care, schools, and the amusements the city holds for the very young. Later, I settled in the barrio of working people and professionals where I conducted a neighborhood study, but that was only one piece of a larger project that was multiply situated.

In still another way this project is multi-layered or multi-sited. I have found during the past decade that Nicaragua has been "good to think" in terms of current political and cultural questions in anthropology and Latin American studies.[11] Through my research there, I have been able to explore issues ranging from the politics of location to discourses of development to gender and sexual identities in a postrevolutionary society. I conceive of this book as a series of essays, a form that allows me to advance most fruitfully several key perspectives as I bring forth a body of research collected over a decade. I do not attempt to offer the sort of detailed analysis of Nicaragua's history and politics that others have done so well[12] but rather to engage in several focused conversations on subjects of current relevance not only to Nicaraguans but to all of us. I hope to show that Nicaragua offers a rich staging ground for discussions of contemporary scholarship and of some of the most salient issues of our day, in Nicaragua and beyond. While my approach is multi-sited, my overall objective is to contribute to an understanding of Nicaragua as a place that not long ago staked its future on a process of

3. *Giant Woman (Gigantona), a popular marionette figure carried by a youth, made an appearance at a women's event.*

social transformation and that in the aftermath of revolution has dared to reimagine itself once again as a more democratic nation.

Chapter 2 sets forth an analysis of the politics of location in Nicaragua and introduces subjects that are developed further in later chapters. I begin with the 1990 electoral loss of the Sandinistas to the coalition government that overturned many revolutionary changes of the last decade and imposed neoliberal measures to return the country to a capitalist path. Then I suggest that despite the initial despair experienced by many Nicaraguans over that outcome and the economic crisis that followed, a number of political and cultural openings have emerged to allow independent social movements to grow in opposition to both the government and to undemocratic practices on the Left. In many cases, women have been central to these developments as those most harshly affected by recent economic policies and as activists in newly organized movements. I consider these apparently contradictory tendencies and call for an analysis that attends to both political economy and cultural politics.

In chapter 3, I discuss the changing face of Nicaragua's capital city in light of post-Sandinista efforts to erase evidence of the revolutionary past and to present a welcoming environment for foreign investors and the national elite. The use of urban space is shown to be inflected by gender and power in the neoliberal era as desires for modernity cause women and low-income residents in general to be removed from public view or located in marginal sites. Ironically, harsh conditions may be catalyzing a more unified response from civil society to address the nation's problems. The multi-layered approach offered here takes Managua as a window through which to view relations with the rest of the country and the world, pointing toward an urban anthropology that considers the city as both location of research and focus of study. Managua is being remade in accordance with powerful interests, but this has not gone unchallenged.

The Managua neighborhood where I lived during my first trip to Nicaragua in 1989 became my home base in visits from 1993 onward. Chapter 4 presents an ethnographic portrait of the barrio and the results of my study of households there. While I draw on interviews with a number of residents, I focus on lengthier conversations and repeated visits with several individuals I got to know well over time, from a woman active with the Sandinistas and a man who is a self-styled historian to members of a large, impoverished household that shared our block in the barrio. I hope to convey a sense of daily life in an urban area known for its mix of working-class and middle-class residents and its varied political support for the Sandinista and post-Sandinista governments. Much of the story revolves around current efforts to survive adversity, when so many are dependent on the informal economy to get by, and what the barrio can tell us about the city and the nation.

Chapter 5 discusses in some detail the consequences of neoliberal policy and structural adjustment in Nicaragua through a consideration of low-income women working in cooperatives in Managua. A number of feminist analysts have brought needed attention to the harsh effects of neoliberalism at the level of the household, where women often bear the burden of maintaining families in the face of rising prices, reduced public services, and privatized health care in the market-driven society. Yet I suggest that while turning to the household and women's unpaid work has brought about a needed change in our thinking about economic development, it is also critical to examine the ways that women are responding to adjustment through their paid work in and outside the home. My contention is that although women often suffer the worst effects of neoliberalism both in and out of the household, they also draw strength from their recent history of social mobilization, which sets them apart from women elsewhere in Latin America.

In chapter 6, I enter the discussion of postsocialist societies that have rapidly altered work relations and organization in order to document how Nicaragua has fared and how it may instruct us. Specifically, I consider the refashioning of cooperatives formed under the Sandinista government into microenterprises that conform to neoliberal standards. I trace the changing fortunes of the urban cooperatives that I followed through the period of my research, which included artisans, seamstresses, bakers, and welders — predominantly women. Once again, we see that while the 1990s have seen the dismantling of many revolutionary projects, the revolution left its legacy, resulting in a productive social tension among urban working women and men who are not ready to give up what they had achieved at such great cost.

Most anthropological studies of development have used a political economy model to examine efforts and outcomes of development programs. In chapter 7, I depart from that model to raise cultural questions concerning ways that discourses of development and nationhood not only reflect different political orientations but also, in themselves, influence practices and outcomes. Nicaragua during the past decade offers a useful example of the way that contentious political economic approaches may play out discursively. I consider the major currents in discussions of microenterprises and the informal sector as development issues and then draw on interviews with working and poor urban residents who articulate a more personal, visceral response to current conditions as these are imprinted on their bodies and minds. My objective is to bring attention to nondominant discourses that point toward alternative approaches and critiques.

In chapter 8, I consider in greater detail the distinctly cultural responses to the political economic transition in neoliberal Nicaragua. Here I discuss those emergent social movements that have gone beyond the party-based organizations of the past decade, raising a number of issues that relate to cultural identity, democratization, and human rights. To different degrees, I examine the neighborhood, women's, lesbian and gay, indigenous, youth, peace, and environmental movements, as well as a formerly Sandinista trade union organization, as these have been influential in calling for a new way of doing politics. Civil society groups, nongovernmental organizations as well as social movements, have been important in supporting these newer initiatives, but Sandinista Party loyalists have also taken note of the new life the movements offer to a nation struggling to reestablish its identity in the postrevolutionary period.

In the last chapter I ask what will be remembered about Nicaragua, as I return to and expand on some questions raised earlier in the context of neoliberal Nicaragua at the close of the century. I reconsider the ways that ideas about Nicaragua have been mobilized in popular "remembering" of the revolution and its aftermath, in the country and outside it, and how the cultural landscape has shifted during this period of globalization. In addition, I seek to discover what cultural signs are on the horizon as the country struggles to recover from the widespread destruction of Hurricane Mitch. Some observers have suggested that the current postdisaster social mobilization in the country is reminiscent of the 1970s, when in the wake of a massive earthquake political tensions led in the direction of social revolution. Without being overly optimistic about the gathering force of civil society in responding to the crisis, we may nevertheless take note of and admire the determination of Nicaraguans to do more than rebuild the same society. Their desire to call upon collective memory and reinvent themselves once again as a nation in the process of becoming more democratic, more tolerant of cultural differences, and more insistent on sustainable development in the interests of both people and environment gives us reason enough to take heart.

Many writers saw in the Nicaraguan revolution a new social movement, which a smaller number called "postmodern," drawing as it did on the collective efforts of a broad array of actors who sought to transform cultural meaning and representation as well as society (Beverley and Oviedo 1993). Yet as the post-Sandinista decade of the 1990s — and the millennium — has come to a close, the conditions of postmodernity under a triumphant global capitalism are still more evident in the wake of the neoliberal economic project and a fragmented Sandinista Party on the one hand and the promising response of civil society and social movements on the other.[13] Drawing inspiration from recent work that brings together the political and the cultural to better understand current developments in Latin America (Alvarez, Dagnino, and Escobar 1998), my work also engages the economic in a feminist analysis of contemporary developments in Nicaragua and beyond. Ultimately, this project is more concerned to raise questions than to resolve them, as the shifting terrain of late-twentieth-century neoliberalism and globalization unsettles our thinking in ways that may prove most valuable in remapping our understanding of Nicaragua in the world.

Chapter Two

NEGOTIATING SPACES

The Gendered Politics of Location

NICARAGUA was at the center of international attention when the revolutionary struggle of the 1970s led into the Sandinista decade of the 1980s. In the social imagination of that decade, especially in the United States, the Central American nation loomed large. When I gave a talk drawing on my preliminary research at an anthropology conference in 1990, a man asked me what was the population of Nicaragua. When I replied that it was a little over three million people, he responded quickly, "I find that hard to believe." Like many who depend on the mass media to frame their views of the world, this man's understanding of Nicaragua as a key focus of U.S. concern—particularly at the time of its landmark presidential election—contributed to a sense that it must have more people and take up more space on the globe. In contrast, when I returned home from a research trip in 1996 and told a colleague about the political campaigns of the numerous candidates in that year's less-watched election (he too asked about the size of the population, which had risen to almost four million), he commented that it sounded like "a tempest in a teapot." Clearly, Nicaragua had diminished in perceived size and importance from the days when it was the imminent danger in "our backyard."

Over the last ten years I have reflected on the ways in which research conducted in Nicaragua is framed by external constructions of the country and, more generally, on the ways in which history alters the politics of location. I have approached my work as a multi-sited ethnography that travels across borders and looks at processes that link local contexts and world systems (Marcus 1998). At this remove from the field experience, these concerns have produced a shift in the analytic orientation of my work. This chapter takes as its point of departure gendered negotiations over social space in Nicaragua, as I explore some of the tensions in a view that attends to both political economy and cultural politics. A number of subjects introduced here, including the urban cooperatives and social movements that were central to my research, are discussed in greater detail in later chapters. In the two that follow most immediately, I consider claims to social space more specifically in Managua and in one of its barrios.

Nicaraguan Revolutionary Claims

Negotiating social, political, and economic space, literally and figuratively, has special resonance in Nicaragua. Two decades ago, the culmination of the struggle against the long-standing Somoza dictatorship led to the emergence of a revolutionary government that laid claim to political space formerly held by a small elite. The Sandinistas transformed the rural landholding system, urban manufacturing, and the distribution of goods and services so that those who formerly had been disenfranchised gained access for the first time to economic openings for a respectable livelihood. Moreover, the social space that was won through the struggle was shared by new players in the Nicaraguan setting, including peasants, low-income urban dwellers, youth, and, significant to this analysis, women.[1]

Women were active participants in the Nicaraguan revolution and in the decade of Sandinista government. They became increasingly active in the grassroots, "sectoral"[2] organizations of Sandinista workers in rural and urban areas during the late 1980s. Although women confronted growing demands on their time in and out of the home during this period, they also found openings to examine their individual and collective gender subordination (Pérez Alemán 1992: 250). Women leaders emerged from the Rural Workers Association (ATC) and the Sandinista Workers Confederation (CST), for example, who would later help to build an independent feminist movement (Criquillon 1995).

The mass women's organization formed by the FSLN before the Sandinistas' victory has been known since 1979 as the Nicaraguan Women's Association "Luisa Amanda Espinosa," or AMNLAE, named for the first woman to have fallen in combat. The association offered support to women in the popular sectors, encouraging their political and economic participation while conforming to FSLN priorities. Under pressure from diverse groups of women, the FSLN and AMNLAE responded to calls for an end to gender inequalities. In 1987, the FSLN issued a public proclamation that recognized the subordinate position of women in Nicaraguan society and their legitimate demands for change. Around this time, AMNLAE also expressed its commitment to gender equality and a willingness to open itself to a more democratic process. This did not occur, however, as Sandinista Party interests continued to set AMNLAE's agenda (Chinchilla 1994).

The gains that were won during the early years of the revolutionary government were challenged later in the 1980s when the Contra war and the economic blockade undercut efforts to bring health care, education, and employment to the broad population. Women's achievements were also threatened as they carried the burden of supporting families when men were drawn off to war or were unable to find work. Moreover, AMNLAE had set aside male privilege and power as issues too sensitive to take on. Thus the space that had opened to women in the process of social transformation began to shrink.

Since the 1990 elections, many of the progressive reforms of the previous decade have been overturned. The UNO government's neoliberal agenda had particularly harsh consequences for women, who often struggled to maintain households and families when economic adjustment policies took away jobs and social services on which they had come to rely.[3] More surprisingly, though, the nineties have also seen growing political participation among Nicaraguan women in the emerging autonomous social movements. These movements, or sometimes loosely organized networks, are taking up issues as wide-ranging as maternal health, violence against women, gay and lesbian rights, the environment, and the economic crisis.[4]

4. *Part of a mural, at Casa Ave María, by Pablo Danilo Téllez and the Grupo Artístico Contraste depicting heroic women in Nicaragua.*

Here I explore and rethink two developments that I had initially considered to be unrelated: the shifting political economy, which with its emphasis on privatization and export-led industrialization has frequently marginalized women; and the expansion of political activism based on a host of concerns that go well beyond the economy to embrace human rights and gender politics at a time when the government has swung sharply to the right. My research in Managua began by focusing on the first of these developments as I followed the changing fortunes of a number of women (and some men) who worked in small industries and commerce in the city. Yet as I documented the grim results of neoliberal policy for low-income urban women, I repeatedly turned with relief to observe (and participate in) feminist activities — meetings, marches, and conferences — that were occurring with increasing regularity in the country. I came to regard this as a "second project" in Nicaragua, to follow the encouraging development of independent initiatives among women in both the middle-class and popular sectors who are seizing a political and cultural space.

Now, however, I want to suggest that there is a significant connection between the changing political economy and the growth of feminist and other social movements in Nicaragua since 1990—a central argument of this book that will be examined further in later chapters. While critics of the former Sandinista government contend that the development of more autonomous movements is the result of a postelectoral democratization process, and partisans of the FSLN call it a continuation of the last decade of social mobilization, I suggest that it is not simply one or the other. Rather, the emergence of more independent social movements is likely the result of a questioning of top-down Sandinista Party politics, strong opposition to neoliberal government policy, continued mobilization under a government that tolerates a degree of political dissent—and a desire to raise issues that had been overlooked or silenced by established political parties both before and after the 1990 elections. In what follows, I discuss the connection between shifting political economies and emergent social movements in terms of struggles for social space in Latin America more generally and then consider the case of Nicaragua.

Struggles for Space in Latin America:
Shifting Political Economies and Cultural Meanings

In recent years, scholars have paid increasing attention to space and place in discussions of how social and political resources and meanings are negotiated in various settings. Cultural geographers and anthropologists have often been the interlocutors in these discussions, sometimes informed by postmodernist criticism of the ways that control of space is gendered, raced, classed, and in general socially constructed (Spain 1992; Keith and Pile 1993; Momsen and Kinnaird 1993; Radcliffe and Westwood 1993). As Keith and Pile (1993: 1) note, the debate centers on "the relationship between time and space; the potential of politics; and the construction of identity." They argue that in the late twentieth century it has been necessary to go beyond theorizing power as "the expression of a singular dimension of oppression, such as class or gender or race" (1). As these authors and others (Beverley and Oviedo 1993; Kaplan 1994) remark, a politics of location must consider the complex relations among all of these dimensions and also link local contexts of struggle to broader systems of power. In other words, attention to the micropolitics of location should be accompanied by analysis of macrostructural relations at the regional, national, and transnational levels.

Moreover, contemporary social relations of domination should be understood as fluid, in a constant process of change. As Caren Kaplan (1994: 138) cautions, "[A]ny exclusive recourse to space, place, or position becomes utterly abstract and universalizing without historical specificity." The value in this perspective, then, is not in returning to a view that takes location as determinant in shaping social processes, a view that supported explanations of gender inequality in terms of women's connection to the private sphere and men's mobility in the public sphere.[5] Rather, a consideration of spatial arrangements and of the meanings attached to the places that social actors occupy, along with attention to how these are contested, can sharpen our understanding of current struggles, wherever they occur.

A particularly well-known and compelling example is that of the Mothers of Plaza de Mayo (known as the Madres) in Argentina, who claimed a public area in which to protest "disappearances" and state terrorism — transforming Buenos Aires's main plaza into a women's space for political expression. The sociologist María del Carmen Feijóo writes,

> The Madres showed a capacity for innovation in the cultural dimension of doing politics. Their originality was evident in their development of new forms of mobilization, such as the walk (*ronda*) around the plaza; giving old symbols new meaning (e.g., the white handkerchiefs); their capacity to resignify a public space (the plaza); and their capability to sustain a political agenda outside the realm of the political parties. (1989: 78)

Arturo Escobar and Sonia Alvarez (1992), writing on social movements in Latin America, trace connections between the democratic openings and economic crises during the so-called lost decade of the eighties and the rise of what have been termed "new" social movements. They identify fundamental links between political and economic change, on the one hand, and collective identity formation, on the other, a key point that has informed my thinking about negotiating spaces in post-Sandinista Nicaragua. As Escobar and Alvarez note, the harsh free market policies introduced to counter the debt crisis and high inflation throughout Latin America contributed to what some call a "reversal of development," with soaring poverty levels and other social dislocations. Despite the fragmentation that this occasioned, however, the period saw new forms of resistance and collective struggle ranging from the organizing of soup kitchens in squatter settlements to environmental, feminist, health, and human rights movements across the continent.[6]

Not only have political and economic conditions given rise to new forms of organizing among new social sectors, but new analyses have appeared that challenge earlier work rooted in modernization and dependency theories. According to Escobar and Alvarez (1992: 3), new research shows that "a multiplicity of social actors establish their presence and spheres of autonomy in a fragmented social and political space. Society itself is largely shaped by the plurality of these struggles and the vision of those involved in the new social movements."

John Beverley and José Oviedo (1993: 1) have commented on the Latin American turn toward postmodernism, which has reinvigorated debate on the Left and led to new thinking about the relationship between local cultures and transnational politics. Escobar (1992: 63) observes (counterintuitively for some, perhaps) that postmodernist insights have caught hold in Latin America more than in other areas, noting that "more clearly in Latin America than elsewhere, the move toward a grand 'theory of social movements' is actively resisted." He describes a crisis of development that may account for both the emergence of new social movements and the theoretical turn toward more pluralist approaches motivated by a desire to embrace cultural differences.

The development models being resisted are those set in place during the 1980s that introduced one adjustment and austerity package after another, producing "a vast landscape of identities of the 'illiterate,' the 'landless peasant,' 'women bypassed by development,' the 'hungry and malnourished,' 'those belonging to the informal sector,' 'urban marginals,' and so forth" (Escobar 1992: 67). Understanding this fragmentation of identities is critical to examining contemporary social movements, which, notably, include the same social actors referred to above. Moreover, we need to understand these struggles as waged not only over material conditions but over cultural and political meanings as social subjects challenge spaces occupied by capitalist states. The production of "new ways of doing politics," or the construction of a new cultural politics, will be seen to have ample force in the Nicaraguan setting.

Racial and ethnic minorities as well as poor and working-class sectors, women among them, are prominent in the new movements in Latin America (Jaquette 1994; Stephen 1997). In addition, feminists, gay men, and lesbians, representing different class and ethnic groups, figure importantly among those forging collective identities and mobilizing for change. The impressive appearance of feminist movements throughout the region during a decade of economic and political crises has been discussed by several authors who have attended the *encuentros* (conference gatherings) held biannually since 1981 by Latin American and Caribbean feminists (Sternbach et al. 1992). Whether because of or in spite of these crises and the obstacles they posed to organizing, the growth of feminism and of lesbian and gay movements has been pronounced since the 1980s (Jaquette 1989; Alvarez 1990; Babb 1997b).

Nicaraguan Contexts of Change

Nicaragua's recent history makes it exceptional in Latin America in a number of respects. The struggle against Somoza's rule drew on diverse sectors that included the middle and working classes, students and professionals, the urban poor, and rural peasants. Women are estimated to have made up about 30 percent of those mobilized in the struggle (Molyneux 1986). Thus the period leading up to the 1979 Sandinista victory was characterized by the coalescence of a broad-based social movement whose participants were in many ways similar to those now forming "new" social movements elsewhere on the continent. Some of the same conditions that propelled social actors in other countries in the 1980s were already present in Nicaragua, affecting the subaltern majority in disenfranchised sectors.

The Nicaraguan revolution was the first in Latin America since the emergence of contemporary feminist movements around the world. This may account for the heavy participation of women in the insurrectionary movement and for the attention to women's concerns later shown by the Sandinista government — although explicit gender demands were often subordinated to party interests. Among the changes brought about by the Sandinistas, the agrarian reform and new urban employment included women as beneficiaries and an ideological campaign against sexism in the media was launched (Padilla, Murguialday, and Criquillon 1987; Chinchilla 1994).

These openings for women were threatened when national defense and economic austerity became priorities in the 1980s. In 1988, the Sandinistas began a program of structural adjustment that brought increasing hardship and loss of support for the revolutionary process (Brenes et al. 1991a). In retrospect, we can say that the 1990 election was decided a year or two earlier, when people were weary of crisis conditions and wanted peace in their country. Women's extra responsibility for maintaining families may also account for the gender gap in the election, with more women supporting the UNO coalition.

While autonomous social movements have emerged in Nicaragua since 1990 in a neoliberal context that is increasingly similar to that found elsewhere in Latin America a decade earlier, there are certain precursors to these movements in the Nicaraguan revolution. As social actors from marginalized sectors were incorporated in the revolution, women became active as combatants and also supported the struggle in other substantial ways. AMNLAE mobilized mothers to support their sons and daughters in the revolutionary process and, later, to join together as the mothers of heroes and martyrs. The mothers have played a strong role in the material and ideological support of the Sandinista struggle—although, ironically, Violeta Chamorro was able to use her image as a mother and her appeal to motherhood to gain support for the UNO government and defeat the Sandinistas (Kampwirth 1996b).[7] We will see, however, that the current social movements are distinguished by their more independent character, their willingness to break away from party politics.

Following Daniel Ortega's unexpected loss in the 1990 election, the FSLN had a valuable opportunity for self-reflection, as the party base called out for more inclusion and democracy. Feminists long active in the party were among the critics who argued for opening up debate. As a result, there was more attention to internal weaknesses in the party, even as the UNO government enacted swift changes that aggravated economic and political problems in the country. Although the FSLN was marked by growing divisions and a number of active members eventually broke away from the party, it drew together to confront the UNO's economic program initiated in March 1991. The program included a drastic devaluation of the currency and the Occupational Conversion Plan funded by the U.S. Agency for International Development (USAID), which sharply cut employment in the state sector by offering workers incentives to start small businesses.

References to social and political space abound in the decade of national-level dislocation since the 1990 election. While the right-wing tendency in the UNO coalition gained substantial space in the government, it also suffered losses in the National Assembly. Sandinistas welcomed the space that became available to the FSLN, and they managed, at the very least, to make their criticisms of the government's neoliberal stabilization and adjustment programs heard. They began to demand alternatives, arguing that "opening economic spaces for the majority is the only way to depolarize the country" (Envío 1993: 10). Women were among those calling for a new political culture, one attuned to the gender implications of harsh neoliberal economic policies.

The Sandinista Party division in 1995 into two political orientations, the FSLN and the MRS, weakened the opposition movement but resulted in more open discussion of the party's failure to respond adequately to its political base (Barricada Internacional 1995a). Activists and scholars (Beverley and Oviedo 1993) who viewed the Sandinista revolution as an exemplary postmodern social movement, offering a heterogeneous and pluralist alternative to existing capitalist and socialist development models, may have been dismayed by the split in the party and by charges of its undemocratic practices (Criquillon 1995; O'Kane 1995). I would suggest, however, that even as neoliberal Nicaragua aspires for many of the hallmarks of modernity, the complex conditions of postmodernity are also in evidence. On the one side, both the Right and the Left have been fragmented since 1990, and on the other, the pluralist social and political currents emerging in civil society offer some hope for a more democratic future.[8]

Economic Spaces in the Urban Terrain

While President Chamorro, better known in Nicaragua as Doña Violeta, tried to put a motherly face on harsh economic reforms, many low-income women and men in Managua were coming to have less and less confidence in the government's ability to improve their lives. The currency was stabilized, but unemployment and underemployment approached 60 percent just as privatization of health care and cuts in social services pulled out the safety net that had protected the urban poor during the previous decade (Envío 1994: 7).

My interviews and conversations in Managua during the years of the

UNO government suggest some ways that new policy directions, motivated by an ideological shift to the right, attempted to close many of the openings that were won under Sandinista leadership. For example, the author of the Ministry of Finance's Occupational Conversion Plan voiced her opinion that cuts in public sector employment would benefit many female employees by allowing them to return home to care for their families (Fatima Reyes, interview, July 18, 1991). Indeed, a disproportionate number of women, and Sandinistas in general, were among those to adopt the plan, which offered employees up to twenty-two months' salary (U.S. $2,000) to leave jobs and establish microenterprises as part of the effort to privatize the economy and reduce social spending. Many women invested in freezers in order to sell soft drinks and ice cream out of their homes, businesses that were destined to fail in an economy already saturated with small, informal enterprises.

The result of this ill-conceived plan to cut back the state sector and favor the private sector has been still-rising unemployment and underemployment. Yet, when I addressed the special obstacles confronting women in small industries and commerce with officials in the Ministry of the Economy who were dedicated to microenterprise development, few were interested in discussing the effects of current policy on these women. Heavier burdens at home, resulting from cuts in such areas as child care, health care, and education, were apparently invisible to the officials, just as the impact of a free market–oriented national economy was apparently invisible as a force driving women's small enterprises out of business. For officials, the "neutral" market may have allowed everyone to compete, but low-income women were finding that they did not share a level playing field.

The rapid decline of women's economic base has been in strong evidence in Managua these last few years. I have followed closely four urban cooperatives that were formed over the last decade in various parts of the city. These working groups were made up of seamstresses, welders, bakers, and artisans, traditional as well as nontraditional occupations for women. All of the seamstresses and welders were women, while both men and women were members of the bakers' and artisans' cooperatives. All of the cooperatives had to struggle to remain in business in the post-1990 period. Two of them, the seamstresses and the bakers, came together in the period soon after the Sandinistas rose to power and encouraged the collectivization of small industries. They organized service cooperatives in which members worked at home but had a central location for selling, holding

5. *Graffiti on a Managua street corner protesting the Occupational Conversion Plan.*

meetings, and other activities. However, by 1993, both co-ops were forced to sell their office spaces because they were unable to keep up payments. Declining sales of bread and locally produced clothing resulting from Nicaraguans' inability to afford even these basics and from changing economic conditions that favor imported goods and larger industries account for these developments. Individuals and families have continued to produce without the support of the cooperatives, but bread production is down as much as 50 percent and clothing production in the co-op I have followed and in many others has nearly ground to a halt.

The other two cooperatives have had somewhat different experiences. The group of women welders, formed in 1991 after a dozen housewives completed a ten-month training program, suffered a number of setbacks and then ceased to function altogether a couple of years later. Working together out of a workshop in a women's center in Managua, these women saw their membership drop steadily as a result of a number of problems, including interpersonal difficulties, resistance of husbands to their wives' working, and lack of steady work. Although they had a space in which to work, they could not be sure that it would remain available to them, making the absence of a secure work environment an issue for them as well. By early 1993, the women had disbanded their organization, and while some sought work elsewhere, others were once again at home with their families. One of the two former coordinators of the co-op, the only single woman in the group, was featured in a short newspaper story and, as a result, received offers to join a couple of male welders in their work. She was ready to join them, but a few months later she told me that opportunities had not come through as she had hoped. She was out of work for an extended period before finding a clerical job in a hospital. Interestingly, the other coordinator had the opportunity to go to the United States with a group of Nicaraguans for technical training funded by USAID, but I do not know what became of this select group.

The cooperative of artisans included several women and men making silver and coral jewelry and two women making decorative wall hangings and other items with bark from the *tuno* tree, found on the Atlantic coast of Nicaragua. The co-op, which was established in 1987, prides itself on its high-quality work. But members have experienced a severe drop in sales as the economy has worsened and as there have been fewer international visitors to buy from them. In 1992, the bark workers left the co-op for family reasons, one woman because her husband opposed her working and the other because she felt that her children needed more attention. Poor sales may well have contributed to their decisions, although this was not expressed directly. The cooperative can be considered successful despite its setbacks. After a long wait, it was able to secure a loan and a grant from a nongovernmental organization (NGO) to construct a spacious new workshop, which was completed in 1992. The co-op was also singled out as one of ten to receive extra support from the national association of small industries (CONAPI) to demonstrate to USAID the promise of small industries in the country. In recent years, the cooperative has sought new markets and tried out new creative techniques, but it is still unclear whether it will succeed in the long run.

The measures that have been imposed since 1990 in Nicaragua follow the same formula applied in other Latin American countries in the last ten years, but the impact may be greater. Mandated by the World Bank and the IMF, administered by USAID, and facilitated by local actors, the neoliberal plan has been set in place more quickly in Nicaragua, with harsher consequences for the majority of the population in small industries and businesses who cannot compete with large industries or with newly imported goods flooding the market. Moreover, the safety net of subsidized production provided under the Sandinista government was eliminated so quickly that even smaller industries with competitive potential have not survived long. To be sure, the government's political negotiations with oppositional groups of the elite as well as the popular sectors have modified the course of neoliberalism in postrevolutionary Nicaragua. Still-mobilized mass organizations and independent movements have won concessions in the areas of worker participation, restraints on repression, protection of the state sector, and ongoing discussions of a national social contract (*concertación*) (Spalding 1994).

For many of those whose businesses have failed or whose jobs in the public sector have been eliminated, the only option is to seek work in the informal sector of small-scale manufacturing, commerce, and services. My research in a Managua barrio encompassed a mix of low-income merchants, artisans, and service workers, as well as a number of professionals who work in a range of activities. I interviewed barrio leaders and middle-class individuals, but I focused on low-income members of the community who were not in leadership positions. Gender and class transected, as many were women in informal employment, unregulated and unprotected, working out of their homes and earning a marginal income. A good number, including some who adopted the Occupational Conversion Plan, had set up front-room stores, but there is such an abundance of these small stores that few do much business. Many women told me of the difficulty they were having feeding their families and meeting other expenses. They spoke of having to "stretch, stretch, stretch" their earnings and of struggling "to survive."

When formal sector employment and child care are scarce, working informally out of their homes may allow women to integrate household and economic responsibilities, an advantage despite low earnings. Notably, these women are also able to straddle the domestic and public spheres, as they literally occupy places at the threshold, in the doorways of their homes. However, according to the Nicaraguan analyst Paola Pérez Alemán (1992), this gendered practice may be enforced by changes in the country's labor code: "[It] institutionalizes the differences between the public and the private spheres, and most importantly it assigns roles for each sex."

A reform of the penal, civil, and labor codes in 1992 introduced a number of measures that contradicted the Nicaraguan Constitution approved by the Sandinista government in 1987. The new penal code reasserts women's primary role in the home and in childbearing. At one extreme, although rape has been made a public crime, the law forces women who have become pregnant as a result of rape to have the child. The law also prohibits sexual relations that are not heterosexual, denying human rights to gay men and lesbians and seeking to enforce normative sexuality. There are a number of forces at play that attempt to limit women's and sexual minorities' participation in public life, although the outcome is unclear, as these groups are resisting and demanding greater entry in social spaces.

Social Spaces and Social Movements

In the years since the 1990 election, an autonomous feminist movement has emerged in Nicaragua. As one activist recently described it, following the electoral defeat, "AMNLAE suffered a crisis, but the movement diversified as the various trends and ideas that had not fit within the organization began to act" (Alemán and Miranda 1993: 23). When AMNLAE did not carry through on the agreement to renew and democratize the women's movement, a number of feminists turned away to build a more diverse and independent movement. Signaling that decision, the Festival of the 52 Percent (referring to women in Nicaragua's population) was held in honor of International Women's Day in March 1991 as an alternative to participating in AMNLAE's national congress.

When I attended this weekend festival, I discovered a vital gathering of representatives of women's centers and organizations, artisans' collectives, and theater and arts groups, among others. Many women from Managua attended, but women came from throughout the country to display their work and share information and ideas. I met women from two of the four cooperatives that I mentioned earlier. High anticipation permeated the three-day event, which took place on the city's central fairgrounds, and it has since been regarded as a turning point in feminist organizing in Nicaragua. The women had clearly staked their ground and claimed a new social space in which to build a movement.

The energy of the festival carried over to plans for a national gathering, or encuentro, called for January 1992. The goal was to bring women from around the country, independent of political affiliation, for three days of

6. *Former President Daniel Ortega sits among a group of women leaders at the* AMNLAE *national congress in 1991.*

workshops and discussions. While the organizers expected a few hundred women, more than eight hundred registered and the meeting was moved to Managua's largest convention center, making a powerful public statement. The theme of the meeting was "Unity in Diversity," and this determination to join across differences characterized the event. Well-known activists and writers mixed with *campesinas*, women from the countryside, who had never before traveled to Managua. We divided into six working groups; the most popular ones focused on the economy and the environment, sexuality, and violence against women. The working groups produced assessments of the situation facing women and concrete proposals for action. At the conclusion of the encuentro, networks were formed to address specific issues. These networks have continued to shape the women's movement, and through them women have gained access to public spaces, including the media.

Coming out of a decade of revolutionary practice, it is not surprising that these women took a long historical view of their current situation. Whether examining the effects of the economic crisis on their lives or the increasing

7. Participants at the women's national Encuentro ("Unity in Diversity") held in Managua in 1992.

reports of violence against women, they traced the problems over the last decade or more and sought to find connections among many apparently disparate questions. For example, in the working group on the economy, women spoke about the psychological cost of the economic crisis, especially for women and children. At a plenary session, the group considering violence against women was called on to expand their notion of violence to include the stress experienced by mothers of heroes and martyrs of the revolution. And, when it was proposed that sexuality is an aspect of all human relationships, participants in the working group on sexuality debated the breadth of the definition of sexuality they would advance.

Another encuentro, this time of women from all of Central America, met in the Pacific Coast resort of Montelimar in March 1992 to prepare for the Sixth Encuentro of Latin American and Caribbean Feminists, which would be held in El Salvador in November 1993. The meeting was charged with the enthusiasm of women who understood the historical significance of this largest of encuentros that would be hosted in Central America for the first time. As Central America is often regarded as a cultural backwater, the strong presence of feminism in the region would dispel some long-held assumptions (Babb 1997b).

During this time, Nicaraguan women representing more than twenty feminist collectives and the networks discussed above formed the National Feminist Committee (CNF). They began working toward the continental encuentro as well as a number of local projects. When they organized activities for International Women's Day in 1993, they focused on the recent setbacks to women's rights as the legislature revised the penal, civil, and labor codes in ways often disadvantageous to women. On March 8, the symbolic burning of these codes at a march and rally expressed the women's rejection of national legislation that "legitimates a discriminatory and sexist society, despite the equality mandated by the Political Constitution" (Alemán 1993: 19).

In more recent years, there have been advances as well as growing pains in the women's movement. Disagreements over political strategy caused the CNF to dissolve in the mid-1990s, but it geared up again during the emergency period following Hurricane Mitch. In contrast to earlier efforts to develop a national feminist agenda, most activity now takes place within smaller groups. The well-funded NGO Puntos de Encuentro (Encounter Points) offers a broad-based approach to research and activism embracing gender, class, race, and other inequalities, while Las Malinches (The Malinches, named for the legendary Indian woman in Mexican history) tends toward a vanguardist, intellectual feminist approach and plays a leadership role in the CNF and the Central American coalition of feminist groups, La Corriente (The Current). The networks continue to be a vital part of ongoing activity, focusing on women's health, reproductive rights, and the campaign against violence.

Just as the feminist movement has grown and seized social space in the years since the election, so has the gay and lesbian movement (and there is considerable overlap in the movements, with women playing a prominent role in both). Although there were private gatherings during the years of the Sandinista government, the party discouraged efforts of gay men and lesbians to claim a public space. The silencing was effective until 1991, when several groups organized and planned the first public celebration of gay pride in Nicaragua. A large cross section of Managua's population turned out for an evening event that featured a film, music and dance, and a panel discussion on the experiences of gay-identified Nicaraguans. The following year, the government's decision to reactivate a repressive sodomy law prohibiting nonheterosexual relations galvanized much of the discussion and debate during several weeks of events held in recognition of the country's gay and lesbian community. By 1993, an entire month of activity was planned, and gay and lesbian organizations continued to grow. Gay groups won public space in the form of several centers concerned with health, sexuality, and AIDS education and also of gay bars for socializing. A frequently heard slogan, "For a sexuality free of prejudice," captured the spirit of the movement: men and women called for equal rights and freedom of expression and linked these rights to broad goals of human liberation. Like feminist activism, lesbian and gay activism has in recent years taken the form of working in small groups, addressing AIDS, homophobia, and human rights. These are recent developments that have only begun to be noticed by writers documenting political change in Nicaragua (Ferguson 1991; Lancaster 1992; Randall 1992, 1993; Thayer 1997).[9]

Toward a New Cultural Politics

In light of the current cultural, political, and economic reconfigurations in Nicaragua, it is not surprising that more analysts are going beyond narrowly applied political economic models to examine cultural questions as well.[10] In 1996, even as the country was consumed by interest in the upcoming presidential election, many Nicaraguans emphasized the urgency of addressing such "cultural" matters as the resolution of conflict in the north of the country—where rearmed groups of former Contras and Sandinista peasants were pressing the government to respond to their demands for land—as well as democratization and the extension of rights to the entire population, before any new economic model or political orientation could be effective. Those who had long been committed to the Sandinista revolution were calling for a new "culture" of peace and reconciliation. As the historian and former adviser to the FSLN government, Alejandro Bendaña, told me, "Neoliberalism fragments society and the question is how people regroup to struggle" (interview, July 3, 1996). He pointed to instances of cultural affirmation, noting that the cultural struggles of indigenous people, environmentalists, and women are offering rich alternatives. He credited the Nicaraguan experience of revolution with enabling some members of society to sustain a consciousness that could democratize the country.

The concern to examine questions of national and cultural identity in a country that has been deeply divided along ethnic lines between the Pacific and Atlantic Coasts as well as along the lines of class, gender, and political orientation is apparent in the current outpouring of literature on the subject. Such recent titles as *Nosotros los nicaragüenses* (We, the Nicaraguans) (Solorzano 1995) and *Identidad y crisis* (Identity and Crisis)(Fundación Internacional "Rubén Darío" 1995) suggest the intense interest among Nicaraguans in such critical self-reflection. One anthology presented the proceedings of a conference on nationalism and identity organized by Nicaragua's Institute of History (Tijerino 1995). Its editor reflected on Nicaraguan identity in relation to democratic reconciliation and national development. She went on to criticize the earlier notion that cultural diversity stood in the way of "modernization," and called for dialogue across differences. The Marxist economist Peter Marchetti (1995), among others, referred to national identity as the key question that emerged at the end of the century and that was likely to remain key in the next decades. He argued that addressing issues of both identity and economic development will be fundamental in Nicaragua if it is to meet the needs of its diverse population.

Recent anthropological research in Nicaragua has brought together analyses of changing political economies and shifting cultural meanings and identities, with attention to gender and sexuality (Higgins and Coen 1992; Lancaster 1992; Field 1999). This approach appears to reflect both the transformed landscape of Nicaraguan culture and politics and the intellectual movement toward pluralist interpretations of history and society. A number of writers have observed that in Latin America generally, many who have been affected most harshly by recent policies are beginning to negotiate the terms of their wider participation in society through forms of collective action (e.g., Escobar 1992: 83).

In Nicaragua, the highly integrated nature of seemingly disparate developments has been evident in the 1990s: the economic crisis, UNO government infighting and political dislocations on the Left, and ideology veering farther to the right under Alemán's Liberal Alliance government, on the one hand, and the emergence of autonomous movements claiming social space, on the other. To account for these related though somewhat contradictory developments we must turn to the historical conjuncture of events following the 1990 elections. First, the Sandinistas' loss brought not only an abrupt political transition but also a more reflective period for the FSLN; forced to acknowledge past errors of a top-down leadership, the party opened the way for more independent organizing. Second, it may be precisely in the context of desperately difficult times that Nicaraguans are seeking not only new lives but also new meanings by which to apprehend their lives. Putting forward gender and sexuality, as well as race and class, as key elements in a new oppositional political agenda is a way that subaltern groups have resisted the conservative government ideology and found openings for collective expressions of identity.

Not all Nicaraguan activists would agree with the weight given to issues of gender and power, however. Women active in the FSLN through AMNLAE and the sectoral organizations sometimes dismiss the issues as irrelevant to peasant women or urban market women (Quandt 1993: 13). Rita Fletes, president of the national marketers' association, former vice coordinator of AMNLAE, and the second woman nominated in Managua as a deputy of the FSLN, was among those who were critical of feminism in the past. But when I spoke with her in 1996, she volunteered a different opinion. A few years ago she thought that feminists offered little to women of the popular classes, whose main concerns were their families and their work, but now she believes that the groups that have emerged since 1990 bring something important to these women as well. She noted that it is necessary to respect diversity and that a coalition of women across political parties could promote women's multiclass interests (Rita Fletes, interview, July 8, 1996). Such a shift in thinking about the complex relationship of gender and class has been evident in the post-Sandinista period.

Of course, debates over the relevance of feminism to women of different social and economic backgrounds are as well known in Nicaragua as elsewhere. Notable in recent years have been the diverse groups of Nicaraguan women — not only privileged middle-class women — who have called for an end to domestic violence, unequal gender relations at home and at work, and subordination under the law. Well-attended workshops addressing these issues in Managua's neighborhood women's centers testify to the broad base of concern. Indeed, the widely felt need to coordinate work on "women's issues" in a feminist context inspired the National Feminist Committee to organize in 1992. Even so, the CNF disbanded two years later when class differences and disagreements over feminist practice produced a split (the FSLN party was dividing into two tendencies at about the same time).

Some of the groups formerly in the CNF, those more closely linked to the popular sectors, later organized a new feminist alliance (*Barricada Internacional* 1995: 17–24). The Hurricane Mitch crisis brought groups back to the CNF, but at least one major feminist NGO, Puntos de Encuentro, chose to remain apart. Given these recent cleavages, it might reasonably be asked whether those Nicaraguans experiencing the sharpest economic and political dislocations and those most active in social movements are in the main nonoverlapping groups, marked by class differences. To a degree there appear to be differences, with intellectuals and middle-class individuals playing some key roles in emergent movements, and certainly the poorest individuals may have too little time and too little hope to be politically active. Nevertheless, Nicaraguans from the working-class and popular sectors participate in various activities and hold leadership positions in a number of women's centers. My research offers some additional examples of women's grassroots participation in social movements, including the women of two Managua cooperatives whom I met first at the Festival of the 52 Percent. Other examples are the urban and rural workers who attended the encuentros; the artisans and market women who participated in a women's center's workshops on domestic violence; the co-op women who joined the feminist and gay communities as they mobilized to challenge the sodomy law; and the women of a sewing cooperative who demonstrated both entrepreneurship and solidarity as they designed T-shirts protesting the five hundredth anniversary celebration of the Spanish conquest of Latin America. Finally, the International Women's Day marches and feminist networks have drawn women from diverse social backgrounds in recent years.

Returning to a point made earlier, I do not want to suggest any new dichotomy whereby political activities in some arenas "count" more than others. As several other writers have noted for Latin America generally, women practice politics and construct new identities in multiple sites, from the family and household to workplaces and the streets (Westwood and Radcliffe 1993: 20). In Nicaragua, current struggles over space are at once political, social, and discursive negotiations over material resources and cultural meanings, and these struggles have no fixed forms or locations. Women workers in urban cooperatives defend their work spaces in order to make their livelihood, while feminist activists take over Managua's largest convention center to convene a national gathering. I have suggested that these are not unrelated phenomena; indeed, they arise from the same current conditions, and there are indications that the more "cultural" movements are breathing new life into ongoing struggles for economic and social justice.

Since 1990 in Nicaragua, there are clear signs that women and other subaltern groups are turning practices honed through more than a decade of revolutionary activity toward collective negotiations over social and political space. In the climate of present-day Nicaragua, despite a repressive economy and national ideology, new alignments and alliances are forming that promise — as feminists have stated — to construct a new way of doing politics and, indeed, a new political culture. Without underestimating the current context of economic despair, the political shift to the right as governments embrace neoliberalism, and the ideological campaign for traditional family values that portrays women workers and activists as "unnatural," there is still reason to expect that emergent social movements in the country will build on new understandings and cultural meanings to enter social spaces that are only now beginning to open.

Chapter Three

"MANAGUA IS NICARAGUA"

Gender, Memory, and Cultural Politics

LATIN AMERICA is often said to receive attention from the United States only when there is a revolution or natural disaster.[1] Nicaragua has experienced both in its recent history, with a significant impact on its capital city, Managua. The Sandinista revolution brought about a process of progressive social transformation in the small Central American country, while earthquakes, volcanoes, and hurricanes have wrought untold destruction there and in neighboring countries in the last decades. The earthquake in 1972 destroyed most of Managua, leaving it a wasteland. Hurricane Joan in 1988 targeted the Atlantic Coast and Hurricane Mitch ten years later concentrated losses in the northwest. Even so, the capital felt the effects of the most recent disaster as the cost of food and other goods continued to escalate because of damaged crops and as many who were homeless and without productive land migrated there in search of shelter and livelihood. National recovery has been painfully slow, and, as usual, women and the poor bear the major responsibility of caring for families in the most precarious circumstances.

In the course of these natural disasters, Nicaraguans have suffered further when governments have failed to respond adequately to crisis conditions. Under the current presidency of Arnoldo Alemán, just as under the Somoza dictatorship that preceded the revolutionary government, deeply entrenched poverty and willful mismanagement have made economic recovery a near-impossibility. Neoliberal policies of structural adjustment mandated by the International Monetary Fund and the World Bank had already cut sharply into social spending, adversely affecting education and health care as well as the country's infrastructure. Now, without a safety net, the majority of those affected face unbearable hardship. Alemán had built his political reputation in the early 1990s as mayor of Managua on projects to modernize the capital city, but populist rhetoric notwithstanding, his attention focused on the interests of the elite. His strongest allies were returning Miami exiles and members of the conservative hierarchy of the Catholic Church. After his election to the presidency in 1996, he applied the same neoliberal development model to the country as a whole — although still concentrating on the capital and giving less attention to the rural areas.

It warrants mentioning here that Managua is certainly not Nicaragua. The title of this chapter is taken from a report prepared in 1984 by Nicaragua's Center for the Study of Agrarian Reform (CIERA). "Managua es Nicaragua" referred to the city as a window through which to view the long history of national development as well as underdevelopment. During the Sandinista decade, efforts to bring about social and economic transformation were in many instances directed to the rural areas but impeded by urban interests. Managua's relationship to the country as a whole was seen as paramount and as mediating Nicaragua's relationship with the rest of the world. The rapidly growing city has had a commanding — sometimes dominating — presence as the product of twentieth-century agrarian capitalism's failure to modernize Nicaragua. As the CIERA report states: "In this double sense (as expression of the past and determination of the future), Managua is Nicaragua" (1984: 3; my translation).[2]

Yet the widely held view that Managua's relationship to the rest of Nicaragua has been detrimental, that it has stood in the way of national devel-

8. *The silhouette of Sandino looks out over the Intercontinental Hotel, two contrasting icons in Managua.*

opment, should be countered with a more balanced perspective. A good deal of concern arises from the rapid pace of urbanization, as those who leave the countryside for the city end up, most visibly although unofficially, in *asentamientos* (squatter settlements) and in the informal economy— contributing to the notion that city dwellers are parasites on the national economy and society. The loss of labor in the rural sector was a concern under the Sandinista government, which tried through agrarian reform to stem migration and increase national production of coffee, cotton, maize, and beans. But some of the revolutionary government's policies, for example, food price subsidies designed to benefit consumers, had the unintended effect of curtailing rural production and enticing more farmers to the city. So, although Managua has had a pivotal role in the political and economic geography of the country, it would be a mistake to hold the city responsible for recent structural problems of development (Massey 1987).

Cities have frequently borne the brunt of criticism for being unproductive drains on economies and even despised centers of corruption (Fincher and Jacobs 1998; Holston 1999). Under the Somoza dictatorship Managua earned a reputation as the playground of a small elite, but the Sandinistas did much to redistribute resources and alter historical inequalities. Now, a small but growing elite is again favored by a government inclined heavily toward rolling back the state sector and promoting the market economy. Managua is being remade to accommodate the consumption needs and desires of the wealthy, while the majority of the city's population is struggling to provide for themselves and their families in marginal, though productive, employment.[3] Ultimately, the government will be accountable for the deepening social problems and economic inequalities that are most painfully evident in the city.

After discussing the changing face of the city of Managua, this chapter considers how neoliberalism has altered the urban landscape in ways that are inflected by gender, class, and power. Even so, I point to some recent efforts to conceive a new urban political culture attentive to gender and power, which have come in response to the social economic reconfiguration of globalized post-Sandinista Nicaragua. By taking Managua as both a subject of study and the context for my research and by remaining mindful of the city's historical relationship to the rest of the country and the world, I suggest a way out of urban anthropology's conundrum as formulated by Richard Fox almost thirty years ago. In a landmark essay, Fox (1972: 205) wrote, "In much contemporary urban anthropology, the city only appears as a difficult, even hostile environment for impoverished, culturally distinctive and historyless populations." My work joins that of other anthropologists who are heeding his call for an approach that goes beyond the study of often-alienated or exotic subgroups of urban populations to embrace the city itself as a fundamental subject for research.

A City Forsaken

In Managua's well-known restaurant Los Antojitos, across the street from the exclusive Intercontinental Hotel, visitors are treated to panoramic photographs of Nicaragua's capital city before the earthquake drastically altered the urban landscape.[4] Tree-lined avenues and tall buildings marked the center of the city before it suffered one of the major disasters in our hemisphere in the twentieth century. Close to midnight on December 23,

Map 2. Managua and Its Barrios. (Monseñor Lezcano, discussed in Chapter 4, is shaded.)

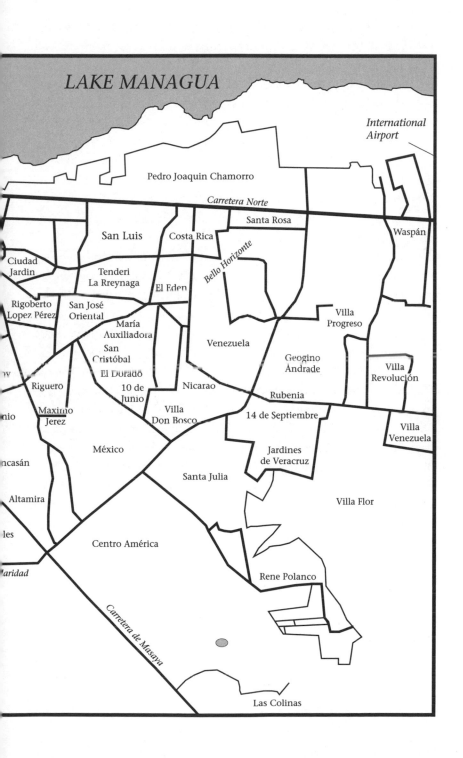

1972, the urban center was quickly turned to rubble and then fires spread. Estimates of lives lost ranged from ten thousand to twenty thousand of the city's four hundred thousand residents, and a majority of those who survived were left homeless. Eighty percent of urban structures were destroyed, including hospitals, schools, and other vital institutions (Gilbert 1988: 1–2). With Managua in shambles, the international aid that came in was substantially squandered by the Somoza government. Instead of rebuilding the city, funds were used to further enrich the dictatorship — and the limited reconstruction that took place was monopolized by the family's economic interests. Poor Nicaraguans, both urban and rural, became even more bitter about their country's state of affairs in light of such a heartless response to their misfortune.

Three decades after the earthquake destroyed it, the city has a feeling of structurelessness, with open spaces where there was once an urban core. Two principal roadways, named Resistencia and Solidaridad by the Sandinistas,[5] pass through neighborhoods that are spread out in a broad semicircle around the ruins of the old city. Other roads radiate from the old center and intersect with the major roadways. The main arteries in and out of the city, the North and South Highways, form part of the Pan-American Highway. Located below sea level in the Pacific region, Managua is surrounded by the country's famous lakes and volcanoes. Lake Managua is its northern limit, while the volcanic Momotombo presents an impressive backdrop. The generally hot, tropical climate of Managua is relieved only by rains between May and October. Although surrounded by lakes, Managua lacks water and must take precautions against its contamination. Until very recently, much of the city has gone without water for a couple of days each week; the poor majority, if they have piped water, hoard barrels of it, while those who are wealthier have their own water pumps and avoid the inconvenience. Like water, electricity is unreliable and in short supply, and power outages are common, especially in poor and working-class neighborhoods. For many in the barrios, the costs of these utilities are prohibitive even when they are available.

Managua's population, which expanded during the Sandinista period as a result of migration due to the Contra war as well as internal growth, rose to over one million, or a third of the national population, by the 1990s. The squatter settlements where most of the recent arrivals live ring the city and lack basic services. Often, great efforts are made by residents to secure housing titles in order to safeguard their property. Even the more established barrios have a confusing appearance to the untrained eye, although their streets are typically laid out in square blocks known as *manzanas*, together forming different neighborhoods. Residents give directions in relation to Lake Managua (north) and by reference to going up (east) or down (west), counting the number of manzanas from well-known landmarks. Sometimes they refer to landmarks that have not existed since the earthquake ("where the little tree was") or to places that shut down long ago but are still remembered ("the León movie theater"), presenting a challenge to newcomers.

The Sandinistas had been determined to make basic resources available to the broad population in Nicaragua and, later, to defend the revolution. Urban renewal was not a priority, but efforts were made to transform cities through popular culture, most dramatically through the painting of colorful murals in Managua and elsewhere. Parks were established in honor of revolutionary heroes and martyrs, streets and plazas were renamed to commemorate the triumph, and so were central places like the international airport, renamed for the national hero Augusto César Sandino. But the old streets paved with traditional hexagonal bricks (*adoquines*), torn up to form barricades during the insurrection, went unrepaired and potholes were rampant. By and large, Nicaraguans were patient during those years, when basic needs took precedence over improvements in infrastructure.

With the electoral victory of Violeta Chamorro and the UNO coalition, a conciliatory presidency made concessions to the Left while welcoming neoliberalism to Nicaragua. During the early 1990s, Managua's mayor, Arnoldo Alemán, embraced the new orientation and won approval for carrying out public works projects in the city. Potholes were filled and new traffic circles and fountains were constructed. The so-called Miami boys returned to Nicaragua to open new restaurants, well-stocked supermarkets, and other establishments. Four-wheel-drive vehicles crowded Managua's already congested streets, while vendors (many of them women and children) were forced away from some busy intersections and began lining the highways leading into and out of the city.

Many of the murals, a hallmark of the revolutionary era, were systematically painted over, obliterated, stripping the city of its only color and popular expression of hope. Under Alemán's orders, city workers participated in a campaign against the popular symbolism of the revolution. A North American scholar writing about the murals lamented:

> None are now safe, despite the law passed by the Sandinista government just before leaving office, declaring as many murals (and martyr monuments) as they could name to be historic patrimony, and therefore untouchable. The murals are a narrative of a revolutionary convulsion the very memory of which the new government wishes to wipe out. (Kunzle 1995: 13)

Just after the UNO government was installed, it erased other symbols of the continued strength of the Sandinista Party. The huge letters FSLN set in stone on a hillside visible from Managua were changed to FIN (end—i.e., of Sandinismo) and then erased completely. A monument commemorating the FSLN founder and martyr Carlos Fonseca first saw its flame extinguished and then the tomb was bombed. Portraits of heroes of the revolution were removed from ministries and other public sites, replaced by photographs of President Chamorro (Kunzle 1995: 14). While mayor, it was politically impossible for Alemán to remove the towering statue of Sandino that dominates the Managua skyline, but he proposed the construction of another icon, a monolithic statue of the Virgin Mary that would stand as a rebuke to the remaining Sandinista monuments. This $5 million project was met with great protest, however, by urban residents who felt the money should be spent on such urgent needs as housing for the homeless. Another of the mayor's projects, to build a huge new cathedral with millions of dollars contributed by Domino Pizza heir Tom Monaghan, went forward after it was met with even louder protest by those who viewed its construction as a thinly veiled effort to impose a post-Sandinista national myth and as an affront to those most affected by economic hardship. In contrast to the solidarity of popular religion and the Christian base communities (CEBs, or lay groups that preached a "social gospel"), the established Catholic Church hierarchy that supported the project was demonstrably insensitive to the cathedral's reception (Linkogle 1996: 220–21).

In the midst of such controversy, large signs assaulted residents and visitors to the city, proclaiming that in the new Managua "The Mayor Gets Things Done" and "Everything Is Changing." Despite Alemán's well-known reputation for corruption, many Managuans were drawn into the

9. *Managua's new cathedral.*

clientelistic bargain of political loyalty in exchange for small improvements
or signs of action, even if the charismatic mayor was unable to truly erase
evidence of continued suffering in the city. All around Managua were pro-
nouncements of the generous funding supplied by the U. S. Agency for International Development for the construction of plazas and parks. Close
observers might also note the scrawled graffiti of those less taken with cos-
metic changes and with the neoliberal turn of government. One wall carried the message, "ESAF = *hambre*," or the structural adjustment program
imposed by the IMF means hunger. Such were the everyday contrasts in
Managua in the 1990s.

The 1996 election of Alemán as president was not surprising given the
success of his urban "cleanup" campaign and the fragmented state of the
Sandinista opposition. Whereas Violeta Chamorro's government sought to
assuage conflict and cultivate the support of the Sandinistas by taking a
middle road, Alemán's Liberal Alliance signaled a more significant turn to
the right. Economic adjustments and political conservatism have meant
worsening conditions for the majority of Nicaraguans. In Managua an estimated 60 percent are unemployed or underemployed. Yet in this period
of shifting alliances, an unholy pact has been established between Alemán,

10. *Graffiti reads "ESAF = Hambre" (ESAF means Hunger).*

widely regarded as the most corrupt of presidents, and Daniel Ortega, whose personal and political reputation has been seriously damaged since his stepdaughter's public allegations of sexual abuse cast doubt on his moral character.[6]

The neoliberal desire to attract foreign investment and cater to middle-class longings is on dramatic display in the changing face of the city. The urban center had remained a void along the earthquake's fault line, but Alemán's stunning project as mayor had been the monstrous new cathedral of stark gray concrete in the forsaken area, its roof of immense spheres clashing perversely with the rectangular slab of the steeple and its interior a garish and jarring mix of bright colors. As president, he was determined to create a city center adjacent to it. Now, a huge traffic circle enhanced with fountains and colored lights stands as a monument to modernity. Alongside it, a commercial mall and a tourist hotel have been constructed. With streets renamed once again, to erase memories of the revolutionary past, there is a great confusion of names and places in the city. One barrio that had been named for a Sandinista martyr was given its prerevolution-ary name, Salvadorita, after the dictator Anastasio Somoza's mother. People resist the erasures by describing locations as "donde fue," where something was before, and by continuing to use names assigned during the revolutionary decade. Some NGOs, women's health clinics, and political offices are maintaining oppositional identities by creating new murals at their centers, but for the most part, urban popular culture has been eclipsed.[7]

Neoliberalism and the Urban Landscape: Gender, Class, and Power

Nicaragua currently faces the dilemma of other Latin American countries following the neoliberal development model. As expressed in a recent report of the research center Nitlapán (*Envío* 1998a: 5), "The dilemma is this: Nicaragua either resolves its poverty building respected institutions and democracy or else anti-democratic authoritarianism will drag it into a bottomless pit of misery, backwardness and social decomposition." Under the Sandinistas, the country was already experiencing great difficulties as the Contra war endured and the state-planned economy depended heavily on subsidies to prop up national production. In 1990, the UNO government introduced structural adjustment measures in a market-driven economy that emphasized export production and cuts in social spending. At the time, Chamorro's government insisted that although the adjustment would be "painful," the country would "get well and soon would be fine" (ibid.: 7). The Liberal Party government of Alemán has continued the same policies, only more ruthlessly, and poverty has deepened.

What has neoliberalism meant for Managua, and how are gender and class differences manifest in the present urban context? As public sector employment was cut back after the 1990 elections, Sandinistas, women among them, were especially affected. The conservative political climate has put pressure on women to leave formal sector jobs and return home, even when most of them must provide for their families' livelihood. Under the government plan, many state employees in Managua accepted severance pay and began to sell items informally from their homes. Thus a result of neoliberal economic policy is that more women are out of the paid workforce and seeking informal sources of income. Ironically, the expansion of the informal sector is regarded as a national problem rather than as a survival strategy for individuals lacking alternatives.

The absence of women in state sector employment is part of a broader departure of women from public culture. Women had been actively organized into urban cooperatives under the Sandinistas, but the neoliberal favoring of larger economic interests and export manufacturing took a heavy toll on these smaller industries, which often employ only about ten workers. While some cooperatives have been refashioned as microenterprises that are more congenial to the market economy, many others have failed. Of the four cooperatives with strong membership by women that I followed through the 1990s, two are closed: the bakers' co-op closed, leaving bakeries to fend for themselves, and the welders' group disbanded because of lack of work and "husbands' jealousy" of their wives' working. The artisans, who viewed their cooperative increasingly as "a museum artifact" in the market economy, sought a new identity as an association of independent producers working under one roof. The last cooperative, seamstresses who sewed at home and then sold their clothing and held meetings in a central place, had lost their lease and continued as a co-op in name only out of loyalty. When I returned to Managua after six months away and looked for the women in their store on the edge of the sprawling Eastern Market, I found that the place had simply vanished. The facade was entirely gone, incorporated in the newly enlarged storefront of a neighboring business.

Erasures of women's spaces in the city were increasingly common as opportunities to participate in the wider economy began to shrink. While women were less active in the formal sector, their presence in informal trades (often hidden from view) and even begging (in public) was greater. One area of girls' and women's involvement that has expanded during the last decade is prostitution. It is not unusual to see young women on the streets near the Intercontinental Hotel late at night and on streets near the main post office at midday. A young mother I had known for some time (and discuss further in the next chapter) appeared to be dressed for this line of work when I saw her during a recent visit, although I could not bring myself to ask her about it directly. She told me that she irons clothes and cleans for a neighbor several times a week, but that would hardly support her family. Meanwhile, boys and men using drugs and in gangs are seen more often on the streets and crime is rampant in the barrios, making the city more dangerous for women as well as for men.[8] In Managua, as conditions produced by neoliberalism leave people with few alternatives, life is indeed hard.[9]

In a city in which almost half the households are headed by women, gender differences in family responsibilities are marked. Education and health care costs are out of reach for many because of privatization and spending cuts, with the result that women have even greater demands on them at home as they pick up the slack of reduced state support. Traditional family values are invoked to shore up the need for private services provided by women who are increasingly removed from the dominant public culture. New school texts produced with USAID funds and introduced during the UNO government's first year endorsed legal marriage and opposed abortion, presenting elementary students with images of mothers caring for families while fathers were out working. The following year, the government's Occupational Conversion Plan cut back on state sector employment and encouraged the proliferation of small family businesses, disproportionately affecting women workers, many of whom began selling items from their homes. The Latin American invocation of the *casa/calle* (house/street) dichotomy, whereby to be respectable women must remain in the private sphere while men may range widely in the public sphere, has made its return to Managua.[10] In the current context of escalating crime and violence in the city, it is notable that families of even modest means are putting up iron bars on windows and doors, and women lock themselves in their homes for their own protection. Unfortunately, recent reports suggest that domestic violence is so prevalent that one in three women in the country is affected, so the home may be no refuge for women.[11]

As other scholars of Latin America have noted (e.g., Radcliffe and Westwood 1996: 134–40), discourses of democracy and nationhood are frequently gendered and claims to citizenship are distinct for women and men. Social movements and political upheavals have often provided the context for renegotiating gender and sexual identities, and these are inflected by race and class differences as national identities are constituted. Thus the Sandinista revolution incorporated women as militants and as mothers of heroes and martyrs and later brought women into 30 percent of the elected positions in the FSLN. This gave women greater access to the public sphere, yet stopped short of transforming gender relations in the family and society. The UNO's conservative gender ideology reinscribed traditional family values, although in a situation that necessarily depends on many women seeking work outside the home. While Violeta Chamorro represented a woman firmly committed to family as wife (she is the widow of the martyr Pedro Joaquín Chamorro), as mother, and, finally, as a maternal figure as president, the inability of most Nicaraguan women to match the ideal of remaining home with family has never been more apparent. Indeed, many women are actively resisting that ideal after a decade of social mobilization under the Sandinistas and with the further support of a growing feminist movement.

Cultural Politics: Shifting Terrain

In recent years, neoliberalism and globalization have brought about notable physical changes in Managua, accompanied by deeper changes in the national political economy and in gender and class relations. Differential access to space and place is more pronounced as the city develops areas that are essentially off-limits to women and low-income people. Jobs are harder to find, street vendors are unable to sell at traffic circles, modern supermarkets carry luxury goods that only the wealthy can afford, and restaurants and entertainment centers cater to the elite. Furthermore, as David Kunzle writes of the last administration:

> How does the UNO government imagine the visual environment of a Nicaragua "rescued" from Sandinista "tyranny"? What new artistic policy is now being offered? A dismally familiar and aesthetically degraded commercial one. Miami is now the model, the true cultural capital of Nicaragua. All the old revolutionary and public-service billboards are gone, swallowed by a forest of commercial advertisement sprouting up everywhere in Managua — even obscuring famous viewpoints — as a veneer of petty enterprise fueled from the United States spreads over generalized and deepening poverty. (1995: 24)

This point is illustrated in the present period of the Alemán presidency by the gala opening of a McDonald's restaurant (Grant Gallup pers. com. 1998). Located at the new Güegüense traffic circle, surrounded by figures of indigenous men in loincloths, the hamburger restaurant's grand opening was attended with fanfare by distinguished guests, including the country's vice president, and by Ronald McDonald, whose arrival shut down the international airport briefly to other travelers. Ironically, the vice president announced that with the opening of McDonald's, "Nicaragua is taking off its loincloth," a candidly racist (and sexist) reference to the nation's indige-

11. McDonald's restaurant lies adjacent to the recently constructed Plaza Güegüense (formerly, Plaza España).

nous peoples, their culture, and their own fast food such as *baho* (a traditional rural dish popular in the city).[12]

The shopping center in the new downtown area, the Metrocentro Commercial Complex, carries clothing manufactured by Perry Ellis and Calvin Klein and has such stores as Benetton, Guess, Levi's, and the Gap. In the mall, a coffee cart serves espresso and capuccino. But there were few shoppers when I visited, and certainly very few Nicaraguan women I know could dream of paying the prices in the stores. Less than a month after Hurricane Mitch devastated the country, one Nicaraguan newspaper proclaimed:

To speak of economic growth, there must be palpable proof that demonstrates the improved economic conditions of a society. And in Nicaragua, the grand opening of the Metrocentro Commercial Complex is a good example of this. . . . The installation of famous international franchises supports that evidence. . . . The effects caused by the devastating power of Mitch can be mitigated by construction such as this, providing a response to the demands for recreation and relaxation — now offered in Metrocentro, all under the same roof. (Rocha 1998: 49; translated from *La Tribuna*, November 26, 1998)

Thus a shopping mall is configured as offering welcome relief from the country's grim everyday realities. Yet as the city center is remade to satisfy the desires of a small elite clientele, a far greater number of women will be found stretching their slight earnings in crowded marketplaces in outlying areas of Managua.

Other changes are occurring in the city to erase the memory of the revolution. Not surprisingly, Plaza de la Revolución (still the site of large Sandinista gatherings each year) has been renamed Plaza de la República. And Alemán issued a decree to rename the national baseball stadium, since 1979 named for the hero who took the life of the first Somoza family dictator, after Denis Martínez, the Nicaraguan-born pitcher who made it to the U.S. major leagues. More surprising, Alemán also declared that a monument to Augusto César Sandino would be erected on the edge of Managua in honor of the revolutionary hero's defense of national sovereignty in the early part of this century. This appropriation, perhaps intended to make Sandino safe for national consumption, was met by silence among the FSLN leadership. Meanwhile, the president's predilection for grandiose projects resulted in the construction of the John Paul II Plaza of Faith, the largest plaza in Central America, as well as a new presidential palace in the ruins left by the earthquake. The palace, built at a cost of several million dollars donated by the government of Taiwan, along with a new three-tiered fountain whose jets of water correspond to computerized musical melodies, was inaugurated at the turn of the millennium (*Envío* 1999a: 28–31).

That women are experiencing the particularly harsh effects of current economic conditions is readily apparent, but the ways in which gender and social class figure in the context of neoliberalism are also revealed in the cultural climate. One of the first policy measures taken by the Sandinista government was the official elimination of sexism in advertising, but early in the 1990s women's bodies were once again on public display on city billboards and in newspapers and magazines. Ads for the Nicaraguan beers Toña and Victoria were notorious for equating women with thirst-quenching "blonde" and "dark" alcoholic beverages. Beauty pageant photos and reportage often made the front page of the national newspapers (including the Sandinista *Barricada*), and the right-wing daily *La Prensa* hailed the Miss Nicaragua beauty pageant as the most important cultural event of the year, commenting that this is "possible only in a real democracy" (1991; quoted in Kunzle 1995: xv).[13] In 1998, Casa Ave María, where I have stayed in recent years, experienced a major fire. The damage included the marring of murals in an indoor patio by a well-known artist depicting heroic women in the country. Whether the cause of the fire was accidental, stemming from faulty wiring, or vandalism, another monument to the revolution (and one of the few dedicated to women) suffered; in this case, fortunately, recon-struction prevented the spread of cultural amnesia that has descended on the country.

The annual festival of Managua's patron saint, Santo Domingo, enacts race relations and the trauma of the Conquest and also serves to illustrate a recent cultural contestation over urban space that is inflected by social class and gender.[14] The most widely celebrated festival in Managua, Santo Do-mingo begins on the evening of July 31 when crowds gather at Las Sierritas Church in the outskirts of Managua, where the small statue of the saint re-sides. After a night of dancing and drinking, the statue of Santo Domingo is taken from the church and carried through the city to Santo Domingo Church, where it remains for ten days. During that period, there are masses and festivities until the statue is returned to Las Sierritas Church. In 1992, fifty thousand people accompanied the statue on its journey between the churches and across Managua. Regarded as a saint of the common people, Santo Domingo attracts a boisterous, costumed following, who take plea-sure in smearing grease on unwitting bystanders, particularly if they appear to be of privileged classes ("tarring" is a reference to African slaves who came to Nicaragua — thus there is a racialized element in this practice). As mayor, Alemán used his power and economic influence to alter the route of the procession so that it bypassed a popular barrio, angering those who planned the event as well as the working-class residents of the barrio. An observer of the festival noted that it is not only a class phenomenon but a gendered one as well; it is "masculine" in the sense that men are freer to engage in the drunken merriment of the street, while women are more of-ten observers or remain at home. Although a certain degree of transgres-sion is expected in the festival, at a symbolic level as well as a practical one, both class and gender differences in the use of public and private space are thus reinscribed (Linkogle 1996: 199–208).

Remaking the City

Returning to Fox's (1972) question of anthropology's contribution to the study of cities, we may ask how developments in Managua shed light on the situation in the rest of the country as well as on the position of Nicaragua in an increasingly globalized world. As José Luis Rocha, a researcher in Managua's Nitlapán institute, inquired in a study of the area affected by Hurricane Mitch's devastation:

> Is this [neoliberalism] the model on which business, the media, and the government are gambling? What possible benefits can such a model bring to the peasants of rural Nicaragua? Will the shopping centers sell farmers' milk or artisans' furniture? Wiwilí milk will not be an ingredient in any of the milkshakes sold there. It will have no chance of reaching the glasses or tables of the transnational fast-food stores. There will be a place for imported perfumes, but not Matagalpa strawberries; for Kerns cold cuts, but not for pineapples and *pitahayas* from La Concha or for Pantasma's bananas; for Quaker oatmeal, but not for Somotillo *jícaro* seeds; for Kellogg's corn flakes, but not for *pinolillo*; for Nike tennis shoes, but not for shoes made in Masaya; for the Rolling Stones, but not for Camilo Zapata. (Rocha 1998: 49)

Rocha concludes by comparing the obstacles facing Nicaragua's poor to an ever-present Mitch and calls on the city to pay heed to the country's predicament. Certainly, the contradictions of the transnational development process for the entire country have never been more apparent than in present-day Managua, when viewed from the vantage point of its growing multinational free trade zone and failing small industries, or its privileged elite and rising unemployment, divided Left, and cultural disaffection.

I believe that we need to reconsider Fox's early call for an urban anthropology that goes beyond the romantic and the exotic in specific locales within cities and pursue a more holistic (and multilayered) approach to cities and (world) society. My larger project considers ways in which Managua, as the capital of Nicaragua, has figured in the imaginations of many beyond its borders and the substantial implications this mythic construction has had for the nation and its people. Within the city, I examine the strategic role of barrios as well as households and workplaces as sites of struggle over democratic participation, but I also consider the city as a whole as a location of negotiation over the terms of citizenship.

Urbanization and a rightward turn toward neoliberalism are both features of post-Sandinista Nicaragua, and in that historical context my research in Managua documents the way in which urban space has become increasingly circumscribed for low-income people and especially for women. There is more to the story, however, as those who are experiencing the harshest dislocations are also participating in social movements that are changing the political landscape. Among the key players in current cultural struggles are members of disenfranchized gender, class, and racial groups. They are often joined by Sandinista intellectuals and other activists who see a need to move beyond the political economic debates of the past and to learn from cultural identity–based movements as a force for social justice and national reconciliation.

Ironically, and in much the same way that the earthquake served to mobilize a popular insurrection against the Somoza dictatorship three decades ago, Hurricane Mitch and the Nicaraguan government's weak response to it may have catalyzed the efforts of diverse groups in the country—social movements, nongovernmental organizations, and unions—to form a broad coalition acting on behalf of civil society. As many as three hundred organizations established forms of coordination around their own specific interests and are working in coalition to propose an integrated response to the national situation. In addition to emergency relief, they are raising concerns that range from health, education, environmental protection, and the economy to community development, children and youth, and women's empowerment and sexuality. The coalition has claimed, "We do not want to build the 'same' country," as they promote a more inclusive, democratic society that attends to the human rights of all Nicaraguans (Envío 1998b: 12–13). As an urban site, Managua has been at the center of discussion of these new forms of social mobilization and of the creative tensions they produce in the city and the society.[15] In Nicaragua as elsewhere in Latin America (Alvarez, Dagnino, and Escobar 1998), we must wait and see how effectively a new political culture is able to challenge the illusion and disillusion offered up as modernity in neoliberalism's wake.

Finally, it may be useful to place this discussion of Managua within the broader framework of cities in relation to nations and the world. Up until this point, I have presented Nicaragua and its capital as fairly exceptional and have emphasized the nation's historical uniqueness. Others who have traveled to Nicaragua have noted their desire to capture the particular features of a location that underwent such remarkable change, much of which is coming undone in the post-Sandinista period. One ethnographer who identified with the revolutionary project expressed well the effort to "salvage what can be recorded before difference disappears" (Martin 1994: 2).[16] Precious though this history may be, we can benefit from the added insights of some recent scholarly analyses of cities.

James Holston and Arjun Appadurai (1999) make a case for redirecting attention from nations to cities as sites for the negotiation of citizenship, democracy, and social inclusion. They offer a postmodern spin to Fox's earlier formulation of studies *in* and *of* the city, noting that "the city can be pretext and context, form and substance, stage and script" (15–16). Their work points toward a more complex approach to cities as strategic arenas for negotiations among social groups and, often, as a staging ground for the project of nation building. While a unified notion of "the city" has now been fractured by richer concepts of difference that acknowledge the multiple experiences of social subjects based on race, gender, class, sexual orientation, age, and so on, cities (in the plural) are the undisputed, paradigmatic places where these differences converge and play out (Jacobs and Fincher 1998). We may be guided by the work of geographers, anthropologists, and others who have drawn on the "politics of location" first articulated by Adrienne Rich (1986) to elaborate an understanding of the ways that the "local" (in this case the city) is always implicated in broader national and transnational processes.

As we map differences in urban sites in an effort to chart not only social inequalities and power differentials but also manifestations of struggles for national inclusion, or citizenship, we may be struck by a question posed recently by the sociologist Saskia Sassen (1999): "Whose city is it?" Clearly, new claims are being made by new social subjects even in the face of globalizing processes of exclusion. But the odds are generally set against subaltern urban players, including women, low-income residents, and racial mi-

12. *Vendors continue to sell their wares at city intersections with traffic lights.*

norities. Struggles over fundamental rights to social participation, economic livelihood, and indeed physical space in which the stakes are particularly high and the risks great are being waged in cities around the globe.
State and civil society will negotiate the terms by which these struggles are
resolved.

As Managua is remade, it is increasingly the space of an elite. The huge
traffic circles (designed only for those with the luxury of traveling in vehicles and dangerous for others) and commercial centers mock a more
thorough and democratic modernization process that has yet to occur. The
renamed city streets and painted-over murals are part of an effort to erase
the past, a time when social and economic differences were challenged and
overturned. The stark inequalities are apparent once again, and the cos-
metic changes to the city cannot hide the poverty and hardship of the majority. The wealthy venture out to urban locations designed for their convenience, then drive home to safe zones at a comfortable distance from sites
of obvious misery. They shield themselves as much as possible from crime
and other social problems, constructing higher walls and better security
systems for their homes and hiring armed guards to patrol their neighbor-

13. A *high security wall now surrounds a middle-class home where I stayed in the early 1990s.*

hoods.[17] In so doing, they create segregated enclaves that, in Managua as elsewhere in Latin America, alter the character of public space and public life and enforce rules of inclusion and exclusion (Caldeira 1999).

To a certain degree, the streets of Managua may be left to those who cannot afford to retreat to enclaves; youth gangs are growing in the city's barrios, beggars gather outside the new cathedral, and gay men who sought a social space in the ruins of the old cathedral have been barred from entering and must meet outside. Nevertheless, as we have seen, the public sector is inhospitable to many who are marginalized in society. Working-class women are among the less privileged groups that are affected most by these changes. While some earn their livelihood in exploitive multinationals in the free trade zone that are now favored over national industries, many others in smaller industries are losing ground. Street vendors, including many women, are still in abundance but are often pushed back from the more central venues. With urban employment shrinking, more women are left without work or with informal employment at home, and some are turning to prostitution or crime as a last resort.

The city of Managua is a rich subject of study as well as a critical stage on which much of historical significance to the nation has been played out in recent years. As the capital and principal urban center of Nicaragua, Managua has engaged once again in a contest over the terms of social participation — a response, perhaps, to a dismal sense that the city belongs increasingly to a small and privileged sector in society. As the city is remade in the image of neoliberal modernity, we may question whether this will serve the long-term interests of economic and political stability or whether, in the short or long term, this latest transformation will produce its own revolutionary consequences.

Chapter Four

A PLACE ON A MAP
The Local and the National
Viewed from the Barrio

R ECALLING Adrienne Rich's words, "a place on a map is also
a place in history," here I offer an ethnographic portrait of a Managua neighborhood that has experienced much of what the city and the country have
undergone in recent decades. Described by one resident as "the flower of
the revolution," Barrio Monseñor Lezcano, in the western part of Managua,
is known for having retained its traditional character after the 1972 earthquake and for its participation in the final offensive in June 1979, but like
some other "combative" barrios, it has since expressed a more pluralist politics. Despite the barrio's earlier support of the FSLN, as in most parts of the
country, the majority voted for the UNO coalition in 1990. As another longtime resident of the neighborhood explained, "This barrio has suffered the
same crisis as the country." The mixed-class inhabitants of this neighborhood represent a wide range of livelihoods, circumstances, and points
of view — regarding their own lives and those of family and the barrio
community.[1]

In the previous chapter, I considered Managua as a site from which to view its relationship to the nation and the world. Here my discussion of one barrio illustrates the way that neighborhoods and their residents in the city are situated culturally, politically, and historically.[2] The British geographer Doreen Massey (1987), writing on Nicaragua from the vantage point of the mid-1980s, presents a similar perspective on the spatial and structural relations of urban and rural Nicaragua and also emphasizes the fundamental importance of the barrio in society and history. As she points out, barrios were central in organizing much of the resistance in the popular struggle against Somoza's government. Most urban Nicaraguans were not organized in major workplaces but rather in small industries and informal economic activities at the neighborhood level. Thus the Sandinistas depended on the barrios to mobilize the population and, later, to protect the gains made by the revolution.

Sandinista Defense Committees (CDSs) were organized by the FSLN before the final offensive and were active in the barrios, mainly carrying out national-level initiatives, through the mid-1980s. By 1988, greater autonomy at the local level was attained as the CDSs evolved to become the Community Movement (Movimiento Comunal), now the most visible barrio-based organization. However, as Managua has grown steadily in recent years and a number of new settlements have sprung up, the neoliberal state has been less responsive in providing needed services and legal recognition, and political activism in some barrios has declined.[3]

When I first traveled to Nicaragua for a short visit in 1989, I stayed with a family living in the outskirts of Barrio Monseñor Lezcano, named for a former bishop of Managua. The barrio was known as a popular, working-to lower-middle-class neighborhood sympathetic to the revolution and to the internationalists who came in abundant numbers during that decade.[4] At that time, the neighborhood committees were still in evidence and the Mothers of Heroes and Martyrs worked actively to organize in the barrio. The Ben Linder House, centrally located in the barrio, named for the young North American engineer who was killed by the Contras, was the gathering place for solidarity workers, who found their way there soon after arriving in the country. It was also where many came for weekly talks after protesting outside the American embassy. The protests, which for years had been held outside the embassy, ended, but the gatherings at the Ben Linder House continued.

Map 3. Barrio Monseñor Lezcano in Northwest Managua.

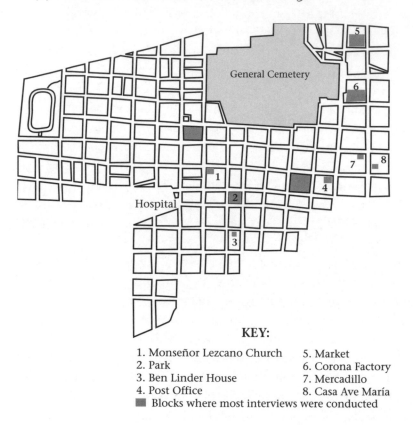

General Cemetery

Hospital

KEY:

1. Monseñor Lezcano Church
2. Park
3. Ben Linder House
4. Post Office
■ Blocks where most interviews were conducted

5. Market
6. Corona Factory
7. Mercadillo
8. Casa Ave María

During my research in Managua in the early 1990s, I directed increasing attention to the barrio, because it seemed to represent a broad range of experiences, especially of those working in the expanding informal economy.[5] Beginning in 1993, Barrio Monseñor Lezcano became my base during visits to Nicaragua and I had the opportunity to know its residents and to collect ethnographic material over a considerable period. Whereas Managua has remained for me a sprawling and fairly unwieldy, though familiar, urban environment, this barrio feels something like home when I return to the country.

Many of the barrio's residents have lived there for at least thirty years, since before the 1972 earthquake. Those who have lived in the barrio for as many as fifty years remember when there was just one, unpaved street and when Monseñor Lezcano Church was a simple structure with a thatched roof. The progressive priests of the parish had the cooperation of the entire barrio in constructing a new church on the same site in the 1960s. This area was fortunate to escape much of the damage suffered elsewhere in the city from the earthquake, and in fact many from the center of Managua relocated to this and other outlying barrios when their homes were destroyed. Thus the neighborhood has experienced a good deal of growth, and it is now one of the most populous areas of Managua, with an estimated twenty thousand to twenty-five thousand residents.[6]

The limits of the barrio are somewhat unclear; the FSLN redefined its boundaries in preparation for the 1990 elections, reducing it to 105 city blocks, but residents generally consider the boundary to lie slightly farther to the east.[7] The FSLN created three sectors in the barrio, which under the revolutionary government corresponded to the party's base committees; now they are devoted to fund-raising, health campaigns, and annual celebrations of the Sandinista victory. The barrio's boundaries are in some flux today and may reflect shifting political interests more than any "natural" divisions. Nevertheless, the residents of Monseñor Lezcano reveal their barrio identity and sense of place vis-à-vis the city of Managua in a number of significant ways.

Major landmarks in the barrio include Monseñor Lezcano Church, Guadalupe Church, the historic General Cemetery, the Western Market (Mercado Occidental), the Corona cooking oil factory, the National Dermatological Hospital,[8] and the San Sebastian supermarket. In addition, there are several public and private schools, evangelical churches, and gas stations and other well-known businesses. A few of these reference points are located close enough to other barrios that their neighborhoods of affiliation are contested, but they are often identified with Monseñor Lezcano. Like other barrios in Managua, Monseñor Lezcano has a central square with a park where children play and adults gather, a post office and telephone service, and so on. Unlike some parts of the city that were favored when Alemán was mayor, this barrio—identified as it is with its former Sandinista character—still had some unpaved streets until a few years ago.

The barrio is known for its residential neighborhood of working-class and middle-class Managuans who have lived together in relative harmony. I came to know best the streets near my home in the barrio, but I also ventured out frequently to other areas where I made the acquaintance of a number of residents, including a retired carpenter and self-styled historian, an elderly woman active with a group of Madres, a local FSLN activist, and a café owner active in the parish. I also selected two square blocks on different sides of the barrio where I visited and interviewed as many residents as possible, with the hope of learning about their livelihoods as well as their views of the barrio and the current situation in the country. And I also made frequent visits to commercial establishments such as the recently reopened Western Market and some smaller shops, including hardware stores, furniture workshops, barber shops, book sellers with just a half dozen paperbacks for sale, and the many *pulperías* (front-room grocery stores).

A Walk through the Barrio

A short walking tour of my immediate neighborhood provides some of the local flavor and rhythm of the barrio.[9] My point of departure is the Casa Ave María, where I stay. It is the home of Grant Gallup, a retired Episcopal priest from Chicago who became a resident of Nicaragua in 1989 and is well known in the activist internationalist community. Fully integrated in the neighborhood himself, Gallup offers room and board to visiting members of delegations and the occasional researcher. The Casa now also houses the Ben Linder library and is widely known for its revolutionary murals depicting biblical themes as well as Nicaraguan and internationalist women.[10] As in most of Managua, this "urban" barrio has a country ambience. One wakes early to the sounds of nearby roosters crowing, the household pet parrot calling, and, at some times of the year, mangos dropping heavily from trees.[11] Activity begins early; the heat becomes intense enough to be uncomfortable, even with the use of electric fans, during much of the year. Some of the barrio's poorest residents have learned to come to Casa Ave María by 6:00 A.M. to receive breakfast at the front gate, and by that hour a local woman has arrived to clean and cook for the house. Gradually, a couple of teenage boys from the barrio arrive to sweep the patio and tend the garden, run errands, and help in other ways. They benefit from their earnings, ample meals, and the opportunity to further their studies.

At opposite ends of the block are business ventures that do an active trade. A woman operates a corner pulpería with a range of items, but it is the nearly pure alcohol, *aguardiente,* that attracts many to her *cantina* as a kind of hangout. Across the street and at the other end of the block is a

14. *Members of a neighbor's family sell fresh foods daily in the barrio's* mercadillo.

small market (*mercadillo*) that for the last several years has offered fresh food daily to barrio customers. A couple, formerly Sandinista and now supporters of Alemán, lives there and operates a store (*venta*); their family along with a half-dozen women, who pay for the privilege, set up tables outside on the street corner where they sell fruit, vegetables, cheese, meat, and fish. Our household made most of its purchases from this small market, benefiting from the convenience, if not the lowest prices available.

Between these businesses are a mixture of others and some private residences. A new pulpería opened next door to the Casa, with just a few items for sale and a few customers. Run by a family of Contra sympathizers who escaped the political violence in northern Nicaragua, the wife operates the front-room store while her husband still has his ranch (*finca*) to tend to in the north. Another house is owned by a police officer and his wife. Although they are middle class by local standards, the wife comes to the Casa asking for financial help until her husband receives his paycheck. Another residence is used by Evangelical Protestants who fixed up the house for meetings and also operate a small store (*tienda*). A lawyer and her parents live on the street as well. A man who lives around the corner is a neighborhood character, an alcoholic with ruined health who offers to sweep the Casa patio in the morning in exchange for breakfast; sometimes he sets up to shine shoes on the patio too. In another household on the street, two gay teenage brothers live with their family and are teased mercilessly by others in the neighborhood. A young man who worked at the Casa until he was found stealing (he still receives financial assistance for his education) lives across the street with his mother, who operates a "unisex" hair salon in her front room, and his brother, his sister, and their children.

Another man who lives on the street sells magazines outside Managua's main post office in the center of the city. He looks distinguished, but I learned that he has a reputation for his use of beer and tranquilizers. More significantly, he was known as a Somoza spy who watched the Sandinista Javier Cuadra closely and reported him when he lived where the Casa is now located. Cuadra was murdered in 1978 and is honored as a martyr, commemorated with a plaque outside the Casa.[12]

Directly across the street from the Casa is a large empty lot where a furniture factory once stood; when it closed, people took away the building materials. The closure meant the loss of employment for about thirty workers in one of the barrio's largest industries. Gallup thought about purchasing the lot to build a cultural center for the barrio's youth, but instead he purchased the property adjacent to Casa Ave María, known affectionately as Casa Otro Lado (House on the Other Side), for music and language instruction. Gallup used this location as a temporary residence when fire damaged his home a few years ago.

In this neighborhood, a high-crime urban area like many throughout Managua, imposing iron gates enclose many houses and their yards to provide security. Nevertheless, there is a lively street life in the barrio. On our street, a group of men often gathers and talks on one side of the street until they move across to the other side to seek shade from the midday heat. In the evenings, children and teenagers populate the street in small groups, moving only when cars pass by or parents call them to come home.

When residents in this part of the barrio want a wider selection of foodstuffs than can be found at the mercadillo, they do not have far to walk. Of course, they could use city transportation and travel across Managua to the huge Eastern Market (Mercado Oriental) where they would find lower prices, but most buy in such small quantity that they find the savings are swallowed up in bus fare. Nearby is the San Sebastian supermarket and food distributor. Although the store had functioned for some twenty years before the revolution, it was closed during the Sandinista period and did not reopen until 1992.[13] This dimly lit store sells both wholesale and retail and carries a range of manufactured goods as well as produce, meats, milk, household supplies, cosmetics, and clothing. It cannot compare to the larger luxury supermarkets in Managua's central plazas, but it carries some of the same products, including imported breakfast cereals, Diet Coke, alcohol, and other goods purchased by better-off barrio residents. More akin to traditional markets, this one has a small flower-bedecked altar to San Sebastian near the cash register.

For about a year in the early 1990s, another supermarket provided some competition for middle-class consumers. La Corona Supermarket, located near the Corona cooking oil factory, was smaller and cleaner and, with ceiling fans, cooler. This store had items that appealed to higher-class customers, including canned fruit and expensive wine and liquor, but the number of people who could afford such goods was inadequate to keep it in business. During the time the store was open, I spoke with several of the workers. As in other larger businesses in the barrio, this one employed few people who are actually from the barrio. When I inquired at La Corona, I was advised to speak to the women mopping the floors as they were the only ones from Monseñor Lezcano. They were also the poorest and lowest-paid employees. In contrast to many I talked with in the barrio and in Managua more generally who lamented that there is an abundance of products in the country now but little money to make purchases, one woman cleaning the floor appeared to identify with the message of neoliberalism: she spoke approvingly of all the goods the store carried. Her income would surely not allow her to buy many items that she so admired, but she expressed the view that things are better now.

Another market in the barrio (actually straddling Monseñor Lezcano and the neighboring barrio, Santa Ana) may have a greater chance of success. This is a covered marketplace known traditionally as the Western Market that takes up a good part of a city block. In the 1980s, the market was named for the revolutionary martyr Leonel Gutiérrez, who died nearby, but it was later closed by the Sandinistas and used as a military base. The market was reopened with fanfare by Mayor Alemán in 1992 after renovations had been made with funds from USAID. At that time, a former name, Mercado Occidental Virgen de la Candalaria, after the saint of commerce, was re-

15. A sign outside the Western Market announces the support of the president and the mayor in renovating and reopening this retail venue.

instituted.[14] The reopening provided a media opportunity for Alemán. The following week he appeared in a photograph posed by the market chapel's Virgen de la Candelaria in a full-page paid advertisement announcing his good work (*Barricada*, July 15, 1992).

I waited with prospective sellers with some anticipation as stalls were painted, a new sign mounted, and an office opened to register new occupants of the market. Sellers who had worked in the market before and others seeking new work opportunities came forward to claim stalls, which required a fair outlay of capital as well as monthly fees. The mayor had promised sellers one month without fees, but this promise was not honored; in contrast to the slogan found throughout the city, "Managua Cambia, La Alcaldia Cumple!" (Managua Is Changing, the Mayor Comes Through!), the sellers were saying "No cumple" (He does not come through). The sellers hoped that consumers would return to the marketplace to make their purchases, but while the market accommodated more than two hundred stalls, it operated at about half capacity during much of the 1990s. A year after reopening, more of the market stalls were occupied, offering the usual range of goods for sale, including fruits and vegetables, meat, fish, eggs, cheese, grains, dry goods, plastic items, and clothing. There was also a small beauty shop, a stall offering simple medical tests, a shoe repair, a bicycle repair, and several small restaurants. One man and his family had sold fruits and vegetables in the market for twenty years before it closed and then sold in the street outside; he recalled the hardships of rationed goods and controlled prices under the Sandinistas and praised the free market policies now in place.

Aceitera La Corona, the cooking oil plant, takes up about three city blocks on the eastern edge of the barrio, near the cemetery. During the years of my research, I made several trips to conduct interviews in the factory, and each time I found fewer workers. The plant hires a very small number of workers from the barrio, about 10 percent according to a woman working in the personnel office, and some from outside Managua. By the 1990s, to remain in business, the company had diversified to produce items such as vinegar, mustard, and mayonnaise. However, like so many other enterprises in the country, this one was suffering from the free market introduction of new products and could not compete successfully. In 1991, a strike over better wages was declared illegal and resulted in the firing of about one hundred protesting workers and the hiring of others who were not organized. Wages rose somewhat, and that, along with the importation of cooking oil, caused the company to lose profits and cut back production. When I first visited in 1992, there were just under one hundred fifty employees, a fraction of the number in earlier years, mostly men in factory production and administration and a few women in clerical and cleaning positions. When cotton production in the country fell off and lowered the production of cottonseed oil for the national market, more workers were laid off. Although barrio residents are quick to mention this factory as one of the largest enterprises in the neighborhood, it has no more direct effect here than in other parts of the city.[15]

Finally, bordering the Corona factory and the Western Market, the General Cemetery takes up an area equal to thirty-six city blocks in the barrio. Also known as the Western Cemetery, construction was begun by Managua's mayor in 1912 when the existing San Pedro Cemetery became inadequate for the expanding city. A decade later the cemetery was inaugurated, and the mayor himself was the first to be buried there (Traña Galeano 1991: 12–15). Among those laid to rest in this cemetery were many who perished in the earthquakes of 1931 and 1972. The former dictators Gen. Anastasio

Somoza García and his son Luis Somoza Debayle were buried in a mausoleum there, but their bodies were quickly exhumed by the Somoza family when the Sandinistas triumphed in July 1979. High-ranking officials of Somoza's National Guard were also buried in a monumental tomb, now in disrepair. Many ordinary citizens have been interred there as well, and by 1988 the number of dead in the cemetery numbered close to 120,000. Outside the enclosed space and the quiet of the cemetery, vendors set up under the shade of trees to sell bunches of flowers to those wishing to pay respect to the deceased.

Venturing Out in the Barrio

Over the course of my research, I made a point of meeting as many residents as possible in the two city blocks I had chosen to study in the barrio.[16] My visits generally included informal interviewing on a dozen questions concerned with individuals' and families' experiences in the barrio, their work lives, and their impressions of changes in the barrio and in the country more generally over the previous decades. I also asked about the gendered aspects of barrio residents' lives. After I had become acquainted with the retired carpenter and autodidact and realized that his block was fairly typical of the barrio, I chose it as one of those on which to focus my research. I chose the second block later, for its location on the opposite side of the barrio and its similarly diverse character. In all, I visited more than twenty households and enterprises on these two blocks.

Managua in general is characterized by a mix of social classes living in close proximity. There are, of course, neighborhoods that are almost exclusively upper and middle class with large homes shielded by iron grillwork or cut glass and barbed wire atop high walls. And then there are working-class and poor neighborhoods with simple, crowded homes that accommodate more people than passersby might imagine. The most destitute often live in the asentamientos that have cropped up in the city's center and outlying areas alike and that lack basic services unless they can tap illegally into electrical and water supplies.

Monseñor Lezcano is surrounded by barrios that are better and worse off than itself, with middle-class Las Palmas and the home of Violeta Chamorro just a few blocks southeast of the Casa Ave María and the impoverished Edgard Lang barrio several blocks south of Monseñor Lezcano

Church. However, within most blocks in the barrio, it is possible to find laborers living next door to professionals, unemployed adjacent to those with steady employment. And it is most common to find households of diverse economic and social standing conducting some informal commerce in their homes. To some degree this may signal the popular democracy of neighborhoods in the city, but it is also an indication of the rapidly changing fortunes of many residents in a period of uncertainty.

The first *manzana*, or square block, where I interviewed includes a wide range of private households and businesses. Households sell ice, soft drinks, gelatin, candy, cheese and milk, used clothing, and *nacatamales* (a snack prepared with corn mush, pork, potatoes, and rice steamed in banana leaves), and a couple of men have a small shoe repair business on the street. There are workshops of a carpenter and a window maker, a chemical supply store, a pastry shop and bakery, a car repair, and a restaurant. In addition, there is a medical clinic, the offices of the Liberal Alliance, and the offices of the Save the Children organization.

Beginning with the home of the carpenter, the friend I will call Don Nicolás,[17] we find a household that, like many others, contains both living quarters and a work site. Don Nicolás, sixty-eight years old when I first met him, was originally from the northern city of León, known for its university and literary heritage, which he proudly called the "city of intellectuals," but moved to Managua with his family when he was eleven. His wife of fifty years had died the year before, and he lived with a son and daughter, three grandchildren, and a family friend in relatively ample quarters located a short distance from Monseñor Lezcano Church. He had been living in the barrio some forty years. Although he described himself as retired, he said that he occasionally was asked to take on a job. He once had as many as eighteen carpenters working for him in his workshop, then six, and then he began working on a casual basis on his own.

All five of his children went to college and have professional training. The daughter who lives with him held an administrative position in the office of the Sandinista *comandante* Tomás Borge. By 1998, her son had started a new business on the block, a printing service that was just getting off the ground, with a professionally made sign outside the door announcing the enterprise. When I visited, he and a few other young people were setting up their equipment in an air-conditioned office. Thus, while Don Nicolás sits next door in his traditional Nicaraguan rocking chair feeling the warm breeze, his grandson represents a generation that is aspiring to a middle-class lifestyle. It remains to be seen if this new business will succeed.

Don Nicolás remembers the time before 1970 when the barrio was populated largely by poor people and laborers from the countryside and the demographic change as more artisans and professionals settled there. He was among those active in the barrio in the early years, organizing the community to perform communal work and to press the city for electrical services, sanitation, and public transportation. He recalls that in 1981, under the Sandinistas, the major streets were paved with adoquines and there was potable water in this part of the barrio. Now there are fewer laborers, and only a small number from the barrio are hired in factories like the Corona cooking oil company. However, he pointed out that there was a wide range of expertise in the barrio: bakers, carpenters, mechanics, shoemakers, tailors, seamstresses, barbers, and hairdressers. Moreover, he spoke approvingly of the wide range of professionals in the barrio: lawyers and doctors (he counted nine medical clinics), teachers, economists, businesspeople, journalists, and accountants among others.

Although the barrio counts many artisans and professionals among its residents, Don Nicolás maintained that their standard of living is not much different from that of workers. He considered those living on his block and said they are all people with some expertise, but it matters little at a time when the majority are suffering. Several members of a household may be salaried, and the household may even hire a cleaning woman (*empleada*), but the economic hardship is widespread. Even so, status differences are evident, and he has experienced the condescension of professionals who look down on artisans. He failed to mention the large number of residents on his block and throughout the barrio who are neither skilled workers nor professionals but participate actively in commerce, whether in pulperías or in small restaurants.

Don Nicolás was generous in his praise for the poorest barrio residents, who had often taken the initiative in making improvements in the neighborhood. Among the examples of local activism that he recalled were residents' participation in the Sandinista vaccination and literacy programs and the efforts to save the Cine León, the barrio's only movie theater, which had been used as a center for military training during the insurrection. Signatures were collected to save the theater, but when the owner left it was closed. The old theater building, its sign still in place, serves as a well-known landmark when residents give directions in the barrio. Don Nicolás also re-membered the construction of a basketball court in a nearby park but re-gretted that the locals did not participate and that the work was done en-tirely by "gringos" volunteering their help. He was more complimentary about the current efforts of the Movimiento Comunal, which had focused its attention on health care and problems faced by youth. Delinquency, gangs, and drug use were issues that he and others mentioned—along with the racialized view that a small number of Afro-Nicaraguans from the At-lantic Coast were troublesome[18]—although popular opinion held that these problems were greater in neighboring barrios. More serious were poverty, hunger, and unemployment. Like others in Monseñor Lezcano, Don Nicolás identified strongly with the barrio, declaring that his neigh-borhood affiliation was more meaningful to him than his identity as an ur-ban resident of Managua.[19]

A longtime Sandinista militant who is nonetheless critical of the party, in 1979 Don Nicolás provided space in his home for a barrio association. He cited this as a historical antecedent to the CDSs and the Movimiento Comunal and said that it was effective because everyone worked together despite political differences. Later, he noted, the Sandinistas established better-structured associations that carried out important projects, but po-litical divisions again emerged. He recalled that a conservative but hard worker was marginalized because he was not affiliated with the FSLN. Al-though political differences are still pronounced and the FSLN is active in the barrio, he was not aware of many current problems at the barrio level. However, like many Sandinista supporters, he was more critical of the na-tional leadership of the FSLN and its failure to provide viable alternatives for the country. As he put it, socialism had failed in Nicaragua as it had failed in eastern Europe, but so too was capitalism failing in neoliberal Nicara-gua. He saw the problem as stemming from the absence of a class identity among Nicaraguan capitalists, which has precluded a national project. In Don Nicolás's well-articulated view, unless capitalism is used to develop the country as a whole, rather than to serve individual and global interests, Nicaragua will continue to have serious problems.

Next door to Don Nicolás lives another retired man and his family. A to-tal of six adults and four children live in the house. As I approached to speak with him, he was sitting in front of the house reading *La Prensa*, the conser-vative newspaper representing the opposition during the Sandinista years and favored by government supporters since 1990. He had once worked for a company that made glass windows. He also worked for a time as a guard and used the money he earned plus some of his wife's earnings from the household production and sale of *mondongo* (a hearty soup) to buy glass and work on his own making windows. His pension gives him about U.S. $40 per month, which buys little. His family eats cheese and beans but not meat. Now, he said, there is so much to buy, yet no money with which to buy it. He charged that governments are alike and that there is no employment for the working class. Originally from a provincial town, he has been in the barrio for more than thirty years and likes the convenience of living in the city. Unlike his wife and children, who are Sandinistas, he has allegiance to no party and complained that the UNO government was led by a woman.

To the other side of Don Nicolás's house is the household of a woman and her mother, brother, and two children. They have lived in the barrio for twenty years and in this house, which they rent, for fifteen years. Throughout these years, they have depended heavily on the pulpería they operate out of their front room. Although her brother works for the Toña beer company, he does not contribute his earnings to the household. Like a number of Nicaraguans, she collapses the past when she tells me that things were better under Somoza and also under the Sandinistas, but now they are worse. Life is especially hard for women, who must cope with hard work, poor sales, and, often, abusive men as well. Her former husband is remarried and lives in Canada; he sends money to the family. Her dream is for her children to live with him and attend a Canadian school.

A restaurant located at the corner of the block had just changed owners when I visited. A woman and her sister operate the place and live there with their husbands and two children. In the past the sisters had a beauty salon, which they regard as their true calling. But for the present they have hired a cook and are trying to make a respectable restaurant of a place that formerly was a bar and attracted what they regard as a bad clientele. They have done some painting and decorating to improve the appearance of their business in the hope of attracting customers, who are still few. Their husbands had other jobs before, but now they help out in the restaurant. The business's future is uncertain because many people lack the resources to eat out in restaurants.

Just around the corner, a woman lives with her husband and young child. She is originally from the barrio and has lived in this house for twelve years. She has worked for seven years in the Ministry of Health and has a better income than many in the barrio. Her husband works in the Ministry of Transportation. They depend on sending their child to a nearby child care center because they cannot afford to hire someone to help out at home. She related that in the past her parents were better off than she and her family are now, but today her mother suffers and needs her help. She can offer food but not money, because her own family is having trouble. But she knows that with two salaries and just one child, she is better off than many of her neighbors. She expressed little hope that conditions would improve anytime soon.

Another home on the block is so small that at first I did not see it between two other residences. A woman and her husband live there with their two young children. She is a primary school teacher, and her husband has been unemployed for almost four years, since the birth of their younger child. She remembers the assistance that the Sandinista government offered with the AFA (a package of basic foods to state workers, including rice, beans, and sugar) and says that now it is not possible for a family to get along on one salary. Although her husband spends more time at home, he lacks experience in housework and performs little of it. Indeed, he has been so deeply affected by his unemployment that he sought the help of a psychologist, then found solace in converting to an evangelical faith.

Another household consists of four sisters, their mother, the husbands of two of the sisters, and ten children. All seventeen live in the space of three rooms plus a kitchen. Like many other poor families, they have a color television set for entertainment in an otherwise drab living environment. Two sisters, who described themselves as *amas de casa* (homemakers or housewives), were home when I stopped by, and they invited me to sit down and talk while they watched a *novela* (TV soap opera). They had lived in the barrio, in this house, for eighteen years. One of their sisters works as a merchant in the Eastern Market and one sister's husband has a wage job. A brother in the United States sends money to their mother, who also receives social security. Referring to their scant family resources, one of the sisters told me that things got worse with the *compactación* (cutbacks in the state sector) of 1988, when she lost her job, and she has not been able to find work since then. Women must work as hard as men, she says, and they also experience domestic violence. Some men, like her brother, do not make a distinction between women's work and men's work and help out at home.

The second manzana in which I conducted interviews is characterized by a similar mix of households and livelihoods. Most places that I visited had some sort of business. These included a couple of hardware stores, a tailor shop, a welder's workshop, a repair shop for household electrical items, a front room selling used American clothing, a carpenter's workshop, several pulperías, a household selling nacatamales, and, finally, a gynecology clinic. While most of those adults living on the block were self-employed, several had professional jobs elsewhere in the city—and others were unemployed. Such was the case of a young man who had received a scholarship and studied international law in Russia but had not found work back home, so both he and his sister depended on their father's earnings as a mechanic to get by.

I spoke with one woman in a comfortable and spacious home where she and her family had lived for just five years although she had grown up in the barrio. Her husband had studied computer science in Mexico and now works for a Nicaraguan company, earning far more than most people I interviewed, about U.S. $800 per month. She had worked until 1987 as an administrative assistant for the Pan American Health Organization in Managua but resigned when her husband persuaded her that the work was demanding and underpaid and that she should return home to care for their three children. Occasionally, she makes cakes that she sells out of her home, especially around Mother's Day, but she devotes herself primarily to managing house and family. When I spoke with her, she was preparing a large pot of mondongo for her family (many others make a business of selling the soup), something she undertakes about once a year.

She counts herself as fortunate that her family has never been wanting and that her children can attend private school. In her view, conditions in the barrio and in the country have improved in the last few years, and she is pleased that there is more to buy and no long lines as in the past. She faults others for not getting the training they need in order to advance and said that "people can't just sit, they need to get out and find work." She herself studied for a while at the university, but she said that her husband is jealous and does not want her to continue her studies; indeed, she must

16. A woman and her child look out from one of the barrio's many pulperías.

have his permission to leave the house. She told me that "machismo prevails in this country."

Another woman devotes herself to her home, because her husband, a man of eighty-four (thirty years her senior), prefers it that way. They live on her husband's pension and their son's income as an importer of Mexican beer. She laments the current economic situation and says it is very difficult to pay for water, electricity, telephone, food, and other needs. Money does not stretch far these days. To cut costs, her husband eats daily at a cafeteria serving retirees, sponsored by the social security administration.

A woman who has not lived long in the barrio explains that a son who lives in the United States purchased the house, where she lives with her daughter and her daughter's two children. Her husband left her twenty-five years ago and rarely offered financial help, and she raised her children alone. At sixty-six, she calls herself a housewife and says that she relies on her daughter's income as a supermarket employee, the first steady job she has had in two years. In previous years, her daughter traveled to Guatemala and Panama to buy clothing and other goods to sell back home.

Next door, a woman of twenty-four lives with her husband and three children, her father-in-law, and her nephew. Her family moved to the barrio when her husband inherited his grandmother's house there. Six months before, she sold ice cream and ice from the house, but she gave it up because there were few sales. Her husband is a truck driver and her father-in-law works in a store, and they also have the help of her mother, who operates a pulpería and gives them food when they need it. Echoing the words of many others, she complains that everything is available in abundance now but people have no money. She recalls that there was no work under the Sandinista government, but now desperation leads women to prostitution and men to robbery.

Another woman on the block lives a still more precarious life, particularly since her brother committed suicide a few months before. He had shared the household with her and her three children and contributed financially, but he was distressed over the worsening situation in the country and its effect on his family. She receives a little help from an older son who has a scholarship to study music in Costa Rica. Since leaving a wage job, she sells ice cream and cleaning products from her home to try to get by. She had grown weary of seeking work out of the home and is using her skills as a seamstress to begin sewing children's clothing as a possible livelihood. Her despair was evident in our conversation, and she shared the view of many others that living conditions are worse for women, who are responsible for the care of their children and often have no men to offer support. As she puts it, "Morning, noon, and night the mother is the one who worries over her children." A sad smile appeared briefly when she told me that before his death, her brother had generously managed to get them a refrigerator and a color TV.

A man on the block discussed the situation of his family. He and his wife have lived in the barrio for almost forty years. He has a primary school education and training to repair radios and televisions, although he pointed out that he does not work for the rich but rather for workers who lack money, so his business is very slow. Referring to his wife as a housewife, he acknowledged that she brings in most of the household income by selling food and drinks from their home. She prepares meals and snacks for sale and also offers fresh juice and soft drinks. When I visited, she was out collecting debts from her customers: many of them must buy on credit until their next paycheck. He was no supporter of the Sandinistas, whose government he described as "disastrous," but now he says things are just as bad, or perhaps worse, because small industry is ruined and there is no work. Despite the availability of new goods entering the market, there are serious obstacles to acquiring them.

The couple's teenage son, a student, and their married daughter with her husband and young child live in rooms separate from the rest of the house but part of the family *solar* (plot of ground). Their daughter had lost her job as a cashier the year before, and although she has looked for work all around Managua, she remains unemployed. Her husband was formerly involved in selling clothing he brought from Guatemala, but now he works as a taxi driver. His mother is working in the United States and sends them money every couple of months (remittances of about U.S. $100), and they are also selling some of her possessions in Nicaragua. They, too, hope to better their lives by going to the United States if they can.

On this block there is a small restaurant rented and managed by a woman who lives elsewhere in the barrio. In the past her husband operated the restaurant, but they went bankrupt and now she is doing somewhat better, although business is still very slow. Her sister, who lives across the street and has a hairdressing business, sometimes helps out. I learned from a woman who lives next door to the restaurant that it is her family that rents out the restaurant as a source of income, but now they have a problem because the manager has not been paying the rent.

A seventy-five-year-old widow shares a household with her two professional sons and a daughter-in-law. One son is a professor at the National Agrarian University and contributes the family's only salary; his brother lost his job in a failed industry two years before. Far more significant than her son's salary, however, is the income she receives from renting a large part of her house to the gynecology clinic. She used to sell food from her home and earned a decent income, but she gave that up because of her ill health, and now, after living in the barrio for twenty-two years, she finds the situation almost hopeless. She complained that, in contrast to the past when everyone worked, today the biggest problem is lack of work.

A middle-aged married couple living with their three children are among the poorest on the block. Both husband and wife have only a few years of primary school education. Before she married she worked as a domestic for many years. Now she works at home, and recently she tried selling food but had no luck. He has worked outside the barrio for four years as a janitor in the mayor's office. They have the advantage of living in the home of his mother, who emigrated to the United States and returns annually with clothing for their family. They have lived in the barrio for twenty-five years and have noticed the growing number of businesses there but believe that most are not profitable.

A sixty-seven-year-old woman lives in cramped quarters with her four daughters, a son-in-law, and five grandchildren. She has been to primary school. Besides doing the housework, she operates a small venta that sells food and soft drinks. During the interview, a Pepsi Cola truck stopped by, and she was unable to buy even one crate of bottles. Fortunately, her daughters have work sewing, cleaning a church in a neighboring barrio, and clerking in a hardware store and a supermarket. She expressed regret that she must be dependent on her daughters, who earn little, since prices are so high now, as is the cost of water and electricity. Everyone has the same story, she added.

A major business on this block is owned by a man who lives in another, higher-class barrio. Since 1973 he has had a large garage and mechanic's workshop where he employs a couple of young men. When the Sandinistas came to power, he and his family emigrated to the United States, where they remained for more than ten years and he worked as a mechanic. He returned alone to Nicaragua and resumed his business. He has a steady clientele of well-off customers, including Comandante Doris Tijerino, former head of the Sandinista police and of AMNLAE, who came by during the interview.

Interviewing people on this block led to my introduction to Elena, a woman in early middle age who has always lived in the barrio. She is a journalist for *La Boletina*, a publication of the feminist center Puntos de Encuentro. Her household of women includes her mother, her two daughters, and a granddaughter. She has long worked outside the home, and her two daughters are university students, yet they are all aware of the vast number of professionally trained Nicaraguans who enter the informal economy, selling lottery tickets and the like, or are unemployed.

Elena has been active with the Movimiento Comunal, which she described as the political arm of the FSLN at the barrio level; despite the official nonpartisan status of the community movement, there is considerable overlap with Sandinista activists. She works mainly in her own sector of the barrio, one of the three sectors in Monseñor Lezcano. She told me that her sector has the most small industry and the least informal commerce but that it also captures the wide mix of livelihoods characteristic of the barrio as a whole. She named a few, including tortilla making, sewing, meal preparation, production of nacatamales, and operating pulperías, and added that it is primarily women who are involved in these businesses. Like others, Elena described the barrio as becoming more middle class since more professionals moved there after the earthquake. She noted some of the barrio's advantages — its better than average infrastructure and its commercial, medical, and educational resources — that have made it attractive to newcomers. Nevertheless, she and her daughters emphasized that the current situation has been a blow to all the social classes in the barrio and beyond, and they mentioned problems of gangs and crime. Elena expressed regret that the FSLN did not coordinate activism more effectively at the local and national levels. She revealed to me with some pride that while she has worked with Sandinista and feminist organizations, she remains independent and does not follow any single political line.

Barrio Lives and Activism

I came upon Doña María's house in the barrio quite by accident. I was taking some photographs in the neighborhood and noticed a wide array of handwritten signs outside her door announcing all manner of items for sale, as well as Sandinista campaign posters left over from the last elections. I stopped at her place to buy a cold drink. When I asked about the many signs in front, she laughed, saying that they really did not have so many things for sale. Over time we formed a friendship and, in a number of conversations, Doña María described her long work history and political involvement in the barrio. She considers herself a seamstress by trade, although she was sewing mainly for her family when we met. She and her husband had always worked together, first selling materials for shoemaking beginning in about 1960. For three years in the early 1970s, she lived and worked in New York as a maid while her husband and children remained in Managua. By the late 1970s, conditions in Nicaragua were worsening and sales were lower, so after the Sandinista triumph they opened their venta, the front-room store they have today. For ten years they sold grains in quantity, but by the late 1980s the national economy was again suffering and they dropped the sale of grains and sold just a few products on a smaller scale:

17. *Old political posters mix with signs for food items sold from the front room of this barrio home.*

bread, cheese, cream, *pinol* (a corn beverage), eggs, beans, oil, sugar, rice, candy, soft drinks, and beer. After she had an accident in the early 1990s, a friend loaned her a freezer, which has allowed her to sell more items. She made a couple of trips each week to the Eastern Market to buy the goods for the venta, and other goods were delivered to her. As an indication of how her sales have declined, she noted that in the past she would sell a case of twenty-four bottles of Coke in a day, but now, because of rising prices, it takes up to three days to do so. She told me that the economy was stalled, and she had been unable to get a bank loan to build her business.

A loyal Sandinista, Doña María recalled that there were problems in the 1980s but that these were largely due to the Contra war and the economic blockade. People at least had more to eat because they could buy basic foods at lower prices. Now the situation is far worse, with higher unemployment and people unable to make a living. The economy favors large business. Small businesses are unable to compete and are going under, with interest on bank loans so high that those who receive them are really just "working for the lenders." She has noticed that people are dispirited by the current situation. As we spoke, a couple of kids came by to purchase Gluglu, a cheap, sugary drink, and she noted sadly that this is often the only breakfast they have.

Doña María became involved with the Madres after her own tragic loss of a young daughter who was struck and killed by one of Somoza's official vehicles in 1970, when María and the girl were taking food to political prisoners. She has proudly framed and hung on her wall a document from the FSLN, "In Recognition, Madre Vanguardia, to compañera María," for her leadership at the national level. Also on the wall are portraits of the national revolutionary heroes Augusto César Sandino, Carlos Fonseca, and Daniel Ortega. After the 1979 triumph, the Madres worked out of the AMNLAE Women's Center "Erlinda Lopez," but several years later they became independent. The Madres' current concern and the focus of their community work is the advancing age and fragile health of many of the mothers. They tried to organize a "popular pharmacy" offering low prices, since the elderly, even those with social security, generally have extremely low incomes. The elderly and the children suffer most, María said, and the Madres have been marginalized since the Sandinistas lost the elections.

While the Madres continued to seek funding for projects and to honor events such as the anniversary of Sandino's death, other political sectors represented in the barrio were less active, according to María. She described the Movimiento Comunal as paralyzed, although she also noted that along with Monseñor Lezcano Church it has been important in the past in giving social and moral support. In contrast to the Sandinista government, which offered the Madres space, the current government has denied their appeal for an office and a gallery for portraits of heroes and would like to see them shut down.

In the early 1990s, there were eight living in Doña María's house, including Doña María and her husband and her son and his family. Her husband received about U.S. $55 monthly in retirement benefits and her son was unemployed, so they were having difficulty making ends meet. In 1994, María left for the United States, where she stayed with a niece in New Jersey and found work in New York. Two years later, her son told me she hoped to return soon to Nicaragua, but at the close of the decade she was still in the United States, caring for a critically ill brother. She was sending money back to her family when she could. Meanwhile, her son had given up the venta in their front room because they were spending more than they were bringing in and customers buying on credit failed to repay them. His wife had a small income working part time in a clinic, and his father, María's husband, was spending more time in his finca growing beans and a few other crops, for the family and sometimes for sale.

In 1993, I was surprised by an announcement in *La Boletina* about a new *cafetín* opening in Barrio Monseñor Lezcano, run "by women and for women of action." I went there and spoke with the owner, Doña Monica. I found a bright and cheerful restaurant with five round tables covered with red-and-white checked cloths, with a breeze circulating through louvered windows along two walls. Monica offered a tour of the place, which is her home as well and also houses a sewing cooperative. The restaurant had opened a few months before, by four women who had completed a pastry-making course, and it attracts a large number of women customers as well as male and female employees from a nearby bank. During this first visit, she told me that a group of fifteen women had just been there for a lunch arranged in advance. By the time I arrived, two men were drinking beer at a table. Rosa explained that while the restaurant was designed to provide a space for women, the men who came were respectful and caused no trouble.

The four women, including Monica, work and earn equally. They divide the café's income in four parts that go toward salaries, items needed in the restaurant, water and electricity, and savings. The café specializes in *repostería* (baked desserts), which they make in their large kitchen and put in display cases in the restaurant, but they serve a variety of simple meals and drinks as well. They derive additional income from catering pastries for women's groups, the social security administration, and so on. They have gone to some effort to paint large, colorful designs of powerful-looking women on the walls inside the café, and Pepsi ads decorate the outer wall along with plantings by the sidewalk. Their location on a major street leading in and out of the barrio has helped to assure them of better-than-average business.

These entrepreneurial women have a strong connection to Monseñor Lezcano Church, where they have volunteered their services over the years. As members of a pastoral commission, they were active in supporting a preschool and a medical clinic and in providing sewing classes and other training. Now their business allows them to help out financially with other church projects. Monica began working with the parish in 1980 and told me that she has always worked for the revolution and for the church. She

18. *The owner of a* cafetín *meant to appeal to women stands by a mural in her restaurant.*

continues to work for the common good, although she emphasized that the government is doing the opposite, which presents a challenge to those doing progressive work. One project was to build a new park, working through the mayor's office to secure USAID funds; when the project failed to get results, the women carried on by themselves, raising funds and getting volunteer labor. Then the mayor's office stepped in with support and the park now bears one of his signs announcing "The Mayor Comes Through." Monica was understandably cynical about that turn of events.

Doña Monica has lived in the barrio since she was fifteen, in this house since 1983. She and her husband have no children, but other family members live with them. They built a new house on the same spot in 1991 and added the space for the cafetín the following year. This is a new line of work for her, as she worked for twenty-four years as a seamstress. She emphasized the importance of women working together and providing a high-quality product in order to be competitive and successful. Her sister employs a couple of other women in a sewing workshop in the household. Monica and her sister were talking about forming an association once the sewing co-op grew bigger, to expand their business and become more visible. However, a year later both their businesses had declined somewhat and their plan appeared unlikely. Reflecting on the changes in the last decade, Monica expressed the hope that with hard work her family and the community would move forward, but she also acknowledged her regret that "the revolution was not revolutionized." She noted that women who were active in supporting the revolution have paid dearly, carrying the burdens of maintaining family and society.

Like Elena (mentioned in the last section), another woman active with the FSLN at the barrio level shared her views on current activism. While Elena cited some of the advantages that drew newcomers to Barrio Monseñor Lezcano, Carmen was more critical of the local consequences of government politics since 1990. She judged that in the early 1990s Mayor Alemán did not want to hear anything about Monseñor Lezcano, as it was still identified as sympathetic to the Sandinistas, and therefore made few infrastructural improvements there. She also viewed the Occupational Conversion Plan as contributing directly to the problems in the barrio; people left state sector jobs with severance pay and purchased freezers or Nintendo games to attract informal business to their homes, but with little success. An architect and party militant in her early thirties, Carmen suggested that her own problems with steady employment under the UNO government might be traced to her political activity with the FSLN. She, like many others, expressed strong opinions about the impact of national politics on her life, the community, and the country.

The Local and the National

Just as the city of Managua can be viewed as a window on Nicaragua, so Barrio Monseñor Lezcano may be seen as a window on the wider urban and national situation. A number of the residents expressed views reflective of national-level policy changes: cutbacks in the state sector had cost people their jobs, privatization of health care contributed to a loss of family well-being, and so on. Residents identified more positively, too, with their barrio. For example, the barrio traditionally celebrates Día de Alegría on July 17, the day in 1979 when Somoza fled the country, and on July 19 barrio residents march together to Managua's Plaza de la Revolución to gather with thousands of others in honor of the revolution. In preparation for these occasions, activists in the barrio often make elaborate plans for neighborhood celebrations, with food, music, and other activities to commemorate the heroic past. The fluidity of residents' participation and social identity is apparent, as they make use of the red-and-black FSLN flags and play popular revolutionary music in the barrio, then march to the city's Plaza—whereupon they become less identified with Barrio Monseñor Lezcano and more identified with Sandinista loyalists everywhere.

My conversations with barrio residents often tacked back and forth between perceptions of the local, the national, and, sometimes, the international. Virtually all those I spoke to felt that conditions in the barrio reflected broader developments in the country, although opinions about these developments varied considerably. At times, I realized that while I was urging people to talk about their experience in the barrio in the hope of discovering something about local identity, some individuals were more interested in sharing their national and even global views, locating their experience in a much broader context. For example, when local Sandinista activists such as Don Nicolás and Doña María described barrio participation in the annual July celebrations, their narratives moved easily from ways that barrio residents were involved to their connection with other people and places in Managua and beyond. Similarly, María's activity with the Madres may be located in the barrio or elsewhere, but it is linked directly with activism throughout the country.

Don Nicolás, who told me that Barrio Monseñor Lezcano "is suffering the same crisis as the country," referred often to the lack of work, rising prices, and higher rates of crime, in the barrio and elsewhere. He talked frequently about the changing social composition of the barrio, as skilled tradespeople, small business owners, and professionals were outnumbering workers. He attributed this to the influx of middle-class residents after the earthquake in 1972 and also to young people attaining higher levels of education than their parents. Don Nicolás appeared satisfied with that development but regretted that at the national level, neoliberalism, with its emphasis on privatization and cutbacks in the state sector, was destroying the labor movement. He felt that workers are now identifying themselves as owners and therefore do not struggle as before. Furthermore, he lamented that the FSLN was a party of entrepreneurs, lacking a program to provide needed leadership for the "masses" of workers, intellectuals, businesspeople, and others. At his most cynical, he told me that the problem was that there had been "no revolution in Nicaragua." Rather, he said, there had been an uprising of all the Nicaraguans who were opposed to Somoza — not necessarily in favor of the Sandinistas. As early as 1980, the people realized that the revolution was not delivering what they had hoped for, and during the course of that decade their disappointment grew.

The globalization that has accompanied neoliberalism in the 1990s can be observed at the level of the barrio as well as nationwide. A number of people commented on the hardship of small industry when imported goods flooded the market at lower prices. A few, like Don Nicolás, were able to draw connections internationally and comment that countries such as Chile, often the model for neoliberal advocates, had had similar experiences, with a majority growing more impoverished in the midst of "modernity" and "development." With the declining population of productive workers in Nicaragua and the growth of the self-employed in commerce and the professions, people are turning to livelihoods that offer the best chance of surviving the harsh current conditions. In Barrio Monseñor Lezcano, for example, an increasing number of households sell used clothing from the United States, which has been underselling clothing produced in Nicaragua. Most of the used clothing is purchased in Miami in bulk, either by individual merchants or by middlemen. For a time, shirts sold for a couple of dollars, and, although they were secondhand, they were considered well made and competed successfully. Later, higher taxes on clothing entering Nicaragua meant higher prices to consumers and made the business somewhat less lucrative.

A sign of the times is the large number of Nicaraguans who wish to learn English. English is taught in the schools, but private tutoring is also common. At Casa Ave María, for example, Grant Gallup offered classes to groups of young people, mainly boys from the neighborhood. Elsewhere in the barrio, I was surprised one day to discover posted outside a modest home a crude notice — like others announcing items for sale and services rendered — advertising English classes; a small chalkboard was hung, just like those reading "Hay arroz" (We have rice) or "Hay huevos" (We have eggs), announcing "Hay clases de inglés" (English classes given). In a rapidly changing world, even people with few resources are hopeful that with a bit of English they might improve their chance of success. At best, many hoped to travel to the United States; at the least, to benefit from an association with the English-speaking world.

Another sign of the times, sadly, is the increasing presence of beggars, prostitutes, homeless, drug addicts, and alcoholics in Managua. I was struck during my visit to the barrio in 1998 by the visibility of individuals on the street who were intoxicated or on drugs and of the poor asking for assistance. A woman carrying a sick child approached me one day, for example, asking (and receiving) a small amount for bus fare to seek help. I was also mugged and robbed and my car broken into on occasion, and this was considered so commonplace that I was only gently reprimanded for not being more careful and for leaving my car unattended on the street. Indeed, few urban residents leave home without someone there to guard the household against theft.

Two final examples from my interviews serve to illustrate the toll that neoliberalism is taking on the barrio and more generally on Nicaragua. Both draw on interviews and conversations I had over a period of years visiting the barrio. The first concerns the experience of a family that has lived in the barrio since the 1960s and has a medium-size clothing industry, known as one of the most successful businesses in the barrio. Their company began operation in 1973 with just two sewing machines and, with hard work, gradually grew to have forty machines. Before the revolution, they had as many as forty-seven workers and produced more than 200 pairs of jeans and 600 shirts daily. Under the Sandinistas, they were considered bourgeois and the family's eleven-year-old son was taunted enough by other children that he was sent to live in the United States. When a majority of workers in their company unionized and demanded workers' control, the family was treated with hostility by others in the barrio. When I first visited in 1992, the business employed twenty-eight women at the machines and three men cutting fabric in a working environment that was made more comfortable with music playing, good lighting, and fans in the two workrooms and air-conditioning in the central offices. Like many work sites, this one had an altar, with blinking lights and artificial flowers. The company produced shirts by the dozens, uniforms for industries, and blue jeans. During my visit, I saw that they had a lot of clothing on hand, with labels in English including "Houston, The Shirt of Destination" [sic] and "Union Bay"; I believe that this was because of the popularity of American clothing rather than the areas where the goods would be marketed. A man carried out stacks of shirts wrapped in plastic that had been prepared for sale. There was also a storeroom from which they sold directly to the public. Just a few months

19. *This small industry in the barrio has seen a steady loss of workers and business since the early 1990s.*

before, the family had to sell a store in the commercial center of Managua because they could not pay the taxes.

A couple and their daughter and son-in-law run the company, which is affiliated with the trade union organization CONAPI. They are worried that both the large textile industries and imported clothing are breaking small and medium-size industries. They recalled that under the Sandinistas the state bought from their company at set prices, although there was no quality control or incentive for companies like theirs that maintained higher standards. Now, they argue, the government is doing nothing to protect smaller industries and the free market is crushing them. Their employees are hired based on their experience, and most come from outside the barrio. They work forty-five hours and earn about U.S. $50 a week. Although they received an international award for the high quality of their work, business began to decline with the structural adjustment in 1988. Living on the premises, the owners unfortunately found themselves in debt and unable to pay their electricity, water, telephone, and tax bills; they are negotiating with the national electrical company to produce uniforms in exchange for cancellation of the debt.

An employee told me that she has worked there since the founding of the company and that she is the only employee from the barrio. The weekly income she reported was lower than that reported to me by the owner, and she had two daughters and three grandchildren living with her who depended on her earnings. We talked at some length about the ways that her family tries to cut expenses, adjusting eating and other habits to weather the economic situation.

A year later, I found the woman owner looking depressed. She explained that the company now employed only a few workers — that day, just three. Most of the orders they received were for uniforms, but with unemployment up the demand for uniforms was correspondingly low. As she put it, "Nicaraguans are against Nicaraguans." People want work, but government policies disfavor national employment. She noted that U.S. companies are sending cut material to assembly plants in Nicaragua's Zona Franca, undermining national development. By this time, her family was counting on the financial help of two sons who live in the United States. Yet she claimed that they would maintain their high standards and would not contemplate selling their sewing machines; invoking a national icon, she stated, "That's our machete."

The last illustration is the case of a large family that lives in especially dire circumstances. I came to know a teenage daughter in the family, Patricia, when she worked at Casa Ave María in 1993. She was small and appeared much younger than her sixteen years. She helped out in the kitchen in the evenings, and the U.S. $4 a day she earned for as many hours of work made her the top wage earner in her family. All the members of the family were devoted Sandinistas; her father had fought with Javier Cuadra, and her mother had been a CDS leader a decade earlier. One day, as I was leaving to conduct interviews in one of the barrio manzanas, she came by to find me and I decided instead to take the opportunity to visit her home. She lived just around the corner in what was a sort of tiny asentamiento which at that time housed about thirty members of her extended family.

As we approached her home, we passed her sister-in-law, who was selling snacks and candy out in front. Once inside, we entered a room that served as a sitting area and also contained a refrigerator that had worked in better times. Patricia called her mother to join us, and then her grandmother and several aunts and their children came in too. In the crowded four rooms off a short alleyway lived these family members as well as Patricia's father and her four siblings, another grandmother, several brothers and sisters-in-law, and their many children. Because they could not pay their bills, they had no electricity (at times they have tapped in illegally) and water had to be carried in pails from a park a few blocks away. Patricia took me on a tour of the living quarters, commenting on the number of people who slept in each bed.

Patricia's father earned about U.S. $100 per month as a police officer. Her mother used to sell ice and ice cream from the house, but she had to give that up when they lost their electricity. Her grandmother used to wash and iron for people, but, again, without power she could no longer do that work. In any event, few people have money to pay for those services now. One brother-in-law works as a typographer and another works as a porter in the Eastern Market, and a sister-in-law works as a cook at the Sandinista radio station. Three of the older children in the family attend university, but most of them have dropped out of school because they are unable to pay the fees or the cost of uniforms and shoes.

The various family units within the larger household obtain food and prepare it separately. They feed the youngest ones first, but sometimes there is nothing to eat. When the price of beans, a staple, went up, they lived mainly on rice, cheese, eggs, tortillas, and coffee. In the past they shopped at a supermarket where the prices were lower, but now they shop at the nearby mercadillo to avoid transportation costs. When I asked how they could afford other needs such as medicine and clothing, they laughed and pointed to their shoes, most of which were old and torn plastic. They said it is difficult to keep children in school; they are sent home if they don't have the right clothes and the required black shoes. Under the Sandinistas, health care, like education, was free and available to everyone, but now they must pay for hospital visits, tests, and medicine. They especially miss the basic food basket, the AFA, that was provided by the revolutionary government. They were unimpressed by the meager improvements in the barrio by the mayor's office, and they described the UNO government and President Chamorro as having "sold them down the river." As Patricia's mother put it, "Now there's nothing. Before, there was unity in the barrio."

When I revisited this family three years later, more of them were living in the same space. Patricia had long since been fired from her job for stealing, and she now had two babies, a two-year-old and a four-month-old, whose father continued to live with his own family; neither Patricia nor the children's father had steady work. At nineteen Patricia still had the appearance of a young adolescent, but like many women her age she found herself with major family responsibilities. Her mother expressed to me the hope that the FSLN would win the upcoming 1996 elections and that things would change for the better.

Of course, the FSLN lost and conditions did not improve for the majority of Nicaraguans. In 1998, I found Patricia's family experiencing still more difficulties. On earlier visits, I was often asked for some small financial contribution just before I left the country. This time, I was asked almost right away when I visited them. They described health problems, including her mother's ulcer and her father's chronic leg problem that had forced him to leave his job with the police. Recently, her grandmother had found a lump in her breast and needed to see a doctor. Patricia is anemic and has an ulcer. They were placing their hopes on sending Patricia's brother to computer school but needed money to do so. There had been a dramatic increase in the number of family members living in the household—up to about fifty, they told me, which I thought must be wrong until they began a count. Overall, although family members continue to find sporadic employment, their condition is desperate.

On my last day in Managua that year, Patricia was dressed in a faux leather miniskirt and close-fitting laced bodice, causing me to think that she might be working as a prostitute, which would not be surprising under the circumstances. I did not ask her about it, fearing I might offend her, and she later appeared at my door wearing a more modest outfit to say good-bye. In a proud gesture, when I gave her a parting gift of clothing she removed her earrings and offered them to me. I accepted, moved by her generosity.

Barrio, City, and National Economy

Barrio Monseñor Lezcano is fairly typical of other parts of the city in its cross section of working- and middle-class residents who participate in the informal and formal economy. As in other third world cities, Managua's informal sector has grown enormously during recent decades, and some estimate that as many as 60 percent of the city's population may now depend on informal economic activities for their livelihood. However, the negative attitudes toward the growth of this sector may be more prevalent in Nicaragua than elsewhere.

I recall the heated conversations I had during my first visit to Nicaragua in 1989 with Sandinistas who were adamant that informal workers were sabotaging the economy by hoarding goods in order to sell at exorbitant prices during times of shortage. Having encountered similar, though milder, attitudes elsewhere in Latin America, I wondered why the revolutionary society did not recognize that only a small minority of informal workers carried out such ruthless practices so successfully — certainly, most appeared to my unfamiliar eyes to be as poor as other marginalized city dwellers. I later came to appreciate Nicaraguans' concern by the late 1980s that the Sandinista government's efforts to favor rural agricultural production and maintain the national economy against increasing odds — especially given the effects of the U.S.-backed Contra war and economic blockade — would be undermined by "unproductive" urban workers.

In fact, some of the revolutionary government's measures to assist rural and urban Nicaraguans had the unintended effect of worsening the situation. Although the agrarian reform should have forestalled the heavy migration to Managua, the subsidized prices and basic food baskets sometimes proved to be a disincentive to rural producers and provided urban residents with a cushion of support. Eventually, lower wages and cuts in the state sector encouraged entry into the informal sector, where individuals might indeed earn more than salaried employees. The government attempted to divert consumers from heavy dependence on the Eastern Market through the creation of new markets and central distribution mechanisms. But right or wrong, public perception remained that marketers and street vendors (e.g., those selling plastic bags of drinking water at intersections) were enriching themselves at the expense of other Nicaraguans.

Yet the assumptions that underlie notions of what constitutes productive and unproductive work are frequently too simple. As Massey (1987) has noted, agricultural production is not inherently more productive than tortilla making and selling, whether part of the formal or the informal economy. Debates over these matters abound in the literature on third world de-

20. A large and impoverished extended family lives in close quarters in the barrio.

velopment, and I do not wish to engage in lengthy discussion except to say that the lines between these categories of work are often blurred. Moreover, when unemployment is rising and people lack alternatives, self-employed workers (informal or otherwise) relieve the state of even higher levels of poverty.

Negative opinions of urban informal workers persisted into the 1990s, when rising unemployment and the Occupational Conversion Plan sent more Managua residents into the informal sector, many as owners of pulperías and other small commercial ventures. Although Nicaraguan scholars (e.g., Chamorro, Chávez, and Membreño 1989, 1991) have begun to study the urban informal sector, showing the heterogeneity of the sector in terms of productivity, income level, and ability to accumulate capital, popular conceptions of informal workers as parasitic within the urban economy and of Managua as parasitic in the national context have gone unabated. Unfortunately, this contributes to a polarized view of city versus countryside. If we are to have a broader understanding of urban-rural relations, we need to move beyond a unitary focus on material production and examine the more complex ways that culture and economy, class and gender, are engaged as people do what they must to get along in neoliberal Nicaragua. The view from the barrio offers a counterpoint to the undifferentiated notion of urban lives and livelihood by showing the manifold ways that individuals and households are coming to terms with new conditions of everyday struggle in the city and the nation.

Chapter Five

UNMAKING THE REVOLUTION

Women, Urban Cooperatives,
and Neoliberalism

P ROGRAMS of stabilization and structural adjustment spread
widely throughout Latin America during the 1980s. In revolutionary Nicaragua, the Sandinista government introduced adjustment programs late in
the decade, but harsher measures mandated by the IMF and the World Bank
came later, after the 1990 elections ushered in the UNO government of Violeta Chamorro. A debate emerged over the consequences of these measures
for the most vulnerable social groups — in Nicaragua as elsewhere, the poor,
women, and children. Yet in Nicaragua the recent history of social mobilization prepared these groups in distinct ways to confront the devastating effects of neoliberal economic programs, setting the country apart from others in Latin America. This chapter shows how low-income urban women,
who are among those affected most by the political change of the past
decade, are actively confronting worsening conditions both at work and
at home.

Several analyses have led the way toward a critical and gendered perspective on the recent effects of development policies that rely on stabilization and adjustment measures (e.g., Elson 1991; Afshar and Dennis 1992; Benería and Feldman 1992). They have called for attention to the household, where women are functioning as shock absorbers for these measures, and they have argued that adjustment plans extend women's unpaid work in the home in ways that must be assessed. I suggest that while turning to the household and women's unpaid work — the emphasis of most feminist research in this area — has brought about a needed transformation in our thinking about economic development, it is equally important to assess the gender-specific ways that women are experiencing adjustment and absorbing the shock through their paid work in and outside the home. Indeed, women's unpaid and paid work are highly interconnected, and just as women's expanding work in the household may constrain their participation in the labor force, their increasingly difficult experiences in earning a livelihood make the new demands at home that much harder to meet. In taking this position, I hope to complement other feminist analyses of neoliberal policy and structural adjustment, demonstrating through my analysis of the Nicaraguan case the need for greater attention to forms of women's economic and political participation that extend beyond the home.

I first consider some of the general consequences of structural adjustment policies for third world women and men and then turn to examine the effects these policies have had in Nicaragua, particularly for women in formal and informal work in Managua's small industries and commerce. I concentrate on the situation of women in the urban cooperatives I followed over the years of my research, presenting narrative accounts of the cooperatives' experiences from their formation to the present. Then I discuss the growing number of women conducting informal activities, often out of the front rooms of their homes in the city's working-class and poor barrios, as a response to the dismantling of urban cooperatives and of the state sector. In concluding the chapter, I suggest that even the best strategies women have devised to confront the economic crisis are not sufficient to withstand the impact of structural adjustment measures and that more thoroughgoing structural transformation may be needed once again in Nicaragua.

Gender and Neoliberal Policy

In her examination of male bias in the development process, Diane Elson (1991: 164) writes that "macro-economic problems, such as large balance of payment deficits, high inflation rates and very low growth rates, have devastated many countries in Asia, Africa, Latin America and the Caribbean in the 1980s." She notes that these problems stem from both internal and external pressures and that many countries have no choice but to look to the IMF and the World Bank for financial assistance. Although it is not my project here, such problems as third world indebtedness and underdevelopment must ultimately be traced to histories of colonialism, dependence on the world market, and the changing structure of capital accumulation. In other words, the global economic problems that are felt most severely in the third world often originate in relations with the first world.

Elson was among the first to challenge the supposedly gender-neutral programs of economic stabilization and structural adjustment that are conditions of international assistance. These programs include plans to reduce inflation, privatize industry, increase export production, decontrol prices, and cut public expenditures. A number of questions could be raised regarding this market-oriented neoliberal model of development, which generally favors elites at the expense of nonelite majorities in societies, but here it is most pertinent to consider the hidden burdens that women must shoulder under these programs.

As Elson and others (Benería and Feldman 1992; Afshar and Dennis 1992) have noted, adjustment programs that are designed to streamline economies and enhance competitiveness are based on macroeconomic concepts that apply to economies overall rather than to particular enterprises or households. Therefore, they rarely examine the disproportionate number of women who are located in the small industries and informal businesses that are apt to suffer most from the new policies. Nor are they likely to notice that when unemployment rises, food costs go up, and health care and education become less widely available, it is women who must adjust to meet pressing family needs. Because the work of stretching household budgets, caring for the ill, and in general managing to get along under conditions of economic and psychological stress are unpaid services that do not apparently affect the market, they are overlooked by development planners.

Yet increasing evidence indicates that women's ability to cushion the blow of economic adjustment is not without limits, and many households are suffering serious consequences from the crises produced by recent policies.

Where men are present as contributors to households in third world countries, they typically offer a smaller portion of what they earn to meet family expenses and keep more for personal spending than do women, even though their incomes are generally higher; in contrast, whether or not women are the sole providers in their families, they tend to turn almost all their income to collective needs (Blumberg 1991). Gender inequality in unpaid service to families is even more apparent; women perform far more of the work of family maintenance. Unequal economic power is frequently accompanied by domestic conflict and violence against women, a serious social problem that is now coming to public attention largely because of women's activism. Thus, if we are interested not only in aggregate measures of economic development but also in equity, we need to examine the household to discover patterns of resource allocation, the gender division of labor, and gender relations in the home (Tinker 1990).

In an analysis that considers the microdynamics of class and gender as the household responds to structural adjustment at the macroeconomic level, Lourdes Benería (in Benería and Feldman 1992: viii) describes the deepening inequalities that are emerging. While she notes the significant absence of proposed alternatives to the neoliberal model, she judges that given women's key roles in the household and beyond, they will be instrumental in efforts to resolve current problems. In fact, Benería and others (e.g., Elson 1992; Pérez Alemán 1992) point to evidence of women's organizing in grassroots social movements in ways that may ultimately transform societies. Nicaraguan women contributed importantly to this process in the revolution and demonstrated a determination to play a similar role even under drastically changed circumstances in the 1990s.[1]

The Nicaraguan Economy in the Sandinista Period

When the Sandinistas came to power after their protracted struggle against the Somoza dictatorship, they faced almost insurmountable problems of underdevelopment, among them an impoverished population, poorly managed resources, and inadequate health care and education. Yet in their first few years in government they carried out a broad program of agrarian reform, created a mixed economy and improved working conditions, made medical care and education available to all, and addressed issues of gender inequality as perpetuated through the media, the law, and other social institutions. Through their mass women's organization, AMNLAE, they worked with women in both the rural and the urban sectors, contributing to the growth of revolutionary consciousness among those women and in the society at large.

Within a few years, however, the conflict with the Contras required the development of a wartime economy that left little in the budget to sustain growth or to further the social transformation that was under way. Analysts have described the Sandinista period as a decade of both enormous hope and deep disappointment as the country struggled to bring about structural change while defending itself against internal and external aggression.[2] Until 1983, the economy experienced growth and social services expanded, but the strain became great enough that by 1985 an economic adjustment was imposed in an effort to stabilize the economy. A key member of the Sandinista government's economic team, Alejandro Martínez Cuenca (1992), describes the commitment to the mixed economy at the same time that measures were introduced to bring down inflation and allow the market to prevail. He notes, however, that the war and the embargo presented obstacles to stability and the economic crisis persisted. As the formal economy crumbled, the informal sector expanded, serving as a safety valve for rising unemployment. Although the government had tried to rein in the informal economy when it appeared to undermine state planning, some Sandinistas came to accept its important role in assuaging the crisis.

Economic imbalances increased over the next few years, with inflation reaching over 1,300 percent by the end of 1987, threatening to become as serious a problem as the counterrevolution in eroding the social base (Martínez Cuenca 1992: 69). The high cost of defending the country and continuing to subsidize social services such as health care and education had contributed to spiraling inflation and a large deficit. Attempting to reverse the trend, the government implemented the 1988 Stabilization and Adjustment Program — shifting from domestic production and consumption to export-oriented production, devaluing the currency, laying off thousands of workers in the public sector (known as *compactación*), and drastically cutting social services. A few months later, the effort to liberalize the economy was disrupted by Hurricane Joan, whose severe damage required costly reconstruction. In 1989, harsher measures were taken, and some critics charged the Sandinista government with inadequate consultation before taking such a "neoliberal" direction.[3] Yet Martínez Cuenca and others argued that the program was not orthodox but heterodox, as the government continued to provide the social buffer of the AFA package to state employees, as well as subsidies for basic needs such as transportation, electricity, and water. Even so, the social cost of the adjustment was high, and women were affected most adversely by the measures both as workers in less secure jobs and as family members responsible for child care and household maintenance (Brenes et al. 1991b).

The strong parallels between these steps taken by a revolutionary government and those mandated elsewhere in Latin America by the IMF and the World Bank are striking. Motivated by similar problems despite the divergent path of Nicaraguan development, the Sandinista government took a long-established route to try to stabilize the economy. In this case, the measures were decided on by the government itself rather than being the result of an externally imposed set of conditions—a significant distinction. From the vantage point of poor and working-class women, however, this may have mattered little at a time of widespread hardship. Even those women who were sympathetic to the objectives of the Nicaraguan revolution expressed alarm when their families faced a steadily rising cost of living and high unemployment.

Contributing to their dissatisfaction were the layoffs in the public sector that caused a growing number of urban women to seek employment in the informal sector. Of the 61 percent of Managua women who were employed at the time of the 1988 adjustment, a high proportion were represented in the informal sector as sellers and providers of other services, and compactación meant still more growth in that sector. Whereas women under the age of forty might have found employment in the formal sector had it not been for the layoffs, they, along with older women and female heads of household, were turning to informal work. Frequently, women needed more than one source of income to support their families (Brenes et al. 1991a).

During this period of economic crisis when households needed income earners, more women sought to enter the labor market. Those pursuing informal employment found increased competition from those in formal sector jobs who discovered that their real wages were insufficient for survival and that they could earn more in informal trade. As early as 1985, 60 percent of employed women were in the informal sector, compared with 49 percent of employed men in that sector (Pérez Alemán 1992: 245). Women continued to experience higher levels of unemployment and lower wages and other earnings than men, an especially critical disparity given the large proportion of female-headed households (conservatively estimated at about 45 percent in Managua). Women were also hit harder as artisans and as workers in small industries, as most available inputs were directed to large private and state industries and credit was tightened.

Thus when the government of Daniel Ortega brought about a devaluation of the national currency and massive cuts in the public sector, the results were severe for the majority of the population and especially severe for low-income women. This accounts in significant part for the Sandinistas' electoral loss two years later and for the gender gap in the vote, with more women than men supporting the UNO. Nevertheless, the adjustment programs adopted by both the Chamorro and Alemán governments have had far worse consequences. Privatization, cuts in social spending, and a reduction of the state sector are familiar by now as key elements of structural adjustment, but in Nicaragua the rate at which these measures have been implemented has been crushing—particularly for a country that had grown accustomed to a state safety net for those in the society who were most vulnerable.

The Post-Sandinista Period

Soon after taking power, the UNO government embraced the neoliberal model in an effort to stabilize the economy. Key components of the program included reducing government spending (cutting back state sector employment and eliminating government subsidies of food, public utilities, and transportation), increasing the sales tax (affecting the poor most, because they spend a greater proportion of their income on goods that are taxed), devaluing the currency, increasing interest rates and reducing access to credit, privatizing state enterprises, promoting assembly plants in the Zona Franca (largely textiles), and eliminating import tariffs (allowing cheaper imported goods to undercut national production). Because of harsh conditions, seven hundred thousand Nicaraguans have left the country to seek work elsewhere, sending home remittances that allow families to escape the worst effects of neoliberalism.[4]

Francisco Mayorga, president of the Central Bank, led the UNO effort in 1990 by introducing a new currency, the gold *córdoba*, but instability continued and he left government service by the end of Chamorro's first year. A more successful monetary plan was introduced by Minister of the Presidency Antonio Lacayo, who announced the major currency devaluation in March 1991 so skillfully that some time passed before opposition was expressed.[5] Nevertheless, the devaluation caused sharp socioeconomic dislocations as real wages fell and prices of many basic goods rose out of reach for the majority. That year, the Occupational Conversion Plan, funded by USAID, offered up to U.S. $2,000 in severance pay to state sector workers who would give up their jobs. Some thirty thousand left by 1993 (25 percent of the total), and many more left in the next couple of years, some to pay off debts and many more to begin selling food and other household items informally from their homes — having the intended effect of shifting workers from the public to the private sector.[6] That the program was directed in particular to women, who were encouraged to seek self-employment in the services and commerce rather than in productive enterprises, was signaled by a television promotion of the plan, which featured a woman owner of a beauty shop and emphasized that her time was her own.

In 1992, the "Year of Reactivation," privatization of industries and export-oriented production proceeded apace. Inflation was brought under control, yet all indicators showed that Nicaragua had never had a worse depression, with levels of unemployment and poverty unprecedented in the country's history. Between 1990 and 1992, formal sector employment dropped 18 percent, as many workers left jobs in health, education, and other public services. Unemployment rose to 19 percent and underemployment to 45 percent in 1992 (*Envío* 1992a: 18–20). The figures reached 20 percent and 54 percent respectively by 1995, making the unemployment rate twice that of 1990 and ten times that of 1984 (Arana 1997: 84).

In 1994, an agreement, the Enhanced Structural Adjustment Facility (ESAF), was signed with the IMF. In return for balance of payment stability, broad and stringent conditions had to be met. At the macroeconomic level, there were signs of growth and recovery, but new problems emerged a year later when the country could not meet the IMF's requirements. The foreign debt reached more than $11 billion, the highest per capita debt in the world. Furthermore, the chasm between rich and poor remained, and poverty conditions persisted. The social cost of the plan came to be viewed as a political issue, and Lacayo's National Project (Proyecto Nacional) met increasing criticism.

Under the neoliberal plan, industrial restructuring has seriously affected workers in small industries and commerce. With the rapid entry of competing foreign industries and products, cuts in credit available to national industry, and the removal of subsidies and price controls, small producers and sellers face a shortage of the primary materials they need in their work and a declining demand for the items they offer for sale. The strategy of establishing free trade zones and favoring large industries that are more competitive in the world market, as well as sharply reducing protective tariffs on imported goods, has driven out many small industries and threatens to weaken many more in Nicaragua. As a result, the informal sector is expanding to absorb displaced workers from industries and from the shrinking, "more efficient" state sector.

Viewed by Western development analysts, the government, and even some Sandinistas as inevitable, structural adjustment has curbed inflation while contributing to high levels of unemployment, declining real wages, and a sharply falling standard of living. Access to basic health care and education, available to everyone in the 1980s, has become a privilege for the middle class. Although many new products, including luxury items, are entering the market, few people have the resources to buy them. Structural adjustment's particularly harsh consequences for women has begun to receive attention in Nicaragua (Fundación Internacional para el Desafío Económico Global [FIDEG] 1991a).

Researchers have noted that the redistributive impact of adjustment has been largely at the expense of women (Metoyer 1997; Stahler-Sholk 1997). Often, men have made up the majority of the newly unemployed, while women are more numerous among those who are underemployed (Renzi and Agurto 1993). Because women made up the majority of state workers, they were disproportionately affected by cuts in the public sector, which sent many of them into the informal sector (Evans 1995). At work and in the family, then, women have often provided the cushion needed when resources are in short supply. They seek new sources of income, stretch household budgets, and take up the slack by offering services that are no longer provided by the state. Thus any success that structural adjustment may have in contributing to "productivity" and "efficiency" depends on a longer working day for women, who carry the major responsibility for maintaining their families. And this, of course, leaves in place the underlying structural basis of economic crises and gender inequality.

As a result of economic restructuring in post-Sandinista Nicaragua, some sectors expanded while others contracted, but throughout the country low-income women struggled harder to earn a livelihood and support their families. In Managua, many turned to small industries and commerce, organized formally or informally and based outside or within their homes. The government did little to assist small and medium-size enterprises or the informal sector, where the majority of Nicaraguans find employment, and instead relied on market forces that favored larger industries. When it did give attention to small enterprises, the impact was limited.

Women and Urban Cooperatives

During the years of the Sandinista government, many small-scale producers were organized in urban cooperatives (just as many were organized in rural cooperatives). According to the Law of Cooperatives, ten members were required to form a *cooperativa productiva* (productive cooperative in which members worked at a common work site) and twenty-five were required for a *cooperativa de servicios* (service cooperative in which members worked at individual sites and came together to organize and to sell their product). One member served as the legal representative of the cooperative, but decision making and other responsibilities were shared collectively. The cooperatives were part of the state project to formalize and collectivize small industries in order to increase production and build class unity among workers. These co-ops benefited from the distribution of low-cost materials and from the state's assistance in marketing their products. Artisans often received special support, as they were strategically located in the Sandinista revival of traditional culture as part of the nation-building project (Whisnant 1995; Field 1998).

Women were drawn into the newly formed cooperatives for the same reasons men were, but also as a deliberate effort to include women in the revolutionary process.[7] Unfortunately, while working-class women were drawn into cooperatives as well as mass organizations (e.g., the CDSs, AMNLAE), traditional gender relations persisted at home, making it difficult for these women to carry out many new responsibilities and avoid men's criticism that they were not fulfilling their family "duty." Many men, even those who in principle supported women's right and responsibility to engage in the wider economy, feared that their wives were beyond their control as they gained access to the public sphere. Implicit or explicit was the traditional invocation of women's proper place in the home (*en la casa*) and not in the "street" (*en la calle*). Some women, including those whose families had middle-class aspirations, bowed to the challenge to their propriety as wives and mothers and left the cooperatives, but many others actively engaged in economic and political work that took them outside the household.

Aside from their token support for microenterprises, the Chamorro and Alemán governments' national policy has not favored small industry in general, as they have encouraged foreign investment and larger industries that are competitive in the global market. Cooperatives, of course, bear the stamp of the Sandinista political orientation—one that is antithetical to the free market economic model now in place. It is estimated that more than half of all small industries nationwide failed in the early 1990s, and those that survived have struggled in the new political economic context (*Barricada Internacional* 1993).

My ethnographic research in Managua sought to provide in-depth local-level studies of working women as a window through which to view the effects of and women's responses to the dramatically shifting policy. Although women working in small industries and commerce make up the majority of employed urban women in the country, they have rarely been the focus of research.[8] The four urban cooperatives I discuss here formed after the Sandinista victory, one as late as 1991 (after the UNO victory). Two of the co-ops were made up exclusively of women, and women figured prominently in the other two. Two of them involved women in traditional gender roles, in the preparation of clothing and food, and the others in nontraditional ones, in welding and artisanry. All felt the impact of the changing economic policies, and the women interviewed noted the adjustments that they themselves were making at work and at home in order to get by. These are frequently viewed as coping or survival strategies, but they should also be understood as women's response to economic policies that are transferring work from the public to the private sector. In their workplaces and in the household, women absorb the shock of the economic crisis, and in so doing they help to underwrite the very policies that marginalize them. Each of the four cooperatives discussed below illustrates points taken up in this chapter. I first discuss the artisans' cooperative, where I spent the most

21. *Jewelers working at the Francisco Estrada Cooperative (portrait of the artisan-martyr hangs on the wall).*

time, was apprenticed, and had the strongest association. Then I discuss the seamstresses and the bakers, two cooperatives that had different degrees of commitment to the ideals that originally motivated their formation. Finally, I consider the welders, an energetic group of women who organized in the early 1990s but never resolved issues of affiliation and commitment before they disbanded just two years later. For all four groups, the struggle to balance work at home and in the cooperative coupled with the increasing force of neoliberalism made work life more precarious.

Francisco Estrada Cooperative

Five jewelry makers and five bark-work artisans came together in 1987, working out of the home of a German woman, Marlene, who had come to Nicaragua in solidarity with the revolution during its early years.[9] They founded the Francisco Estrada Cooperative (Cooperativa Francisco Estrada), named for an artisan and national hero who was a general in Sandino's army in the 1920s and whose portrait hangs prominently on the wall. The men and women who made up their workshop included experienced jewelers who worked with silver, malachite, and black coral, resources found in the country, as well as women who specialized in making ornamental wall hangings and other items from the bark of tuno trees found on the Atlantic Coast. Marlene and one of the men, Ivan, who had been a jewelry maker for twenty-five years, worked together before they founded the cooperative. One of the women, an experienced artisan, trained several other women who joined the cooperative to work with bark, although she soon left to work independently. Three women, Carmen, Paola, and Blanca, whom I met in 1991 at the Festival of the 52 Percent, had come more recently. Despite the high quality of their work, sales remained low, limited to foreigners in Nicaragua seeking unusual artisans' crafts and the small number of Nicaraguans who could afford ornamental items. Two men, jewelry makers, left the co-op in 1992; the other members explained their departure by saying that the men could not accept the crisis conditions that they were facing collectively.

I spent the most time with the bark workers, Paola and Blanca, and the jewelry makers, Marlene and Carmen. I got to know the men, too, but at the outset I made myself useful by helping out with cutting and gluing pieces of bark for wall hangings, place mats, coasters, and other items under the close supervision of the two women bark workers. This elementary apprenticing gave me an opportunity to spend longer periods in casual conversation and observation in the workshop, a space at one end of Marlene's house, which is in a wooded area in central Managua. Members of the cooperative were always generous with their time, and, as in the case of the other cooperatives, I visited occasionally in their homes as well. Once, to celebrate Semana Santa (Holy Week), the co-op members and I took a day trip to Granada in my truck. We hired a boat to take us to a small island on Lake Nicaragua for a picnic and relaxation. And the women in this cooperative greeted me warmly whenever I returned to the country. Thus I came to regard members of this group as close friends.

Marlene had been an artisan in Germany before she emigrated to Nicaragua in 1981. She worked as a technical assistant with the Ministry of Culture and later with a group of artisans, including Ivan, before they formed the cooperative. Paola had worked as a nurse before her young children demanded her attention, and she appreciated that she could leave the co-op to take her children home from school for lunch and bring them with her to the workshop if her husband was not at home; she had dreams of attending business school. Blanca joined the Sandinista literacy campaign in 1980 when she was sixteen, then worked in a government ministry until she was hospitalized for six months because of exhaustion; later, she attended university but ended her studies to seek work and earn a living. She sometimes brought her husband's young son from an earlier marriage to the co-op where he could eat with the group and play outside, and she dreamed of leaving on her own to seek work in Canada as her brother had done. Carmen had joined the co-op a couple of years before, first working with bark and then learning the craft of jewelry making, which she prefers. Several of the male jewelers as well as a woman who cooked for the co-op were part of the same large family. In general, members of the co-op were congenial and identified with Sandinista politics, although Paola always felt somewhat out of step as her husband opposed the FSLN, and she tried to remain friendly but politically noncommittal. The cooperative was an active member of the National Chamber of Medium and Small Industry (Cámara Nacional de la Mediana y Pequeña Industria, or CONAPI), which allocated supplies and offered other support.[10]

For the artisans' production of bark items, tuno bark is purchased in large pieces that have been pressed flat and which they iron to make smoother before the cutting, gluing, and sewing is done. The natural shades of the bark, ranging from off-white to dark brown, allow them to make abstract or naturalistic designs (sometimes indigenous patterns, a reference to the people who first used the bark on the Atlantic Coast) that are highlighted with top-stitching. The women have experimented with making purses, eyeglass cases, wallets, lampshades, room screens, pillow covers, and other personal and household items. Blanca and Paola had been working in the cooperative only six months when I met them, but they worked in a relaxed yet efficient way. They sat at a table to cut and glue the bark, used their one functioning sewing machine for stitching, and, finally, employed the ironing board or pressing machine to smooth the finished item. It could take up to six hours to make a wall hanging that would sell for about U.S. $5. The process involved tracing a pattern on the bark, cutting it out and arranging the parts on another piece of bark, gluing the pieces on and ironing them flat, sewing the pieces on and ironing again, pasting on another piece of bark as backing, trimming the edges, stitching around the edges, and ironing once more. One of the first projects I observed was commissioned by AMNLAE; it was an intricate design that included 141 small letters (at one point knocked to the floor by one of the young boys) commemorating the Mothers of Heroes and Martyrs. Sales of the bark work were always slower than those of the jewelry, which kept the workshop afloat.

The jewelry makers do most of their work around a rectangular table. Marlene and Carmen, along with the men they work with, sit at carved-out semicircular places that are fashioned with wood blocks on which to do their work. To do detailed work and protect their eyes as they use blowtorches, they use magnifying goggles. When they work with coral and semiprecious stones, they go to another area of the workshop where they have equipment for cutting and polishing. They make a variety of rings, bracelets, necklaces, key rings, and other items and also do repairs. Their work is displayed in enclosed glass cabinets for protection and for customers to make selections. In the early 1990s, the cooperative counted on word of mouth to bring buyers to their somewhat out-of-the-way workshop.

Under the Sandinista government, like other cooperatives, these artisans benefited from state-subsidized materials and assistance in promotion and marketing. In fact, the government guaranteed them a market, and co-op members joked that for a time all the Sandinistas were wearing black coral and silver jewelry from Cooperativa Francisco Estrada. A good deal of bureaucratic paperwork was often required of the co-op, to which members objected, but they remained loyal to the FSLN and political posters still decorate their walls. The situation changed with the UNO government, of course, and to make matters worse, the artisans could not afford the high interest rates on loans provided through CONAPI that might have allowed them to improve their artisanry. So they have cut back on production and earn what they can, according to how much they produce and sell. When two artisans collaborate on a piece, they share the earnings. Some weeks they sell nothing and therefore take home only a small advance in pay. Occasionally, conflicts arise over the way that tasks are distributed (generally all tasks are shared, although one man specializes in the preparation of coral for the jewelers) or how well a member is carrying out responsibilities (as in the case of a former member who was an alcoholic), but these problems are generally resolved within the group.

In spite of the difficulties they faced in the early 1990s, members told me about the advantages of working in a cooperative. Paola said that she appreciates the sharing of risk as well as income beyond what each artisan makes from individual production and sales. She noted that cooperatives generally bring together people who are responsible and have a commitment to the group, who join out of a sense of solidarity. They also learn from one another and teach new skills to others. In their small group, nearly everyone has a specific role, as coordinator, treasurer, secretary, or record keeper for inventory. In principle, monthly meetings allow all members to participate harmoniously in making decisions, although in practice this cooperative, like many others, had lost members who were not comfortable sharing collective tasks or who became frustrated when sales declined.

As in the case of the sewing cooperative Obreras Unidas Textil, discussed next, members of this co-op substituted time spent in marketing their products for production time. Often, several members would take an afternoon off to visit hotels or shops that might consider selling their jewelry or bark items. They also explored the possibility of exporting their work to European markets; however, these efforts have not resulted in many opportunities to expand their sales. Another strategy has been to try new techniques and designs to capture the interest of the buying public. This approach has sometimes backfired, as when Paola and Blanca invested many hours and costly materials to create several folding room screens with detailed bark work and the client, who had commissioned the work with a down payment, failed to come up with the remaining money owed.

The co-op considered whether the bark workers should be apprenticed as jewelers (Carmen already had been), since jewelry sales were somewhat better. Up to that point there had been a commitment to produce bark items as a local industry that made use of indigenous materials, thereby promoting "authentic" Nicaraguan artisanry. In 1992, however, the two remaining bark workers left the co-op to return to their homes. Both said that they needed to spend more time with their husbands and children. Blanca, who had long appeared depressed and often had headaches, was under pressure from her husband to stay at home, to cook, clean, and care for his young son while he held down a job at a supermarket.[11] And Paola's son's difficulty at school was the precipitating factor, along with her husband's preference that she leave her job (even though she lived within sight of the cooperative, so her family could easily locate her when she was needed) and rely on his income as the owner of a small hardware business.[12] Certainly another factor in the women's decisions was the very low level of their sales. They had virtually been subsidized by the jewelry makers for some time and may have considered themselves a liability to the co-op. In better times they might not have faced this difficult decision.

That same year, the cooperative sought and received financial support from a Norwegian NGO to build a separate workshop and expand its productive capacity in the area adjacent to Marlene's house. Following months of effort requiring many visits to various offices, CONAPI and the NGO authorized the loan that the co-op needed for construction, which was completed in mid-1992. The artisans hoped that as their visibility and productivity grew, so would their sales. They added several new women apprentices in jewelry making (with financial support from the NGO) and stepped up efforts to find markets outside Nicaragua.[13] Marlene acknowledged that they were taking a calculated risk in incurring debts as they expanded production, but business and morale improved as they enjoyed their spacious new workshop and the new equipment they acquired, and she held out hope that the co-op would become self-sustaining. She also expressed the view that the Sandinistas erred in offering workers too much assistance, so that they did not work to become self-sustaining. She was concerned, perhaps, that history might repeat itself if cooperatives became overly dependent on NGO support. Indeed, despite their vigorous efforts, the cooperative members were not able to repay their debt by the end of the 1990s.

Since its founding the Cooperativa Francisco Estrada has participated in CONAPI. Although members have criticized the recent administration for top-down leadership that pays insufficient attention to the base, they have been more steadfast than many others in attending meetings and supporting the organization. Marlene and Carmen have been the most active and are viewed by CONAPI as the spokespersons for the cooperative; Marlene commented to me that everyone who meets Carmen "falls in love with her," and she has been called on to represent the co-op as a result. In 1993, Carmen was sent with other CONAPI artisans to Costa Rica to explore marketing opportunities. A couple of years later, she accepted an invitation from CONAPI to travel to Ecuador for additional training in jewelry production. When she was elected as CONAPI's vice secretary of the Third Region (Managua), she was pleased to become more active, but after a trial period during which she saw her production and earnings decline, she stepped down.

By 1996, Marlene and Carmen were the only women still working in the cooperative, and nine men worked there. They continued to experience low sales, depending on customers coming to the workshop and selling at the occasional fair, so problems with indebtedness have been a constant worry. To adjust to the changing situation, they began working more autonomously as individuals rather than cooperatively, each one managing his or her own sales and bookkeeping; Marlene described this as a practical decision rather than an ideological one, although it is in keeping with the individualism of the market economy. She continued to serve as the cooperative's legal representative, while Carmen served as the coordinator.

Two years later, I found that in Marlene's view Francisco Estrada was no longer a cooperative but an association of members who paid monthly fees to rent space and equipment from her. She spoke more cynically than before of the unwillingness of some co-op members to take personal responsibility and said that under the new organization everyone necessarily took such responsibility. Since they have not been able to repay CONAPI or the NGO, they are no longer affiliated with CONAPI and are not technically a cooperative. There were different understandings among members of the group as to whether they were all collaborating to pay off the debt or whether Marlene had assumed the debt. Apparently, there was not one moment when the co-op ceased to function, and according to some members, they are "less" a co-op now but still have some of its features. A couple of men who joined recently praised the group for being "like a family" working together. During this period of transition, the different stakes of members evidently are being negotiated.

By this time, Carmen had left the co-op and was operating a small venta out of her home where she sold soft drinks, milk, candy, bread, sugar, toiletries, and a few other items. She told me that after ten years with the co-op, sales were too low for her to continue there. She was beginning to do sewing, including frilly items for bathrooms that she hoped to be able to sell to stores in Managua. She and I took some samples of her work to Francisco Estrada to show Marlene, who was politely disinclined to take on the work, as well as to a couple of stores whose owners said they would consider commissioning Carmen's sewing projects. She told me that she was bored working alone at home and missed the artisans' workshop.

To make ends meet and with future retirement in mind, Marlene had undertaken a new venture with a friend from Costa Rica who helped with financing. They had built several *casitas* (small houses, with bedroom, kitchen, and bath) on the wooded land around her house, which she intended to rent on a short-term or long-term basis. The enterprise has not been quick to take off in the last few years. Of the other women who had left the co-op, Paola had started preparing mondongo at her home, which she offered at lunchtime to about six men who are bus drivers and mechanics for the school her children attend (she told me that it is hard work and the men make her house dirty, but it adds needed income for her family); and Blanca had not visited the co-op but was reportedly still at home with her stepson and husband, although it was known that he had another woman.

This cooperative, like a couple of the others I discuss, has had some internal problems, but in general members have worked hard to build a successful working environment and viable business. The Francisco Estrada artisans are recognized for the high quality and design of their products, but sales are down because there are fewer international visitors to Nicaragua, Nicaraguans rarely purchase such ornamental items, and those who do find better buys in imported jewelry and other artisanry from neighboring countries. If they have survived longer than many cooperatives, it is because of the quality of their work, their lack of alternatives, and the fact that they have been favored in recent years by international assistance through an NGO. By now, however, Marlene describes the cooperative as a "museum artifact" in neoliberal Nicaragua. While some government officials claim that so many small industries are failing because of the poor quality of their products and poor managerial skills, the example offered here suggests that new policies favoring larger industries and imported goods undermine even the best efforts of many small producers.

Women's United Textile Cooperative

The Women's United Textile Cooperative (Obreras Unidas Textil, or OUT) was established in 1983 as a service co-op, the result of the Sandinista government's urging small producers to organize. The women in the co-op sewed clothing at home that they then sold from a central location. They came on a rotating basis to sell from their small store in Managua's Eastern Market district, where they had about four racks of clothing, and each earned according to the sales of the clothing she had made. Their selling area included space for meetings, a small altar with the Virgin set on top of a table, and a kitchen. The cooperative's coordinator, Elvia, and four other

22. Members of the Women's United Textile Cooperative stand outside their store, which was later dissolved.

elected members held one-year terms that were renewed during most of the 1990s. Elvia generally came to the store every day, and meetings of all members were held there monthly to decide on the rotation of tasks. A large poster showed the names of the two women who were responsible for the store and the four others who would function as support staff each day.

As in other service co-ops formed under the Sandinista government, members benefited from the availability of lower-priced materials, in this case fabric and thread, and the central location for marketing their products, while retaining the right to sell from their homes as well. They enjoyed the friendships they made with other women workers, and like many other cooperatives they joined CONAPI. The cooperative began with sixty-eight members (including two men), but, as a result of the economic downturn following the structural adjustment of 1988, membership dropped to twenty-nine women, a number that has held steady in principle, if not always in practice. Many of the remaining women were among the founders, now middle-aged or older women, who regard the co-op as a sort of family to which they owe their loyalty. Like others in small industries, they identified the problems they were experiencing as stemming from the post-Sandinista governments' support of large industries and elimination of assistance to small industries in the name of the "free market." The garment producers were particularly hard hit, however, as imported new and used clothing from the United States and elsewhere began flooding the market and underselling them. One of the women told me, "The free market is affecting us and we don't sell." Many members left in the late 1980s to seek other work. Those who stayed have lowered their production because of poor sales. Slower sales and stalled production led some of the active members to seek additional sources of income. Some began to sell soft drinks or other items from their homes, and some, ironically, began to sell used clothing. As one woman put it, "The compañeras understand that I do it out of necessity." Several women had rather reluctantly begun selling clothing on a daily basis from nearby market stalls where more shoppers passed by, sewing at home in the evening. Among these women, some sold from the store as well, in this way diversifying their marketing strategy.

When I first met these women, they were discouraged because the UNO government was offering little support to small producers or to CONAPI, which in turn could offer little assistance in the form of loans to its membership. Moreover, with more people turning to self-employment and small industry, the competition was greater. The favoring of large industry and imported goods, especially clothing, hurt them the most. Some reported selling just a single item, or nothing at all, in a week's time. They continued only because of their hard work, and their "love of the cooperative."

Within the group, there were some significant differences in age, education, family status, and social class. Elvia, the coordinator of the group, was an older woman of humble background who lived with her family in the northern part of Managua. Teresa, active in CONAPI as a volunteer at the regional level, was a middle-aged single mother and also of working-class background, highly motivated but finding herself caught in a difficult economic situation. One of the oldest members, Julia, was seventy, a widow, and had worked as a seamstress for thirty years. She had seven sewing machines in her home that she and her daughter, along with employees, had used; until the early 1980s, she had enough work to sew at home and take her clothing twice a day to a seller in the Eastern Market. Now the machines are largely idle and she sells used clothing and soft drinks in the front of her house. Yet another woman, Margarita, was younger, married (her husband was working as a welder in Canada and sent the family re-mittances), and was the most educated, having attended college for a year. She was in a far more secure economic position, and she hired her sister and four other women to sew with her in her home so that she could pro-duce and sell shirts by the dozens. Although she sold some of the shirts from the co-op store out of loyalty, she sold most of them to intermediaries who took them to rural markets. The majority of women were heads of households, and they generally had in common their commitment to the cooperative and to Sandinista politics.

Elvia traced the cooperative's difficulties to 1988, when the Sandinista adjustment and greater competition from the free market led some forty members to leave. The next few years were "precarious," she said, but in 1992 they "drowned." That year, according to CONAPI, only twelve garment cooperatives remained of the thirty that existed in 1988. When I visited the store that year, I saw that the racks of clothing were nearly bare, and there were very few customers. The women continued to take turns coming to the store, but they did so mainly to safeguard their property and to share a midday meal that they prepared together; everyone ate, regardless of abil-ity to pay, and they had each other's company at a time when the mood was grim. They laughed and agreed when one woman told me that in Nicara-gua "the rich are becoming poor and the poor are becoming wretched [*des-graciado*]." Some expressed resentment that CONAPI had used them as a "battle horse" for the organization, praising the women's relatively long his-tory and commitment but when times were hard offering no assistance. As Teresa explained, they were particularly bitter because the new president of CONAPI had been in the garment industry himself but changed to an-other business in time to avoid the problems they were facing. They felt that he had had a responsibility to advise them but instead had only looked out for his own interests.

The cooperative dealt in isolation with the difficult question of whether to sell its store and dissolve the co-op or hang on a while longer. By this time, only Margarita was sewing and making sales on a regular basis. When I re-quested a white school shirt for my son, a woman who had not sold anything in some time responded quickly by sewing a shirt for me the next day. On my last visit to the store that year, I found the women in low spirits, feeling defeated, with a single rack of clothing for sale. Sadly, the items were imported secondhand clothing from the United States. The women blamed the foreign textile companies in the Zona Franca for taking business from national garment producers like themselves. They did not appear to expect customers that afternoon, and none came. Elvia summed up the situation: "The truth is, our chances of surviving here are slim."

Indeed, when I returned to Nicaragua early in 1993 I was surprised to find that the store had simply vanished. Upon questioning, I was told that the co-op members had sold the store to a neighboring clothing retailer, who had absorbed the space to enlarge his establishment. While accounts differ, Elvia maintained that in late 1992 the co-op had begun renting the store to neighboring store owners. However, in recent months the rent had not been paid, and the store owners rationalized that the co-op members were not legal owners but had received the store in the Piñata (a Sandinista giveaway of state property just before the UNO took power). Although the women had the title to prove they were the owners, they lacked resources to hire a lawyer and press the case.[14] Over the next few weeks, I located members who still identified actively with the cooperative and worked on some basis from their homes or in the streets. These women spoke of trying to find a new space in which to work together again, but in the meantime they were changing leadership and preparing to conduct business from the new coordinator's home. Teresa, whose energies had been devoted to volunteering with CONAPI, had agreed to take on the function, but over the next few years it appeared that Elvia continued as coordinator.

Although the co-op's clothing production has dropped off sharply, some members have put more time into selling from their homes and from market stalls in the streets. Some have added shoes or other merchandise to their offerings. Still others concentrate on meeting the seasonal demand for new school uniforms or for dresses for Semana Santa. Those who continue to sew are finding that acceptable-quality fabric and thread at reasonable prices are more difficult to locate and that they have to spend more time searching for supplies. Several women travel regularly to other Central American countries to purchase sewing supplies or ready-made apparel at lower prices.

By 1993, when the women no longer had a central location in which to meet regularly and conducted limited business from their homes or from kiosks in the market, I began to hear of some disagreements among them.

Several expressed dissatisfaction with Elvia because she did not attend meetings at CONAPI and so could not keep the members informed of opportunities as they arose. The somewhat younger women who expressed this view favored Teresa as coordinator because she had long-term contact with CONAPI and could keep the membership apprised of meetings, workshops, resources, and credit programs. As it was, some complained that there was no point in gathering for meetings as a co-op if there was no useful information to be shared. But they expressed the hope that the group could regain the unity they once had.

Later that year, the women rented a small space in the commercial area around the CONAPI offices, where they hoped to sell clothing. This did not appear to be a successful strategy, however. They were not attracting customers and the space was being used for storage. Teresa, who was finally asked by Elvia to take over as coordinator, agreed and expressed the opinion that the best prospect for the women would be to find a central workplace where they could sew more efficiently. Once, as an example, she took me to visit such a sewing cooperative that had ample room for its members to work.[15] She told me, "Women are claiming the space they have a right to," holding out the hope of reactivating Obreras Unidas Textil. I found during visits in 1996 and 1998 that the cooperative did not undergo any significant change but continued in name and under the shifting, nominal leadership of Teresa and Elvia. At times there was slight tension between the two, as I found when I drove Teresa over to visit Elvia's house and the former was openly envious of the older woman's good fortune in acquiring a loan and maintaining her health — two things that Teresa had failed to do despite her best efforts.

Adjustment policies that contribute to unemployment and higher food prices severely reduce the cooperative's customers' ability to buy clothing and threaten to put it out of business. At a time when large garment factories and imported clothing are favored, the women are struggling harder to maintain sales — extending their hours of work, diversifying their production and their market, and traveling greater distances to purchase materials and sell. In all these ways, they not only support themselves and their families but also underwrite the process of structural adjustment through their resolve to work harder and withstand the difficulties it causes. For the majority, who are older women, there is no security for the future other than the social support they offer one another. As Julia put it, "We're paralyzed by this government."

Industrial Bakers of Managua

The largest service cooperative of bakeries, Industrial Bakers of Managua (Cooperativa de Industriales Panificadores de Managua, or COOIPAM), was established in 1979. More men than women became members, but many had wives who worked closely with them, and a number of women owners of bakeries were represented as well. They benefited from the co-op's provision of basic materials such as flour at lower cost and also joined CONAPI after the trade organization was formed in the 1980s. The co-op owned ample office space in a working-class neighborhood adjacent to Barrio Monseñor Lezcano where meetings were held regularly by the leadership. When I first visited the office in 1991, the central coordinator, Tomás, told me that 162 bakeries throughout the city belonged to COOIPAM (there had been more than 400 a few years before); he noted a concentration in certain barrios, for example, in Ciudad Jardin near the Eastern Market. The bakeries I came to know best over the years were concentrated in another barrio on the eastern side of the city, Bello Horizonte.

As a service cooperative, member bakers generally work out of their homes. By the early 1990s, most were finding it difficult to obtain financing and reasonably priced materials. Tomás compared that time unfavorably with the Sandinista period, when there was more support for small producers. Their co-op of bakeries was the only one remaining in the city, as ten others had failed. Tomás attributed their ability to survive to their willingness "to demand their rights." Under better circumstances, the cooperative, in collaboration with CONAPI, would offer more services to members, such as social security, health care, transportation, and assistance to families at the time of death of members. The main benefit for members at that time was access to lower-price materials, including flour, sugar, and shortening; members did not pay fees but were expected to buy with the cooperative, which supported administrative expenses.

Bread producers would seem to have the advantage of engaging in a business that has a constant demand. Yet as more bakeries open there is more competition, with larger enterprises having more chance of success. Some bakers reported changing with the times and offering popular items

23. *A woman works in bread production at a bakery.*

like pizza or sweet pastries. In one bakery where I conducted interviews, the family was proud of its college-educated daughter, who handles the bookkeeping and manages the enterprise, no doubt contributing to its success. Another family in the bakery business (discussed below) has cornered the market in one city neighborhood, with the mother doing business near a major traffic circle and her daughter managing her own bakery just a block away. The daughter has space for half a dozen tables where customers can sit down to enjoy pastry and something to drink. But even in these more fortunate enterprises production was declining sharply and the loss of income was threatening families' economic survival.

In exceptional cases, the experience has been much different. One of the bakeries I visited had been in business for twenty-five years. The owner had twenty-six employees plus family members working for him and possessed two buildings and four trucks. In this case, the owner reported that during the Somoza period he produced 200 *quintales* (20,000 kilos) of bread each week, which was reduced to five quintales under the Sandinistas, and in the early 1990s production was back up to 120 quintales. Although the bakery joined COOIPAM, he no longer felt a connection to the cooperative. He complained that under the Sandinistas "they wouldn't let us work," and he resented the cooperative structure. In another bakery, large enough to have advertising on billboards in the city, the owner's daughter described the current situation. With family and sixteen employees working, the bakery has been in business since 1978. Mainly men are hired to do the heavy (and higher-paying) work around the ovens, while both women and men work in the mixing of the bread dough, and women do the packing. She explained that COOIPAM failed because of debts owed to the bank, and their bakery is thinking of joining CONAPI or another trade organization directly. Having a college education, she was consulted by her father about what affiliation, regardless of political ideology, would be most useful to them. At present, their bakery is receiving assistance from an NGO, which has allowed her to pursue a business course at the university.

In early 1992, COOIPAM ceased to function, having been driven out of operation when suppliers of flour began selling directly to the bakeries at favorable prices. Unable to compete, the co-op put its offices and equipment up for sale, and the bakeries I visited began viewing their enterprises as independent.[16] They saw little advantage in affiliating with a trade union organization that was itself struggling for survival. A year later the co-op's property remained unsold and they were still trying to sell some twenty calculators, ten typewriters, and file cabinets. The formerly active coordinator, Tomás, came periodically to sell a small quantity of bread there, half hoping that the co-op could be revived, and meetings of the leadership were occasionally still held. He suggested that if they sold the office building they could pay off their substantial debt and consider purchasing a smaller office space. In his view, even though the cooperative was unable to carry out all of its intended functions, it continued to defend the rights of bakers, to protest rising costs, and to provide some materials below market prices. He gave some examples of rapidly rising prices (at a time when five córdobas were worth about one U.S. dollar), including that of flour, which had cost 70 córdobas for a quintal in October 1992 and rose to 105 córdobas in January 1993 and 125 córdobas in March that year. Similarly, sugar cost 93 córdobas in December 1992 and rose to 125 córdobas in March 1993 (the cooperative sold it to members for 120 córdobas). With rising prices and the increasing cost of gasoline, bread was becoming an expensive commodity for low-income and unemployed consumers.

Tomás spoke passionately of the potential of small enterprises, which he pointed out employ a majority of Nicaraguans who hold jobs, for the country's development. But he told me, "Neoliberal policy and unemployment don't allow people to gain a livelihood." He went on to say that whereas the Sandinistas gave special attention to small industries, "now the government is asphyxiating small industry and only helping big industries." He asked me if I didn't agree that everywhere else governments protect their national industries, but not in Nicaragua. Now it is only the largest bakeries, like La Panaderia de Plaza España (centrally located, with a posh area for having pastry and coffee), with thirty-eight employees and distribution to many supermarkets, that do well. Bakery owners in general were divided between those who adopted the attitude of the neoliberal government regarding the desirability of open competition and others who looked back nostalgically on the more protective Sandinista years. All, including Tomás, appeared critical of CONAPI, noting its lack of support for the co-ops, whether or not they favored the continuation of COOIPAM. And all were demoralized by the economic situation that further reduced bread consumption as many families bought tortillas and plantains as cheaper substitutes.

Two bakeries owned by women that I followed from 1992 through 1998 are illustrative of those that remained viable through the decade but were struggling to remain in business. Located on a street in eastern Managua where I had lived for several months, the bakeries are operated at the residences of a mother and her daughter. The mother, Luz, sees a steadier flow of customers, due in part to her bakery's location near the barrio's main traffic circle. She has seven employees, five men and two women, plus help from family members. In her late fifties, she is married to a retired man with whom she has three children, and she has had the bakery for close to thirty years. She told me that her husband never wanted her to work for a living and has never agreed with her decision, but she seemed proud to have been successful to this point. She was selling directly to the public and also to three supermarkets, with the use of a truck she owned. She enjoys the work and says she has no problems with workers but does find that the current lack of credit under the post-Sandinista government makes her job difficult. Luz noted that her bakery produced ten quintales per day in the past and now produces three or four quintales. An avowed Sandinista who had participated in COOIPAM and CONAPI, she nonetheless claimed that the loss of connection with these organizations was insignificant in terms of her business, since they could no longer provide materials at competitive prices or offer other assistance. She did, however, miss the solidarity of membership with them and the ability to confront the government over such issues as the high cost of taxes, electricity, and water to small industries. Summing up, Luz described the situation as "worse than under Somoza," the worst in all her years.

Less than a block down the street, Luz's daughter Laura has a somewhat smaller bakery with restaurant seating in front that she was operating with the assistance of three employees, two men working at the oven and a woman selling. I lived next door for some months and purchased bread and other items for the family I stayed with long before interviewing there. Laura herself buys ingredients at the market two or three times per week, participates in production, and manages the bakery. She has specialized in making pizza and calls attention to it in the name of her establishment, Pizza Pan. Along with ordinary bread and pizza, she makes pastries and sells soft drinks as well to customers who stay to sit at one of several tables.

Laura has lived for the last twenty years in Managua and has had the bakery since 1990. She studied in Spain, earned a high school diploma, and lived for two years in Washington, D.C., before rejoining her family and working in her mother's bakery. During the 1980s, she worked in a sewing cooperative but left when the economy contracted and used clothing poured into the country. She is thirty-four, married to a man who is professionally employed, and has two children who attend private school. Laura regards the bakery as independent and says that there is no point in belonging to a cooperative now, when she can get better prices buying directly from flour companies than through COOIPAM or CONAPI. However, she misses the workshops and gatherings and finds that the competition of the free market is undercutting her business. She offers lodging and meals as well as wages to her employees, and to offset her costs she must keep the bakery open seven days a week (workers get one day off) rather than six as in the past, but still her income is lower than when she began.

By 1993, Laura let two employees go to reduce her costs and tried to capture more customers by providing greater variety, something she announced in a large banner over her door. In addition, she had acquired a color TV (which attracts some who come to watch novelas) and hanging plants when they remodeled a year before, in another effort to appeal to a wider public. Despite the renovation and new offerings, including popcorn, candy, cig-

24. *A sign announces the sale of the office building of the Industrial Bakers of Managua,* COOIPAM.

arettes, and magazines, she said that business was terrible (*malisimo*). Pizza was still selling reasonably well, but bread production was down considerably. Like her mother, Luz, she was committed to maintaining quality even if smaller loaves of bread were sold, and that way she retained some loyal customers. Yet she said that sales were so low not just because of competition in bread production but because Nicaraguans' consumption of bread had dropped as the economy worsened. Although Laura might be considered middle class by local standards, she limited her family's expenses by buying less expensive food, eating out no more than once a week, and going to the beach only once each year as recreation. Virtually all her time is put into the bakery and restaurant, from 9:00 A.M. to 10:00 P.M.

My visits to these two bakeries in the late 1990s found Luz and Laura managing to stay in business by "holding on by their fingernails" while small industries were "strangled" in the neoliberal economy. Luz reported that she was producing 20 percent of what she had in 1990, and selling just to the public rather than to supermarkets. With fewer employees, her day has lengthened to twelve hours, from 6:00 A.M. to 6:00 P.M., and she works "like a burro." She recalls a time when she could drive a car and go to restaurants or the movies, but now she has no car and can't afford to go out. She told me that "for the grace of God" she goes on. Laura's most recent strategy was to give up making pizza and turn instead to preparing lunchtime meals for customers. She expressed the hope that she could still send her children, now in Catholic school, to university.

COOIPAM's office building was finally sold to a car repair enterprise, and no new facility was acquired. The cooperative's experience suggests that while some individuals place responsibility for their present difficulties on CONAPI or on the bakers' co-op itself, their problems clearly stem from increasing competition and lack of state support in the new market-driven economy. Long-standing food preferences might predict that consumers would continue to patronize local bakeries, but economic circumstances dictate that many turn instead to cheaper manufactured bread like Pan Bimbo (produced elsewhere in Central America) found in supermarkets, or to other food substitutes. Like the garment producers, the bakers are highly resourceful, yet both groups are reporting that production is being cut dramatically, often in half, as sales dwindle for those fortunate enough to remain in business.

Welders' Cooperative

The welders' cooperative formed in 1991 after a dozen formerly unemployed women completed a trade school course. The women's program consisted of ten months of technical training in welding and consciousness-raising workshops organized by the vocational program SINACAP (later known as INATEC, National Technical Institute) to prepare them as women for nontraditional work.[17] They continued to receive assistance from this state organization, particularly from the director of the women's section, a woman named Gabriela, who was devoted to providing women with skills outside the usual "female" trades in sewing and food services. She followed up in her work with nontraditional women workers after their training because, as she told me, they often lack support from their families and communities.

Just after these women began working together, a sample of their work was on display at the Festival of the 52 Percent, where I met several of the women for the first time. Two months later, they held the customary inauguration of their workshop, which was located in one of AMNLAE's women's centers in Managua. Marking the importance of the occasion, the national coordinator of AMNLAE, Gladys Baez, had been invited to speak and cut the ritual "ribbon." Some items made by the collective were arranged in the center of the room, including several chairs, a table, and a kitchen shelving rack, along with their equipment (much of it donated by international organizations), including soldering torches, an anvil, a vise, an electric bench grinder with polishing wheel, hammers, saws, files, safety shields, eye goggles, work aprons, and gloves. More chairs were lined up along the walls for us to sit on, and refreshments, prepared by the welders, were set up in the back. Red crepe paper tied in bows decorated the doorway — the bars at the door were also made by these women — and the work space. The coordinator of the AMNLAE center, Isabel, who served as an adviser to the welders, welcomed us. She introduced one of the more senior women in the collective (the majority were in their twenties and thirties), who spoke movingly about the importance of the welders' training and the opportunity they had to work together. Then Baez greeted everyone and spoke of the value of these women doing nontraditional work, noting that "work has no sex." She went on to criticize President Chamorro's policies for their assault on working people and drew a connection with Western imperialism. She then led the way to the entrance, where she cut the crepe paper to inaugurate the workshop. Afterward, loud music played on a boom box and food and drink were offered. That afternoon, I met the two co-coordinators of the welders' group, Doris and María Elena, as well as other women in the collective.

In high spirits, the women began their work, making wrought-iron chairs and tables, plant stands, and security bars for windows and doors. Some job opportunities came from their supporters, including SINACAP (CONAPI and the Casa Ave María also expressed interest but did not hire the women). At the outset, four women worked all day and another six worked half days because they had young children to care for (two others quit after the training for personal and health reasons). The arrangement may also have been an accommodation to the available equipment and space. Unfortunately, the group disbanded just a couple of years later, ending the "colectiva" (as it was called, since the women never agreed on a name). Jobs kept the women busy in the early months, but then work tapered off and broken equipment slowed them down. Not infrequently, I stopped by the workshop to find just a couple of the welders talking or making a meal because something had arisen that kept them from working. If the women's absences were not work

related, they were often family related, a child's illness or a husband's insistence that his wife remain at home.

When there was work under way, the women generally carried it out
with enthusiasm and a sense of purpose. All were proud to have learned
every aspect of the work, so that tasks could be divided each day on a rotating basis depending on available tools and equipment. The women were
seeking loans to enable them to purchase more metal and other materials.
I asked what would be involved, for example, to make a door of about six
by four feet, the kind of door with security bars that is typical of many Nicaraguan homes. Doris told me that it might take all ten women about a
week to make such a door. First they would need to acquire the required
eighteen-foot lengths of iron from a hardware store, then measure and cut,
hammer and shape, and solder all the parts, before finally painting the
door. Making a fairly simple fruit stand (which looks like a wire bicycle basket) could take a couple of women all day to finish. One of them would
hold the wire pieces to be soldered by a second woman. They would stop
periodically to place the stand on the anvil to hammer it into shape and
then smooth it on the polishing wheel. The work is painstaking, as the solder must be applied in just the right way so that the work is not ruined.
Since a fruit stand cost about 30 córdobas to make and sold for 50 córdobas,
each woman might earn about 10 córdobas (U.S. $2) for her effort. They
told me that they all earned equally based on the collective work they did
and tried to divide earnings weekly.

In addition to the elected co-coordinators, the collective had a secretary
and a treasurer, and members spoke of a need for someone to specialize in
marketing. Doris and María Elena explained that they did the same work
as all the welders but had added responsibilities too. They told me that they
liked the work, the independence it offered, and the flexibility of the hours.
There was evident friendship among the women, expressed by the warmth
of their conversation, the sharing of cigarettes, and the touching, laughing,
and singing as they spent time together. The opportunity they had to work
was especially valued at a time when the economic situation was so difficult and unemployment was high. And, as María Elena put it, "women are
hit hardest, always, always, due to low income and family responsibilities."
When I asked about the difficulties they experienced, I often heard that the
problems were external to the collective and they just needed time to get
on their feet. Later, however, when there was more trust between us, I

25. The co-coordinators of the women welders' collective, at a work site.

learned about internal problems in the group over how work was distributed by Doris and María Elena. Some felt that the co-coordinators were
lacking in leadership skills.

Other differences emerged when CONAPI sought their participation by
having three male representatives appear at the workshop to talk to the
welders. Headed by Antonio Chávez, then vice president of CONAPI, the
men met with eight welders and Isabel, the coordinator of the AMNLAE center who acted in a self-appointed advisory capacity. Sitting in a circle, the
men discussed the advantages to be gained by formal membership in
CONAPI, including assistance in locating a permanent workshop, acquiring
further training and loans, and advocacy for small industry in negotiations
with the government. For a monthly fee of five córdobas, or about a dollar,
members also received a card entitling them to health and other benefits.
Isabel interrupted to say that the women's affiliation with SINACAP was sufficient to meet their needs and that CONAPI might not be adequately attentive to the problems faced by the welders. She appeared to be arguing on
feminist grounds that the women would lose their autonomy under the

male-dominated leadership. After the men went on to say that the decision was in the hands of the collective, the welders, beginning with Doris, expressed their interest in joining CONAPI. Chávez was describing the trade union association's women's section when Isabel intervened again to say that CONAPI concerns itself only with women's economic problems and not other gender issues. As she persisted, the others looked impatient, and finally the meeting broke up.

Just after the meeting, Isabel expressed to me in private her view that CONAPI was very *machista* and that the real problem the welders had was one of coordination as they are poorly organized. Her attitude toward the welders was condescending and assumed that they could not make their own informed decision. Then, as I went into the workshop, the welders included me in their confidential conversation. They told me that they were ready to join CONAPI and that they had benefited from the support of SINACAP and the AMNLAE center but that they themselves needed to make the collective succeed. Although they were determined at that point to be in contact with CONAPI, their membership was never formalized. They later related to me their view that CONAPI might need them more than they needed CONAPI, pointing to the failure of so many cooperatives; they decided to remain independent and to continue using space at the AMNLAE center until they were established enough to have their own workshop.

During that first year of their work together, the welders had visits from others who volunteered to help the women attract more business. A woman from the United States who was a technical adviser came with a Nicaraguan businessman to consult with the welders about publicity and finding buyers. As the man spoke, he was also interrupted by Isabel, who referred nostalgically to the revolutionary past. He argued that while it was fine to recall the past, small industries needed to organize in new ways, since "capitalism is the force and the reason to exist in this world." When Isabel went on about her own role and that of her husband in the revolution and said that she wanted the "muchachas" to have another analysis to consider, the welders looked amused, then impatient, and began talking among themselves. The technical adviser proceeded by saying that the welders would be selling not only their product but themselves as well, and they needed to develop effective personal styles. She offered to help the women come up with a name to advertise their business. Her colleague added that the welders should not refer to themselves as a "colectiva" but rather an "empresa" (enterprise), select a "capitalist name" (for example, Tecnoarte), and use business cards. The welders seemed to take these suggestions seriously but did not follow through on them, saying that their first priority was to obtain financing.

Over time, it became clear to me that the welders were being pulled in various directions, advised differently by Isabel at AMNLAE and by Gabriela at SINACAP (the latter thought that the group could benefit from affiliation with CONAPI and that Isabel opposed it because she was afraid of losing control over the collective). The welders themselves made efforts toward greater independence from their advisers and from a series of technical assistants, but they were confronting other problems as well, from work difficulties to family matters. A few months after the inauguration of their workshop, four women had left for reasons of health, family, and lack of work, and the remaining six had only sporadic work, often from those seeking to offer them support. Many days, the women came to the workshop just to see if any work was coming in, then went out together to purchase food to prepare for their lunch (much as the women of Obreras Unidas Textil had done before they lost their store).

By late 1991, only three welders from the original group remained active in the collective. Family responsibilities and a lack of jobs kept the other women away, including a few who had hoped to resume their work later. The older woman who had spoken passionately at the inauguration left to care for her five children (the youngest of whom had health problems) plus two others who live with her and her husband, although she felt "suffocated" staying at home. Another woman, with three children at the age of twenty-three, left when one of her children was sick and then she herself became sick. The youngest member of the collective, just sixteen, married a man who did not allow her to continue working and she was soon expecting her first child.

Eight new women had begun a training course, and when I met with them they seemed enthusiastic. But within a few months only three of them remained. Doris surmised that the cost of transportation to the training center was prohibitive when the women lacked paid employment. A few months later, Doris's co-coordinator, María Elena, judged by some of the welders to be too much of an individualist for the collective, left to work in partnership with a male welder. She had revealed to me in private her doubts about working in a collective, especially one made up entirely of women — and she was not the only woman in the groups I followed who expressed the dominant cultural view that women do not work well together. The women no doubt continued to experience discrimination in their nontraditional work, although this should have been offset to a degree by the view that women welders were more careful and did a better job.

Despite these setbacks, the remaining welders devised several strategies for the survival of their group. Besides continuing to integrate newly trained women, they consulted with more individuals regarding the promotion of their work. A woman in the collective was designated advertising manager, and she polled the others concerning ways of becoming better known around the city. The women continued to receive a few jobs by word of mouth and through INATEC. Given the competitive nature of work in welding, the future looked uncertain. Those remaining in the group depended, for the most part, on other sources of family support to get through that difficult period. They might have reconsidered incorporating as an official cooperative in order to be eligible for loans through CONAPI, but with their reduced number that was not possible. The women talked about refashioning the collective as a microenterprise, a legal entity of up to five workers receiving some promotion by the government, to increase their likelihood of receiving a loan.

During this time, a couple of Peace Corps volunteers from the United States approached the welders with an offer of assistance. The two women, one of whom had experience in welding and the other in microenterprises, discussed working with the group. They offered to give workshops designed for women in small businesses and also encouraged the welders to apply for loans or development grants. The welders could apply for USAID funding of up to U.S. $2,000 for the workshop, administered through the Peace Corps, but needed to demonstrate their willingness to meet together and prepare a proposal and budget. To do this, however, the women would have needed to invest more unpaid time before seeing a return, something they could ill afford, especially as husbands and families were losing confidence that they would ever have a viable business. They also needed a permanent location for their workshop, something that was increasingly uncertain as AMNLAE discussed different uses of their facilities. The welders had more problems at about this time: some of their equipment was apparently stolen from the workshop. The welders' ambivalent attitude toward participating in yet another series of training workshops was evident from the number of times that the Peace Corps volunteers, earnest young women who clearly wanted to make a difference (but were becoming impatient with the welders' apparent lack of seriousness), scheduled workshops only to find that just one or two welders showed up, often very late. After many attempts to schedule a session on microenterprise development, the volunteers brought in training materials one morning, but no welders came. Looking over the materials, I observed that the emphasis was on finding a marketable product, illustrating with the "Case of Cleo," a woman who successfully produced and marketed tie-dye shirts. I could not help thinking that the cultural misunderstandings in these intended encounters were enormous and that whatever "training" the welders might be offered was unlikely to remove the structural obstacles they faced in both their work and at home.

The Peace Corps volunteers and I were surprised when the welders suddenly announced that they were to receive an interest-free loan of U.S. $2,000 from INATEC, contingent on their agreement to take a two-week course in loan management. The volunteers expressed frustration because the welders had not consulted them in making the decision. About two weeks later, it came to light that the new women's training course had been suspended because they were not attending regularly. Personal reasons were cited to explain the women's absences, for example, one woman's husband would not allow her to go because the classes were held at night (at first, he had insisted that her seven-year-old daughter accompany her). Nevertheless, Isabel reprimanded the women harshly, bringing one of them to tears, telling them that if they did not complete the course they would not be able to join the collective or receive their loan.

By 1993, the welders' collective had disbanded. Pointing to the family obligations of the other women, the former coordinator Doris (the only single woman in the remaining group) expressed disappointment at their failure to continue working together. The lack of jobs, the missing (presumed stolen) equipment, the uncertainty over the use of space in the women's center, and Isabel's recent demand that the welders turn over to the AMNLAE center half of what they earned surely entered into the women's decision to return to their homes, although Doris emphasized the "jealousy of husbands." Her own passionate commitment to working as a welder and the visibility she gained through a short article about her in the daily newspaper *Barricada*, led her to join briefly with several male welders. A year later, however, she had taken a clerical job in Managua's women's hospital. I learned that María Elena had accepted an invitation to travel to the United States with a group of Nicaraguans who would receive technical training, and another woman found a job working in a Taiwanese assembly plant in the Zona Franca. Most appeared to be at home, and several told me of their sense of isolation and frustration.

A brief comparison of the current statuses of the cooperatives examined here reveals both differences and similarities. While the bakers' cooperative COOIPAM ceased to function, a number of bakeries stayed in business independently, although with significant adjustments in both work and household. The welders' collective was the only one of the four that disbanded entirely, due in large part to family needs and expectations that drew women back home and away from paid work. In the case of Paola and Blanca who left bark work in the Cooperativa Francisco Estrada, family needs were also cited as critical in the decision to leave. The seamstresses of Obreras Unidas Textil continued to identify with their cooperative, but it is notable that most of the women were older with grown children, lessening the pressure to give up their work (which in any event was generally done at home). While these examples of the household and family demands experienced by women in small businesses and cooperatives might be interpreted as the result of individual circumstances rather than changing economic and political conditions, I would maintain that the two are closely intertwined. As I have noted, structural adjustment has often resulted in heavier responsibilities for women at home when social services are cut, health care and education costs rise, and household incomes drop. The competing demands on women's time and energy, often divided between the family and the workplace, become especially acute under conditions of austerity and adjustment. At a certain point the day can be stretched no farther and women must negotiate "personal" solutions. While the Sandinistas did not end male privilege, the post-Sandinista conservative ideology of the family more actively supports it, and issues of gender and power are closely connected in the changing political and economic context of neoliberalism.

Women in the Urban Informal Sector

As women in cooperatives and other formal sector employment are losing ground in Managua, many are turning to a precarious livelihood in the urban informal sector. There, small-scale production and commerce, often based in the home, do not benefit from protective legislation or the representation of a trade union organization. While earnings are typically quite low, there is great diversity within the informal sector in terms of economic activities and the individuals who perform them (Chamorro, Chávez, and Membreño 1991).[18] What is striking, however, is the preponderance of women in the sector and the added burdens they experience as a result of the gender division of labor. Summing up gender differences in the urban informal sector throughout Central America and the limitations placed on women, J. P. Pérez Sáinz and R. Menjívar Larín write:

> [T]he presence of men and women in the informal sector differs. For men, individualistic motivations and a small contribution to domestic labour allows them in some instances to involve themselves in dynamic informality. By contrast, domestic and family considerations seriously limit such possibilities for women and confine them in most cases to a subsistence informality. Thus, factors associated with gender differences, as expressed in the reproductive sphere, extend their influence to the informal world. (1994: 447)

The urban informal sector has for some time included about half of Managua's economically active population, but there has been significant growth in recent years. Under the Sandinista government, some informal workers were "formalized" when they joined cooperatives and state enterprises. The early efforts became more aggressive, and those who did not leave informal work were scrutinized, licensed, and taxed, and consumers were cautioned to report instances of hoarding and speculation. Yet while a few informal sector merchants were growing rich, the majority were subsisting at best. The scapegoating of the informal sector was such that it was represented by the government as causing major economic problems and also constituting the bulk of political opposition to the Sandinistas. As a consequence, the official discourse maintaining that the informal sector was counterrevolutionary may have alienated an important base of support (Speer 1997).

Now that employment in cooperatives and the state sector is being reduced in the interest of streamlining the economy, people are falling back on independent and informal activities. Recent policy has had the effect of transferring even more workers from the public to the private sector. The

Occupational Conversion Plan was introduced to encourage public sector employees to leave their jobs and set up small businesses. It appears that many who left public sector jobs were Sandinistas, considered undesirable by the new government, or women, viewed as appropriately turning their attention back home. Home is no refuge, however, when women must work double time to take care of families and earn incomes by undertaking a host of small-scale informal activities in manufacturing and commerce. Far from supporting sustainable enterprises, one result of the plan was an abundance of freezer purchases by people planning to sell bottled drinks or ice out of their homes.

Many women in Managaua, including Barrio Monseñor Lezcano, operate small restaurants or engage in selling small quantities of fruit, vegetables, soft drinks, or other goods out of their homes' front rooms. In the poorest families, children add to the family income by selling in the streets or by asking for tips for guarding parked cars. And many others go to extraordinary lengths to support their families. Some of the women who formerly worked in cooperatives have returned to their homes — to families and also to informal work. For example, they prepare mondongo for sale to workingmen in the neighborhood, sew clothes to sell on consignment, or operate household ventas.

To some degree, those turning to private small businesses may be viewed as a hallmark of neoliberalism. Their success appears to rise or fall on their ability to judge the market and enter it with motivation and hard work. But the market is influenced sharply by government policy, which currently favors larger business and foreign investment. Thus the discourse of "freedom" to participate in the economy unencumbered by the state overlooks the structural inequalities that beset small business and the informal sector. Not surprisingly, studies show that despite its heterogeneity, those in this sector are deeply dissatisfied with the orientation of post-Sandinista governments (Speer 1997).

Structural Adjustment or Structural Change?

Many women I talked to in Managua commented on the ways in which they were coping at home and at work with low earnings, rising prices, and inadequate social services. Nearly all of them noted that their families' eating habits had changed; instead of waking up to large meals of rice, beans, eggs, and cheese, they had just a bit of *gallopinto* (mixed rice and beans) and coffee. Instead of having three abundant meals, including meat, each day, they included meat in their diet only about once a week. They looked longer and harder for less expensive foods to buy. Other women cut back on transportation costs, opting to walk to places where they had formerly taken buses. Some who had the resources in the past to hire other women to wash and iron their clothes were doing this work themselves. Those who had always done this work themselves were doing it less frequently, just once or twice a week to save on soap and electricity. In addition, with an apparent deterioration of physical and mental health in the country, women were taking on the care of family members in ill health. These household responses to the crisis conditions wrought by adjustment policies in Nicaragua have parallels in a number of other third world countries.

What is distinct about Nicaragua is the way in which the fast pace and devastating effects of these policies have eroded the benefits of the Sandinista revolution. Yet also distinct is the readiness of the population to mobilize in opposition to these policies. The decade of broad participation left a legacy of expectations that has been challenged but not eliminated since 1990. The determination of Nicaraguans to take part in the political process and to retain their hard-won rights expresses itself in everyday strategies of resistance to the economic crisis, as well as through political statements by the FSLN, organized protests of popular organizations, and policy research conducted by independent institutes.

I suggested at the beginning of this chapter that we need to reexamine women's strategies for confronting crisis conditions in their paid work as well as at home. By offering examples of women working in urban cooperatives and in the urban informal sector, I have shown that even in instances in which production and sales have slowed, working women often step up their efforts to get by. They often work longer hours to find affordable materials, to acquire the skills they need, and to gain access to markets for their products. The strain of surviving under conditions that are driving many small industries and commercial enterprises out of business also affects their ability to carry out family responsibilities. Therefore, we need to examine the interconnectedness of women's unpaid and paid work as both are extended in response to neoliberal policies.

Almost half of the households in Nicaragua's cities are headed by women, and women make up at least 44 percent of the economically active population. Policies that do not take gender into account will have particularly serious effects on the health and well-being of these women and their children. My work and that of others (Elson 1991; Afshar and Dennis 1992; Benería and Feldman 1992) reveal that structural adjustment is cushioned by women whose discretionary time and energy are already extremely limited. The human cost of recent policies will be seen in the long term if the consequences of these policies are not considered now.

Structural adjustment, by introducing new competition and reducing national demand, has led to the decline of many urban cooperatives and small industries established under the Sandinistas. A report by CONAPI (*Barricada Internacional* 1993) indicated that some 7,000 small and medium-sized industries and services closed in 1992 alone, leaving just 3,000 shops registered with the Ministry of Economy. Since women have been disproportionately represented in the co-ops and industries, the decline has hit them especially hard.

Some writers have argued that more humane approaches to structural adjustment would lower the high cost exacted among the most vulnerable sectors in third world countries (Cornia, Jolly, and Stewart 1987; UNICEF 1989). However, these writers overlook the adverse effects of adjustment programs on both men and women in broad sectors of the population and the ways in which the programs are dependent on structural inequalities of gender, class, and race. We have seen that women, in particular, underwrite the cost of neoliberal development through their extended workdays. Other analysts have been more critical of structural adjustment and have called for discussion of far-reaching structural transformation (e.g., Gladwin 1991). While scholars and activists have long called attention to the harsh effects and antidemocratic practices of neoliberalism and global capitalism, a renewed discussion involving policy makers and planners could be informed by the experiences of Nicaragua — a country that broke away, for a time, from the dominant economic development model.

In Nicaragua, a nation that has seen the hard-won structural transformation of the last decade rolled back to a significant degree since 1990, there has been discussion of a "national project" and alternatives to the neoliberal economic model (*Envío* 1992b), although in more recent years the emphasis has simply been on softening the blows of adjustment. Not surprisingly, women are among the most vocal in questioning the current economic model and calling for some relief. As active participants in the Nicaraguan revolution, they claimed a space in which to assert their rights to full citizenship. In the late 1980s, these women found new ways to organize and confront difficult conditions as the demands on their time increased both in the labor force and at home. Although women's participation in neighborhood organizations declined, their engagement in sectoral organizations of the labor movement grew stronger (Pérez Alemán 1992: 250). In the post-Sandinista period, we may observe openings for women's participation despite the deepening problems the country is facing. While AMNLAE no longer plays a strong leadership role, emergent feminist and women's organizations are flourishing along with other independent groups and social movements. As we have seen, women in Managua's urban cooperatives and informal sector are experiencing and responding to neoliberalism through their workplaces and their homes, but these women also live within and actively construct a broader political culture of opposition that continues to grow.

Chapter Six

FROM COOPERATIVES TO MICROENTERPRISES IN THE POSTREVOLUTIONARY ERA

T HE RAPID dismantling of socialist economies over the last decade, as the Soviet Union and eastern Europe have undergone dramatic transformations, has led to intense debates on the perceived failures of socialism and, for some, the inevitability of capitalism and the rule of the market. In such discussions, comparisons with China are sometimes drawn, but little mention is made of Latin American experiments with socialism. This also holds true for recent discussions of the politics of gender relations after socialism, which have focused productively on eastern Europe and Russia but generally do not consider the Latin American region (Gal and Kligman 2000). When attention does turn to this part of the world, it is most often to Cuba that analysts direct their gaze (Weisskopf 1992). Predictions of the imminent failure of that forty-year experiment in socialist development have been more frequent since the collapse of the Soviet Union.

Nicaragua has rarely figured in the discussions of postsocialist transitions to neoliberalism and global capitalism. Of course, the U.S. government took a keen interest when the revolution was under way, and so did a number of third world countries intent on overcoming histories of underdevelopment and gaining greater independence in the international arena (Enríquez 1991: 1). A landmark collection of essays on problems of third world socialism written by leftist academics during that period took its inspiration from the Nicaraguan experience (Fagen, Deere, and Coraggio 1986). Yet a more recent collection of essays concerned with diminished states and open markets in Latin America (Rosen and McFadyen 1995) barely mentions Nicaragua. In the book's foreword, the Salvadoran political scientist and former presidential candidate Rubén Zamora points to the fall of existing socialism and the rise of neoliberalism — signaling a return to free market economics — as global processes that frame current struggles in Latin America (Zamora 1995). He goes on to argue passionately that popular movements and civil society more generally in the region present the Left with alternatives to the old party structures and organizations linked to them. He could be describing postrevolutionary Nicaragua, but the country is referred to only in passing (7–9).

In the introduction I noted that I had arrived late for the revolution in Nicaragua, and, to be sure, most scholars inspired to carry out research in the country got there earlier and many left soon after the demise of the Sandinista government in 1990. What appeared at first to be a late start, however, turned out to offer the opportunity to witness the transition to an important new phase of Nicaraguan history. In this chapter, I consider several approaches to postsocialist transitions and what they may contribute to an understanding of Nicaragua, and then I examine how work has been restructured in the country, focusing particularly on the refashioning of cooperatives as microenterprises in the neoliberal era. I close with a brief consideration of new forms of social mobilization that counter this period's harsh effects.

Postsocialist Transitions

Latin Americanists have had a predilection for studying twentieth-century examples of revolutionary change in the continent, and, more often than not, they have identified closely with the progressive political orientations of the places where they have worked — whether revolutionary Mexico or Cuba, Allende's Chile, or Sandinista Nicaragua. This is not to say that scholars have failed to take a critical view of some policies and practices of revolutionary governments, but they have frequently held anti-imperialist or socialist views, making them sympathetic to struggles against injustice and inequality that are often the by-products of neocolonial and capitalist regimes.

In contrast to the race to observe and document Latin American revolutions, it was the *fall* of the Soviet Union that produced an influx of social scientists to Russia and eastern Europe who were keen to witness the transitions from socialist societies to capitalist economies and liberal democracies. Unlike approaches taken to Latin America, current studies of the former Soviet Union are less concerned with what has been dismantled and tend to take as key moments the collapsed state and the opening up of the market, viewed as auspicious or inauspicious, depending on the viewpoint—similar to differences of interpretation that emerged in discussions of the Nicaraguan revolution.

In a recent collection of ethnographic studies from the postsocialist world, the volume's coeditors, Michael Burawoy and Katherine Verdery (1999) raise questions about the nature of transitions to the promised land of capitalism and democracy in eastern Europe and Russia. They note that, with few exceptions, researchers and policy makers have held to either the "revolutionary" notion that former "totalitarian" societies must make a sharp break to follow the neoliberal path or the "evolutionary" view that postsocialist societies require a more gradual, institutionalized approach to enter the market economy successfully. In both cases, the "shock treatment" of economic adjustment is seen as necessary to pave the way for capitalism, with or without social buffers to assist vulnerable populations. To be sure, the anthology presents more complicated accounts of the micropolitics of everyday life and considers the uneven and ambiguous ways that societies experience transitions from socialist to postsocialist periods. The authors find that even as family, community, and work are being refashioned to meet the needs of the market, political opposition is expressed to neoliberal government programs. Thus it would be a mistake to rely on reductionist positions that see the success and failure of transition in monolithic terms.

The alternatives offered in this scheme by revolutionary and evolutionary theorists of transition closely parallel the Latin Americanist schools of neoliberals, on the one hand, and advocates of "adjustment with a human face," on the other. What is lacking in the scheme, however, is a place for those who favor socialist over capitalist orientations or who seek alternatives to structural adjustment, which many view as a bankrupt development model. Burawoy notes, "[O]ne is hard-pressed to discover such powerful Marxist treatments of postsocialism," and he wonders "how long it will be before disillusionment will lead back to Marxism's critique of markets and liberal democracy" (1999: 307, 308). Perhaps in the long run indigenous theorizing in the countries in question will replace the traveling grand theories from the West, but for now capitalist triumphalism appears to be carrying the day. Burawoy writes the following of the former Soviet Union, although he could be addressing the postsocialist world more generally:

> As socialism retreats into the past, the danger is that we will become ever more enthralled with a single model—an ideal typification of liberal capitalism—against which to compare reality, inevitably making of the post-Soviet world a black hole. We will lose sight of alternatives, whether alternative capitalisms, alternative socialisms, or other utopias that offer novel lenses through which to interpret the present and the past, as well as the future. (309)

Unlike the former Soviet Union and eastern Europe, where socialism has met its demise, or Cuba, where a more dogmatic socialism has been challenged by economic crisis, or other examples of Communist Party–directed socialism, Nicaragua's socialist-oriented Sandinista government was less orthodox in its plan of social reconstruction following revolutionary insurrection (Vanden and Prevost 1993). The Sandinista National Liberation Front sought a democratic pluralism and nonaligned politics as well as a mixed economy, private enterprise alongside an expanded state sector. Unlike state socialism in the Soviet Union or eastern Europe, Nicaragua's effort was to develop a popular, participatory form that broke from the dominant, authoritarian models. For this reason, it is looked to less often as an example from which to draw lessons about the past, present, and future of socialism. But the Nicaraguan revolution brought about a program of social transformation that went far enough to attract both international acclaim and a rather predictable reaction from the United States—which, through its economic embargo and its funding of the Contra war, contributed significantly to the problems that brought down the Sandinistas after only a decade in power. As Vanden and Prevost (1993: 47) describe it, "The ideology of the Nicaraguan Revolution was at once the recuperation of a long history of popular national struggle and the specific Nicaraguan manifestation of the new wave of revolution that was sweeping the Third World."

Nicaragua went through two major transitions in a fairly short period: from a market economy dominated by the elite Somoza family to a state-regulated economy under the Sandinistas, then back to a market-driven program under the government of the UNO, mandated by the IMF and set in place by USAID (Spoor 1994: 517). These were not simple shifts back and forth between capitalist and socialist models but rather negotiated processes that often allowed for unexpected economic juxtapositions. The Chamorro government continued to bend somewhat to the interests of the Sandinistas, who despite their split into two tendencies represented a powerful political force in the country (*Barricada Internacional* 1995). While state intervention in the market characterized the Sandinista decade, the subsequent period was also marked by a significant degree of economic regulation by the government. At the same time, the market liberalization and structural adjustment that are generally associated with the UNO regime actually began under the Sandinistas. Thus the Nicaraguan economy presents a far more complicated situation than the apparent "state versus market" dichotomy would suggest (Spoor 1994).

The "neoliberal turn" in Nicaragua might suggest a simple reversal of political direction and of economic policy after the 1990 elections. Indeed, some evidence supports the argument that there has been a systematic undoing of economic reforms introduced by the Sandinistas. Whereas the FSLN promoted the distribution of available resources among the general population, succeeding governments adopted a neoliberal plan that supported the privatization of industry, health and education, and cutbacks in state-provided services, subsidies, and basic food packages. In the competitive context of the 1990s, former landowners reclaimed their holdings and large industries drove out smaller ones that were no longer protected by the state. Low-income women and men have been disproportionately affected in the process. Nevertheless, the revolution left its legacy and Nicaraguans have not passively allowed their hard-won rights to be taken away. Although it was widely expected that the revolution would be "undone," the transition has been more complex. Indeed, as Rose Spalding (1994: 157) has noted, if the revolution transformed Nicaraguan society, it should "build strong buffers against the neoliberal tide."

Economic Restructuring under the Sandinista Government

The Nicaraguan revolution sought to break with the agroexport economy of the Somoza period and to establish a redistributive economy that would benefit a population that had long suffered from international dependency. Heavy reliance on coffee and cotton production made the country vulnerable to price fluctuations, and the Somoza family had done little to promote economic development. The Sandinistas' broad program of agrarian reform and policy of economic redistribution was accompanied by nationalized production in key sectors of the economy and the introduction of import and exchange controls. However, economic planning allowed for continued support of the private sector to a significant degree, and generous loans were made available to capitalists willing to reactivate their enterprises (Walker 1986: 68). Whether the model would have succeeded is uncertain, as structural problems inherited from the Somoza period and the Contra war undermined the nation's development (Spalding 1987: 4).

Even so, the early years of the revolutionary government saw notable structural change. Outstanding initiatives in the areas of health care and education, rural land reform, and change in the urban sector stood out as critical elements in economic restructuring. New policies awarding land to squatters and efforts to bring water and electricity to their settlements attracted labor to the cities, especially Managua. When low-paid urban workers turned to employment in the informal sector, where earnings were sometimes higher, the government countered by raising wage levels in formal sector jobs. Provision of basic food items and subsidies of imported goods continued until the government could no longer afford to underwrite the basic consumption of the entire country and turned to offering incentives to the most productive sectors of the formal economy (Gibson 1987: 40).

The Sandinista government encouraged formal sector employment primarily in the state sector and in services, rather than in industry, and tried to attract those informal traders who swelled the markets to new work sites. Nevertheless, an abundance of workers continued to produce and sell needed goods in small, independent associations of fewer than a dozen individuals. If we count small industries of up to thirty workers, more than half the industrial working population in 1985 was employed in an estimated ten thousand workshops (Laenen 1988: 380). Some had begun work in small businesses after the 1972 earthquake destroyed much of Managua, and with it a major part of its industrial and commercial infrastructure. These workers were encouraged to organize collectively and were offered state-sponsored training and lower prices for primary goods needed in their cooperatives. Programs to provide training for women in nontraditional employment were among those introduced. In many cases, the state bought and sold the items produced by the cooperatives, enabling small producers to remain in business.

Surprisingly little scholarly attention has focused on small industries and urban cooperatives during the Sandinista period.[1] An exception is the extensive study of small industries, highlighting the case of clothing producers, carried out by Arie Laenen (1988), a researcher from the Netherlands who later headed the NGO MEDA for several years. His detailed research showed that just as the Sandinista years were characterized in general by a mixed economy, so was small industry characterized by a variety of relations to state and market.

> In the Nicaraguan small industry we find: private producers of small capitalist workshops, independent producers with one-man workshops, wage labourers of small workshops without social security or organization in a trade union, family labour which can or cannot be paid, outworkers who work for a small workshop, labourers/members of cooperatives who are in possession of the means of production, wage labourers of state collectives who know social security, and, finally, wage labourers in cooperatives and collectives. (Laenen 1988: 388)

While there was little articulation between small and large industries, a stronger articulation between the state and small industry developed as workers were encouraged to organize in production and service cooperatives. In the former, the means of production (e.g., sewing machines in the case of seamstresses) were brought to a common site by individuals who before had worked at home or in small workshops. In the latter, the means of production remained the property of individual members who worked at separate sites but benefited from services such as the joint purchase of materials, application for credit, or sale of produced goods. The production cooperatives, which better suited the revolutionary project of establishing new social relations through collectivization, were favored with more raw materials and social services. With technical assistance and materials supplied to them, both types of cooperatives organized in large numbers in the early 1980s, until the Sandinista government became concerned about the sector's rapid growth and began emphasizing productivity and quality of goods in existing cooperatives rather than the creation of new employment. However, quality was not improved significantly as a result of the state purchasing and marketing the bulk of the cooperatives' output. In this way, as small businesses the cooperatives were protected from direct competition with larger businesses, although larger enterprises were ultimately supported in other ways by a government that was eager to promote industrialization and modernization.

As work was reorganized, there were disjunctions between the expectations of the government, on the one hand, and those of cooperative members, on the other. The Sandinista Ministry of Industry called for cooperatives to hold monthly *asambleas* (assemblies) of members as decision-making bodies, but the hierarchical structure was intended mainly to carry out the will of the government. CONAPI was not actively organized and working with cooperatives until the late 1980s, and until then there was no trade union association to build solidarity among them and mediate between cooperatives and the government. The service co-ops, by virtue of being spread out in individual work sites, were particularly difficult to organize. Furthermore, as Laenen aptly notes:

[T]here is a fundamental contrast between the logic of the State and the logic of the small industry. The logic of the State in Nicaragua is to provide for a production of basic consumer goods for the population in as cheap as possible a way. Because of its share in this production, small industry was considered from the beginning a socially and economically important element in the intended economic process of transition toward socialism. But also in a political sense small industry had a right to exist, as many small producers had supported the FSLN and had fought in the war of liberation. (1988: 394)

The Sandinista government recognized the political importance of the small business sector, just as it recognized the political importance of the informal sector, in terms of the large population it included and the early role it played in supporting the revolution. In the end, however, there was insufficient recognition of the economic importance of the sector and insufficient space was provided to small industries for autonomous, self-sustaining development to occur.

By the mid-1980s, efforts toward social and economic development had been seriously undercut both by the U.S. trade embargo imposed under the Reagan administration and by the need to defend the country in the face of the Contra war. Nicaraguan economic policy moved from a revolutionary planning process to a program aimed at stabilization. In 1988–89, the Sandinistas' response to hyperinflation and declining economic growth was to cut back on employment in the public sector and on state spending in general. Nominal wage increases, intended to soften the blow, were inadequate to protect the poorest Nicaraguans from the harsh effects of the adjustment measures (Ricciardi 1991).

Reorganization of Work under Chamorro and Alemán

If the Sandinistas' stabilization and adjustment program was hard on many Nicaraguans, the IMF directed neoliberal agenda of the UNO government was far more crushing. New structural adjustment measures were introduced quickly after the 1990 elections in a country whose former revolutionary government had provided a safety net of support. Privatization, the withdrawal of protective tariffs, and cuts in social services were some elements that clashed loudly with the policies of the Sandinistas. Yet the measures promoted by the UNO government met resistance from some business elites as well as from the popular sectors, with both groups fearing they would lose from the withdrawal of economic support (Spalding 1994: 158). Thus the neoliberalism endorsed by the U.S. government and some privileged Nicaraguan sectors was modified as a result of mobilized opposition by diverse segments of the population — a convergence of cross-class interests that has been seen in the country's recent history.

The devaluation of the currency in March 1991 escaped strong opposition, and soon afterward twenty-eight thousand state workers who agreed to leave their jobs were granted generous severance pay funded by USAID under the Occupational Conversion Plan (Spalding 1994: 169). These and other efforts to win public acceptance paid off as many former state employees were mollified long enough to set up small independent businesses — although a large number of them were failing by 1992, the so-called Year of

Reactivation. Other concessions to neoliberalism's opponents included the provision that workers in former state farms and industries would be allowed to control a quarter to a third of the newly privatized businesses. These concessions did not necessarily lead to significant worker participation or empowerment but received approval from enough Sandinistas to lessen dissatisfaction over the economic model.

Nevertheless, the deepening economic crisis during the 1990s took a great toll on small producers in the country. The majority of small producers and businesses experienced increasing competition as larger industries — both national and foreign — were favored by policies of the Chamorro and, later, Alemán governments. No longer having the benefit of favorable terms of credit or protective tariffs on imported goods, cooperatives and other small businesses failed at higher rates. Meanwhile, foreign interests were welcomed to Managua's Zona Franca, where they could employ workers at relatively low wages (although often higher than earnings in the cooperatives). Many low-income women and men in Managua came to have less and less confidence that the government would bring about better conditions in their lives. As noted earlier, the currency was stabilized in the 1990s, but unemployment and underemployment approached 60 percent at the same time that privatization of health care and cuts in social services eliminated state protection of the urban poor (*Envío* 1994: 7). Since 1990 there has been a gradual erosion of small industries and an expansion of the informal sector, particularly as the state sector has been cut back.

Some members of the business elite were also disadvantaged by the neoliberal restructuring of the economy when government accommodations to the industrial sector were insufficient to enable them to compete successfully under new conditions in the international market (Spalding 1997). Both large and small producers in many cases expressed a desire for a renewal of state support that was eliminated after the Sandinistas lost power. Likewise, some members of the elite opposed the IMF structural adjustment and called for a reconsideration of harsh economic policies. Spalding (1997) notes that restructuring was particularly detrimental to the poor and nonelite but that it also threatened the growth potential of the elite. She points to a need for support for all levels of producers, cooperatives, and workers' enterprises, as part of a more inclusive development program. But now let us turn to the particular consequences of changing economic policy for urban cooperatives and small businesses.

Urban Cooperatives in the Transition
from Revolutionary to Neoliberal Nicaragua

In the political and economic transition following the 1990 elections, many urban cooperatives and small industries shrank, collapsed, or were reconfigured as microenterprises — perceived as more in harmony with neoliberalism. Numerous women workers have been affected, and while some have benefited from new employment opportunities, others have experienced less positive outcomes. The Nicaraguan case may be considered alongside other formerly socialist countries in which women were set back disproportionately to men as work was transformed to meet the requirements of the neoliberal capitalist development model (Einhorn 1993).

The worsening situation of low-income women is illustrated in my research on the four urban cooperatives discussed above. Two of the cooperatives, the seamstresses and the bakers, came together in the period soon after the Sandinistas rose to power and encouraged collectivization of small industries. They organized service cooperatives, in which members worked at home but had a central location for selling their product, holding meetings, and other activities. However, these two co-ops were forced to put their office spaces up for sale when they were unable to keep up payments. Some individuals and families stayed in business, but declining sales of bread and locally produced clothing have resulted from Nicaraguans' inability to afford even these basic goods and from changing economic conditions that favor imported goods and larger industries. The collective of welders working out of an AMNLAE women's center suffered a number of setbacks and ceased to function after just a couple of years. The women gave some thought to identifying as a microenterprise, securing a loan, and marketing their work more aggressively, but they had inadequate personal and collective resources to follow through. For their part, members of the artisans' cooperative have remained committed to high-quality work, but they too have been challenged in recent years. The cooperative had been singled out as one of ten to receive extra support from CONAPI, enabling its members to seek new markets and try out new creative techniques, in an effort to demonstrate to USAID the promise of small industries and to attract more external support. Now, however, the artisans' viability depends on the degree to which they turn from a Sandinista-identified work organization to a "microenterprise" orientation and compete successfully in the open market.

Indeed, all four cooperatives made efforts to navigate the rough terrain of the transition from Sandinista to post-Sandinista governments. All accommodated to some extent to the new economic terms of the neoliberal period. The bakers diversified production even as they reduced output, to compete more effectively against the ever-available Pan Bimbo. Although many were longtime Sandinistas, as small business proprietors they felt that their cooperative, COOIPAM, was no longer able to assist them with lower-priced materials or better terms of credit and had become an unnecessary part of the bureaucracy. The seamstresses of Obreras Unidas Textil, many of whom were older founding members whose children were grown, had fewer family demands than some younger women workers, and when they lost their store they nonetheless continued sewing at home. When sales dropped to an extremely low point because of competition from larger and global industries, some began selling used clothing or other items out of their homes. Like the bakers, they developed strategies to cut costs and market their products, in their case traveling across national borders to acquire lower-priced materials and selling seasonal items in the streets where more customers came to shop.

The collective of women welders was torn between remaining independent or joining CONAPI, which could have signaled an oppositional stance in relation to the UNO government in the early 1990s. On the one hand, this collective was under pressure from INATEC and AMNLAE to be an exemplary group of women workers in a nontraditional industry. On the other hand, they were encouraged by NGOs and Peace Corps volunteers to refashion themselves as a promising young microenterprise in order to compete for jobs in the capitalist marketplace. In the end, their indecision as to what direction to take combined with insufficient work opportunities and excessive family demands and they disbanded.

Finally, the artisans present an example of a cooperative that has moved gradually toward microenterprise status, as a result of interpersonal relations (the desire for all to take responsibility for their work and frustration when this did not occur) and increasing reliance on NGO support as opposed to assistance from CONAPI. Both internal and external pressures have promoted individualism in the workplace and a willingness to accept the terms of neoliberalism in the marketplace. The jewelry artisans who remained after the bark workers left the co-op sought out new designs to appeal to the limited number of customers who came to their workshop as

well as new venues for marketing their products. Members of the group offer different assessments of the degree to which they continue to operate as
a cooperative or now function as an association of independent artisans
working under one roof. What is as true of the artisans as of many others in
the current period is that the break with the past has not been altogether
sudden or absolute but rather a negotiated process.

To the extent that CONAPI remains at all effective in representing the cooperatives' membership, it generally labors on behalf of small businesses to
persuade the government to soften the blow of neoliberal measures rather
than present strong opposition to the measures. Small industries like the
four discussed here are attempting to ensure their survival by not relying
solely on that association formed under the Sandinistas — now relatively
weak — but also redefining themselves in order to remain viable in the current context.

From Cooperatives to Microenterprises

In this decade of transition, the Chamorro and Alemán governments as well
as several NGOs promoted the development of microenterprises. With up to
five individuals working together, these units were smaller than the cooperatives sponsored by CONAPI. But the microenterprises — whether composed of former members of co-ops or of newly organized workers — often
involved people carrying out similar productive activities in areas such as
food, clothing, leather work and shoes, woodworking and furniture, and
artesanía (crafts). Typically, individuals working in an area such as food
preparation or shoemaking would join together to qualify for certain benefits as microenterprises.[2] In relatively modest but growing numbers, microenterprises were given loans to begin operating, and in some cases women
were targeted as recipients. The new Office of Small Industries and Microenterprises within the Ministry of the Economy was established to oversee
development of these enterprises, providing loans and technical assistance.
NGOs offering support to microenterprises have often been more forthcoming in acknowledging the high failure rate of the microenterprises, many
of which have been unable to repay loans and have gone out of business.
The post-Sandinista governments, however, were intent on replacing cooperatives, which represented the persistence of Sandinista work organization, with microenterprises that would symbolize the success of the free

26. *Artisans come monthly to Managua's Cultural Center to sell at a micro-fair.*

market model. It was no doubt feared that without assistance (and the appearance of promotion) numerous small businesses in the country would fail and this could lead to unrest. To forestall that outcome, the government conducted large-scale publicity campaigns and held highly visible fairs for the sale of items produced by microentrepreneurs.

The Office of Small Industries and Microenterprises was created with support from the Netherlands by the minister of the economy, Silvio de Franco, whose earlier interest in the informal sector and microenterprises included attention to low-income women.[3] However, contradictory government objectives were expressed to me by María Hurtado de Vigil, who was named director of the office. While she stated that the government sought to support those small enterprises that were most likely to succeed, she acknowledged that even those promising industries stood little chance of success in a context of shifting policy that favored the entry of imported goods and increased competition in a global market. Stressing the benefits of liberalizing the economy, she said she had not considered the implications for women microentrepreneurs deemed "likely to fail" (Hurtado de

Vigil, interview, May 8, 1991). Her response was typical of government officials I spoke with concerning how women are managing the double burden of household responsibilities and work in microenterprises. Even when
prompted by my comments about the many women I had met whose family duties and husbands' attitudes had made steady participation at work
difficult to sustain, nearly all appeared unaware of the gender-based problem. If I went on to ask if child care or other support was ever made available to level the playing field for women, most looked at me blankly. Yet
this problem that women faced was as apparent in the microenterprises as
in the cooperatives.[4]

During the years of my research, I made a number of visits to the office of
the National Program to Support Microenterprise (Programa Nacional de
Apoyo a la Microempresa, or PAMIC), a division of the Ministry of the Economy. In its first year, it issued a report that analyzed microenterprises in
Managua (PAMIC 1991) and laid the groundwork for the program's initiatives. The report characterizes microenterprises[5] as growing in the capital
city in response to rising unemployment and views them as an opportunity
for self-employment among low-income urban residents. While both the
cooperatives in CONAPI and the microenterprises are concentrated in similar areas of production, CONAPI reports a majority of women in its constituency whereas PAMIC's study found that women constituted just 15 percent
in the microenterprises counted. The women were located mainly in food
and garment production, the most vulnerable sectors of the economy. The
report acknowledged that gender was not included as a key variable and
that women may have been underassessed. Indeed, the finding that total
participation regardless of gender in microenterprises—taking into account the formal economy but not the informal economy—was 12 percent
suggests that the sector as a whole may have been underassessed.

Between 1991 and 1993, I had several interviews with the Dutch economist Stefan Platteau, head of the PAMIC office at that time. As he explained,
PAMIC's objectives were to offer training, credit, and promotion and to negotiate with NGOs and the Banco Popular on behalf of microenterprises. He
shared a view held by many others, including some Sandinistas, that the revolutionary government had "spoiled" workers by offering handouts and support without providing the training that would make them self-sustaining.
Moreover, he maintained that many who failed were lacking in commitment or that they produced low-quality products. Thus he was intent on

finding highly motivated individuals to train in microenterprises in order to make his program a success. In 1992, a year after his job was created, he was still optimistic that individuals with management abilities and determination could succeed with credit and training (Platteau, interview, February 24, 1992). By mid-1993, he revealed much more cynicism about the prospects for the five thousand microentrepreneurs his office had assisted. He noted a problematic "work culture" in Nicaragua, in which people feel that it doesn't pay to work, that he traced to the last decade and the Sandinistas. He said he now tells people that if they want loans and want to succeed, there will be "blood, sweat, and tears" — a remark he repeated several times for emphasis. While his cynicism extended to doubting that the growth of microenterprises would turn around the economy, he felt that much was at stake in demonstrating the good results of his program (Platteau, interview, July 23, 1993).

During this time, María Hurtado made occasional appearances at CONAPI assemblies to represent the government's response to small business and microenterprise. In general, she presented the view that the government was doing everything possible to support small businesses, but she was received with some impatience by a group demanding greater protection in the face of neoliberalism. Antonio Chávez, a leading official in CONAPI, viewed her office's interventions as a political move to counter the opposition symbolized by CONAPI and offered a different perspective regarding the impact of recent economic measures on small industries. Chávez reported that the sector had been particularly hard hit and that women, 54 percent of its membership, were the most affected. The majority of women workers, located in the garment and food industries, experienced great losses as import tariffs were lowered on goods entering Nicaragua. He acknowledged that the decline in the sector began under the Sandinistas, but he argued that the current "shock treatment" is far worse (Chávez, interview, May 8, 1991). CONAPI reported that some 7,000 small and medium-sized industries and services closed in 1992, leaving just 3,000 shops registered with the Ministry of the Economy (*Barricada Internacional* 1993). Chávez summarized his view by stating that "PAMIC doesn't so much as offer aspirin for the migraine that small industry has now."

This grim outlook was held by some NGOs assisting microenterprises in the early 1990s. One of them, MEDA, was experiencing difficulty finding

27. *Headquarters of* CONAPI, *the National Association of Medium and Small Industry.*

suitable enterprises to support as many were failing or deemed unlikely to succeed. With funding and direction provided by the Netherlands, only one in five enterprises that MEDA approached was offered a loan, and among those receiving loans many were still foundering. While MEDA had targeted productive groups in the leading areas of clothing, leather, wood and furniture, food, and crafts, it began sponsoring service and commercial enterprises as well. The Dutch director, Arie Laenen, who was preparing to leave the country and turn over control to Nicaraguans, told me that women were experiencing higher rates of failure than men, particularly since they were located in the more vulnerable areas of production, and more of them were turning to services and commerce. He said that self-sustainability is achieved by a few microenterprises that offer products of better quality, while 20 to 30 percent of microenterprises were failing altogether at that time. Laenen's (1988) extensive studies of small industries in the mid-1980s suggested to him that of 10,000 to 11,000 small industries in the country in 1985, only about 5,000 had survived until 1992.

28. PAMIC, *the government office for microenterprises, hosts a fair for microentrepreneurs to sell to the public.*

By 1993, efforts increased to promote products made by small industries and microenterprises. While CONAPI had campaigns, complete with bumper stickers and key chains, to "Buy Nicaraguan," PAMIC organized fairs and disseminated posters stating that "From Microentrepreneur to the Consumer, Everything Is Cheaper!" Despite the promotion of national cuisine like nacatamales and clothing such as *guayabera* shirts, the fairs brought out a limited number of buyers. Indeed, when I attended a fair that year that was sponsored by PAMIC, the Banco Popular, and NGOs, far more stands were set up for the sale of beer and food than for products made in Nicaraguan microenterprises. The cost to participate would have been prohibitive for many small businesses and the entry fee may have deterred potential customers who had little money to spend. The largest number of customers came late at night to eat, drink, and go on carnival rides. Although the advertising had suggested that some two hundred fifty microentrepreneurs would be at the fair, there were in fact far fewer, and those businesses in attendance represented much larger ones as well, such as a company of one hundred employees manufacturing factory-produced clothing and a vendor of the *Encyclopedia Britannica*.

Even so, contests for product design and fairs open to the public continued to receive wide media attention over the following years. Newspapers
ran features on PAMIC's efforts to make microenterprises more competitive
in new markets (e.g., *La Prensa*, June 19, 1996). In addition to sponsoring
fairs in Managua (including monthly artisan fairs that attracted international visitors) and throughout the country, the government sponsored
Nicaraguan microentrepreneurs' travel to fairs elsewhere in Central America to generate interest in local production across national borders. A poster
showed the globe with North and South America featured and bold rain-
bow stripes shooting out from Nicaragua. María Hurtado was quoted as
saying that more than half the employed Nicaraguan population earns its
income in microenterprises and that during the past year PAMIC offered
seminars to twenty-five hundred people in microenterprises, including
60 percent women. PAMIC continued to receive funding from the Netherlands, and also from Norway, Switzerland, Sweden, and the United Nations Association in Nicaragua.

In 1996, I interviewed Luis Carvajal, who had taken over Platteau's functions at PAMIC. By this time, its emphasis was on subcontracting work to
NGOs that would assist microenterprises and much of its own effort was in
technical assistance and training rather than in the provision of credit. It offered assistance in product design and marketing, giving particular attention to improving quality, going beyond Managua to the rural sector. Carvajal noted the new concern with the environment and also with women's
participation as artisans in such areas as ceramic and garment production.
He was pleased that Nicaraguans had recently traveled to participate in
fairs in Honduras and Panama. He also commented that PAMIC's relationship with CONAPI was a good one and that, leaving politics aside, the difference between their concern for cooperatives and microenterprises is less
significant; nevertheless, he acknowledged the historical antagonism of interests between them.

While Carvajal avoided explicit mention of the changed political context in the country, he welcomed many aspects of neoliberalism (and at
the end of our conversation he allowed that as the national elections approached he thought the Liberal Party of Alemán would be best for the
country). He shared the view expressed by others that under the Sandinistas small industries were protected in a captive market but quality suffered. Now the situation for some small industries and microenterprises

is precarious as they continue to expect the government to solve their problems. But the change is good insofar as people begin to take charge of their lives and work and reclaim their self-esteem in small industries. They must "be competitive or die"; passive attitudes won't make it. In his view, the failure rate of small enterprises is artificially high because it includes those like himself who left voluntarily and others who formed microenterprises in recent years but lacked the training and experience necessary to succeed. Now he sees things turning around and more microenterprises succeeding.

Two years later, CONAPI and PAMIC continued to vie for small businesses' participation. Notwithstanding the government's rhetoric, collaboration was strained as CONAPI officials perceived that Alemán's administration would like to see an end to the trade union association formed under the Sandinistas and to advance its own interests through PAMIC. When I returned to the latter's offices, I found Alemán's portrait looming large where Chamorro's had appeared before. Announcements displayed on bulletin boards revealed the attention to such issues as women in microenterprises, the environment, and sustainable development, clearly reflecting the concerns of international funding agencies. A poster read "Microentrepreneurs promote enterprises that are efficient, competitive, and environmentally sound. Together we will make the change. PAMIC. Nicaraguan government." The continued refashioning of PAMIC as a modern response to conditions of globalization was evident.

Carvajal was confident that the new government was committed to microenterprise development as its number two concern, after agricultural development. PAMIC had been promised an elevated status as an institute (and its name would be changed to Instituto Nicaragüense de Apoyo a la Pequeña y Mediana Empresa, or INPYME), with more specialists and resources. The concern with public relations in an open market was signaled by the new corporate image of the office. Carvajal stressed again that a process of "natural selection" was inevitable, and their office provided assistance in marketing techniques to those microentrepreneurs with the vision and competitive edge to find their niche in the market. Garment producers were no longer assisted because they were not regarded as competitive in the economy, but others, in leather goods, furniture, artesanía, and specialty foods, were meeting more success. "A new type of entrepreneur who manages the tools of the market" will make it, he told me, while others will expire, or "die," as a result of globalization. Although there will be a contraction in small business, he viewed increased specialization in a competitive context as a positive value. When I asked about PAMIC's work with women, he proudly showed me recent reports indicating that a majority of those the organization serves are women. Interestingly, in its reports PAMIC had adopted a practice I had seen only that year at Puntos de Encuentro, using the symbol @ (understood as *o* or *a*) in certain words to avoid gender bias in the Spanish language. While steps had been taken to address women's interests, he agreed that a very small number of women had actually benefited from programs to support microenterprises.

The current neoliberal climate has generated a great deal of attention to microenterprises, and it has come from a wide range of sources. At the Nicaraguan women's encuentro in January 1992, the working group devoted to discussing women in the economy appealed for more support of women in microenterprise development. At a time of high unemployment, this was regarded as a strategy to enable women and their families to weather the economic crisis. That same year, Marlene, of the Cooperativa Francisco Estrada, expressed the view that there would soon be more studies of microentrepreneurs than microentrepreneurs themselves. She laughed when I said it was the classic dilemma of anthropology and other social sciences, inundating subjects of study to the point of being an annoyance. The point that she and others were making was that it might better serve the interests of Nicaraguans to offer assistance more directly to those in need.

In an economy in which the majority of urban and rural workers are located in small industries and microenterprises, it is politically advantageous for the Nicaraguan government to give the impression of concern and support for workers in this sector (Leguizamon 1990). The new administrative apparatus for and discourse on microenterprises seems designed to offer hope to the most vulnerable economic sector at the same time that neoliberal policies further undermine its chance of success. At this point, the difference between the Sandinista-organized cooperatives (no longer benefited by government protection and low-cost materials) and the microenterprises promoted by the Chamorro and Alemán governments is largely ideological—the former based on the principle of state-led development and the latter based on the model of free market competition. In terms of their material conditions, everyday working experiences, and future prospects, both forms of organization are suffering.

Alternatives for Social Mobilization

The changes in Nicaragua's economy and in the organization of work since 1990 have been in some ways transformative and in other ways illusory. Two decades ago, as noted by the political scientist David Close (1999: 19), "Sandinista Nicaragua began life as a more open, tolerant, and pluralistic system than any prior socialist revolutionary state." A private sector with large, medium, and small enterprises coexisted with state-supported cooperatives in the rural and urban areas. Today, the unexpected juxtapositions remain, with elements of both state-directed and market-driven development—although the latter is rapidly gaining force. The Nicaraguan revolution brought substantial changes to a small, underdeveloped nation, but rather than follow an orthodox model of socialist development, the Sandinistas allowed for a mixed economy and heterodox policies and practices. When the Contra war demanded increased defense spending and an austerity economy, measures were introduced that bore resemblance to structural adjustment mandated by the IMF elsewhere in Latin America. However, the FSLN remained committed to delivering basic needs and services to the population—an orientation that was sharply reversed after the UNO coalition came to power.

The neoliberal project ushered in by the Chamorro government and furthered by the Alemán government called for a reorganization of work as the state sector was cut back, industry was privatized, and national production was challenged by conditions favoring imports. Even so, Nicaraguans were vocal in their criticisms of the harsh consequences of the new free market orientation and they won some important concessions, including assistance to small-scale producers. The post-Sandinista governments' support for microenterprise development, at the same time that urban cooperatives and small industries in general are seriously undermined by neoliberal policy, reveals a determined effort to contain the opposition of a large population in urban Nicaragua. However, judging from the continued failure of so many small production units and the downturn of the economy overall, it will take far more to quell the opposition.

The collapse of the Soviet Union and subsequent events in eastern Europe were watched closely in Nicaragua, as in the rest of the world (Hoyt 1997: 148–55). The FSLN was sobered by the historical significance for socialism and the Left and reexamined its own previous political practices; indeed, the unsettling events in that world region may have foreshadowed the divisions that emerged in the Sandinista Party in the next few years. The Nicaraguan election in 1990 marked the loss of another "historic model" of socialist-oriented development, ushering in a fitful political transition and a worsening economic crisis in the country. Yet the loss also presented an opportunity to follow the response of the Left and of emergent popular movements to the challenge of neoliberalism in one small Central American nation. And, in the last decade, we have watched as Nicaragua has experienced the productive tension of a society demanding democratic and pluralist approaches to national development. Without a doubt, social revolutions of the future will be different from revolutions of the past, and we can learn as much from current struggles as we can from historical ones. As the old debates over state sector versus private sector development and over loyalty to a political party line subside, today's social movements in Nicaragua and elsewhere may prefigure, in all their uncertainties, alternatives for the future.

With the FSLN Party greatly weakened and in the absence of a viable economic program advocated by those critical of neoliberalism, what are the alternatives for economic and political change? In concluding this chapter, it is useful to turn attention briefly to new forms of social mobilization in evidence since 1990.[6] I have focused up to now on the changing organization of work from cooperatives to microenterprises, but this decade has also seen growing political participation at the grassroots level on a range of issues. Breaking from party lines, autonomous social movements, or sometimes loosely organized networks, have taken up concerns as wide-ranging as the environment, health, women's rights, and, not surprisingly, the economic crisis. There is a notable relationship between the changing political economy, with the new emphasis on privatization and export-led industrialization, and the expansion of political activism on issues of human rights and gender politics, at a time when the government has swung sharply to the right. There is disagreement over whether this activism is a continuation of the social mobilization under the Sandinistas or the result of a post-Sandinista democratization process, but, as usual, the social reality is more complex.

Many Latin Americans who have been affected most harshly by recent policies are beginning to negotiate the terms of their wider participation in society through forms of collective action (Escobar 1992: 83). In Nicaragua, the economic crisis and political dislocations, on the one hand, and the rise of autonomous social movements, on the other, are related though somewhat contradictory developments in the post-Sandinista period.

Chapter Seven

NARRATIVES
OF DEVELOPMENT,
NATIONHOOD,
AND THE BODY

I N July 1993, at a meeting held in Managua for women working in cooperatives, the participants listened patiently as one man after another addressed them about the need to develop political consciousness during a
period when the country was experiencing the harsh effects of capitalism
and globalization. Finally, a woman stood up and confidently exhorted the
assembled group to organize against the oppressive forces of neoliberalism
and postmodernism. I never learned what led her to include postmodernism as a capitalist threat although she clearly viewed it, along with neoliberalism, as emblematic of the late twentieth century. Her words serve as
a challenge as I consider what postmodern approaches to the cultural politics of late capitalism have to offer to our understanding of the everyday
misery and long-term prospects of so many in Nicaragua and elsewhere in
Latin America.[1]

Studies of development and nation building in Latin America generally
have used a political economy model, although a few have departed from

29. Banner reads "Women Cooperativists of Nicaragua for economic democratization, development, and defense of our human rights" at a gathering in Managua.

that approach to raise important cultural questions concerning ways in which discourses of development and the nation influence practices and outcomes differently across societies. This chapter contributes to the latter project by approaching two subjects rarely discussed together: discourses of development and body politics. Nicaragua during the 1990s illustrates the way in which contentious political economic approaches may play out in cultural practices and discourses in a nation in transition from the revolutionary Sandinista past to the neoliberal present. While the neoliberal model of market-driven development is now dominant, the Sandinistas' discourse continues to question the political underpinnings of that model. Drawing on my research among women and men working in small industries and commerce, and the scholars and policy makers who have attended to them in Managua during the past decade, I consider the national-level debate on "microenterprises" and the "informal sector"—terms that are ideologically charged in the Nicaraguan setting. Then I suggest that working-class and poor urban residents offer more personal, visceral discourses based on local-level experiences of the body and personhood, often inflected by gender, to account for the difficulties they are facing. A case will be made for attention to nondominant discourses that invoke gender and the body as sites on which current conditions are inscribed and that may point the way toward alternative approaches and critiques. At stake is the way Nicaraguans (and others) apprehend and struggle over "development" and "nationhood."[2]

Doubting Development

Going beyond criticism of Western models, I am interested in how the views of scholars, policy makers, and ordinary citizens regarding "development" and a "national project" work in the context of Nicaragua and elsewhere.[3] To that end, I examine the dominant models and discourses of economic development in Nicaragua to see what these models *do*, even when they fail in their stated objectives. Then I turn to the narratives of women and men in Barrio Monseñor Lezcano and in urban cooperatives in Managua, whose words and lives embody an alternative discourse, and suggest that a great deal may be riding on the contest over the terms of this debate.

My rethinking of development derives from several directions. The writings of Marx, Foucault, and feminist theorists have influenced the work of a number of anthropologists and others reexamining development. Arturo Escobar's (1992, 1995) theorization of social movements and what he terms "the development encounter" is joined by the work of other scholars concerned with the post–World War II construction of development and consequences for the "third world" (e.g., Ferguson 1990; DuBois 1991; Pigg 1992; Moore and Schmitz 1995). Several feminist writers have entered the fray, including Sallie Westwood and Sarah A. Radcliffe (1993) and Marianne H. Marchand and Jane L. Parpart (1995), whose work also challenges the modernist assumptions behind most development (as well as gender and development) thinking.

Following Foucault, Escobar (1984–85, 1995) and Marc DuBois (1991) consider the dynamics of discourse, power, and knowledge, particularly as they have been constructed in the first world and imposed in the third world. They show how discourses of development have worked to consolidate the power of first world countries as they constructed the notion of "underdevelopment" and then set forth to build an apparatus to deal with it. At the same time, other discursive practices based on the local knowledge of third world peoples have contributed to social movements that challenge the dominance of singular accounts of development and underdevelopment. An understanding of power as diffuse, exercised from the bottom up as much as the top down (by state apparatuses), enables us to see how local-level initiatives may unsettle what appear to be fixed social structures.

These writers recognize that such problems as underdevelopment have a concrete historical basis but contend that "without examining development as discourse we cannot understand the systematic ways in which the Western developed countries have been able to manage and control and, in many ways, even create the Third World politically, economically, sociologically and culturally" (Escobar 1984–85: 384). Indeed, development as discourse is also "a very real historical formation" even when it is built around fictitious constructs (ibid.: 389). As such, the development paradigm needs to be reexamined, and for that to occur, development must be challenged as a natural category. James Ferguson (1990: xv) shows how development in southern Africa has failed in its stated goal of modernizing economic and social life, "all the while performing, almost unnoticed, its own pre-eminently political operation of expanding bureaucratic state power." He traces the social effects of ideas of development, arguing that a conceptual apparatus can bring about significant structural change. "The challenge," he writes, "is to treat these systems of thought and discourse like any other kind of structured social practice" (277).

Several authors (Parpart 1993; Westwood and Radcliffe 1993; Marchand and Parpart 1995) have drawn together feminist and postmodernist critiques to examine gender, development, and social movements waged over the right to national inclusion and full citizenship; in their view, these critiques' allied focus on difference disrupts universalist thinking about women that has represented them singularly as a gender without recognizing the specificity of their race, class, and national origin.[4] As Parpart (1993: 439) points out, some scholars of third world development have rejected these critiques as first world preoccupations. Yet she and others argue that both feminism and postmodernism have wide resonance and can move us beyond the "metanarratives of both Enlightenment and Marxist thought," based as these are on universalist assumptions about history and society (ibid.). Indeed, these privileged and monolithic discourses are most likely to be shaken in those places where there is attention to power and difference, often in the third world. Feminist and other writers who examine discourse as social practice are nonetheless keenly aware of the difficulty of offering accounts that "deconstruct Eurocentric views" while they are tied, "by convention, to many of the terms that promote this unitary vision" (Westwood and Radcliffe 1993: 2).

In the second half of this chapter, building on the postmodern feminist critique of development, I bring further attention to the body in the construction of the nation. Nations sometimes stand in for ideas and meanings in the global imagination, for example, India for postcolonial nostalgia (Appadurai 1996) and Brazil for third world poverty and modernity (Scheper-Hughes 1992). In a similar way, the human body may stand in for the health or sensibility of a people or a nation; for example, Puerto Ricans may suffer the illness of colonialism and seek the cure of nationalism (Negrón-Muntaner and Grosfoguel 1997), and Guatemalans emerging from a devastating period of civil war speak of their nation as a wounded body (Nelson 1999). As Margaret Lock and Nancy Scheper-Hughes argue, in a critical-interpretive approach there may be three "bodies": the individual, physical body; the social or symbolic body; and the body politic. While the materiality of the body is central to any analysis of the human consequences of neoliberalism, it is also important to understand "talk about the body" as "talk about the nature of society" (Lock and Scheper-Hughes 1990: 61).

I will suggest that while the dominant discourses of development in Nicaragua invoke the health of the body politic in the abstract, nondominant discourses reveal that nonelite Nicaraguans are thinking politics through their own bodies in a much more immediate way. Drawing inspiration from literary and historical studies, I agree with Francine Masiello, who writes:

(Neo)liberal rule was never a disembodied process. . . . [I]t is not surprising in this respect that a large number of Latin American social movements insist on the body as a point of departure to defend human rights and economic advancement; that powerful activists congregate today around issues of sexual choice; that informal sectors reveal a high female component, with housewives unions in barrios placing successful claims on democratic rule through negotiation with the market. (1997: 231)

As she urges, we will need to bring the gendered body as an "originating point of discourse, community, and action" to our discussions of neoliberal development and nation building.[5]

From Revolution to Neoliberalism

Over the last decade, I have followed the rough transition from the revolutionary government of Daniel Ortega and the FSLN to the U.S.-supported governments of Violeta Chamorro's National Opposition Union (UNO) and Arnoldo Alemán's Liberal Alliance. My main concern has been to trace the effects of this transition in the lives and work of low-income women in small industries and commerce in Managua and the women's responses to increasingly harsh living conditions. This period saw the introduction of measures designed to stabilize the economy through sharp cuts in state sector employment and social services; privatization of industries, health care, and education; devaluation of the currency; and market liberalization.

Although 1990 marked a significant reversal of policy orientation and a neoliberal turn, I have argued that the political transition should not be viewed as unilaterally "undoing" the changes brought about by the Nicaraguan revolution. To be sure, the FSLN government was less orthodox than many socialist-oriented governments and it had developed a mixed economy based on land reform and an expanded state sector along with continued private enterprise. But it carried out a broad program of social transformation, and the revolution's challenge to U.S. political interests was sufficient to prompt the Reagan administration to support the Contra war and impose an economic blockade. By the time of the 1990 election, Nicaraguans were frustrated by worsening economic conditions and longing for peace, and Chamorro's presidency offered to compromise with diverse political interests, particularly the still-strong FSLN. While her government represented a turn from state intervention in the market to a free market economy, the process was negotiated and the transition was complex (Spalding 1994). The 1996 election of Arnoldo Alemán marked a further turn to the right and harsher neoliberal measures, but even then the legacy of the revolution provided protection against extreme reversals of policy (Walker 1997).

Dominant Discourses of Development

In 1991, I had an affiliation with the Central American University in Managua, where some of the most important work on the economy was being carried out. Like most intellectuals in Nicaragua, the academics at the UCA were largely identified with Sandinista politics. The Fulbright program, which sponsored my work that year, urged me to have a second affiliation with the Central American Institute of Business Administration, which modeled itself on and had ties with Harvard Business School in the United States. In contrast to the UCA, the INCAE had faculty and trained business students who were by and large sympathetic with the government's neoliberal turn. My double affiliation offered an ideal vantage point from which to observe the production of two quite different discourses to account for and remedy the problems facing the country. Indeed, my interest in discourses of development had its origins in the discussions I heard and participated in at the UCA and the INCAE — especially those related to my research in small industries and the "informal sector" of unregulated economic activities. From the humid offices of a national university in the city's center to the unnecessarily air-conditioned offices of the small but lofty campus of the business school, built at an elevation high enough to escape urban discomforts, the intellectual as well as physical distance was substantial.

Here I will relate what these two dominant discourses of development have offered in conversation and in print regarding the situation of small industries and commerce, which constitute the bulk of economic activity in the urban area. The INCAE came to serve as a think tank for the UNO government, with its highly educated economists and other social scientists offering analyses of the current situation and training an elite to take on positions of economic and political leadership. The school's director at that time was a Colombian economist well known for his studies of small and medium-sized industries. The author of an analysis of the small business sector in Central America, Francisco A. Leguizamon (1990), has written that through 1990 there was little attention to the small and medium-size business sector in the region. This neglect occurred even though more than 90 percent of the businesses in Central America could be classified in this category (up to fifty employees, managed by no more than three persons). He claims that current interest in the sector reflects the onset of the worst depression since the 1930s and the recognition that this sector is key for Central American economies. Leguizamon considers national strategies and barriers to development in the region and proposes what he calls a "radical change," a reference to a firmer commitment to the free market and capitalism as a force for economic development and "democratization." He judges that small and medium-size businesses have the potential to play a greater role in the national economy and adds that as they do, women will be among those who have more opportunities to enter the formal economy.

Leguizamon argues that in the Central American region, Sandinista Nicaragua suffered the most precarious conditions for development in the 1980s and now is most in need of change. He is critical of the way that private investment was limited, cooperatives established, and businesses decentralized. Blaming these factors for the drastic drop in national production, he maintains that Sandinista policy did more to restrict than encourage small and medium-size businesses — although he acknowledges that 40 percent of the budget went to defense against the Contras by mid-decade and this produced a severe economic depression. Writing his analysis just after the elections, he concluded that the prospects for democracy and economic development in Nicaragua were improved under the UNO government.

Nevertheless, when I interviewed Leguizamon at the INCAE in 1991, he was less optimistic. He stated that he had so far seen little change in the economic situation and little improvement for small industry. Although the Ministry of the Economy had created a new office of microenterprises and small industry, it had scant power to introduce change, and Leguizamon saw instead the continued growth of informal activity, along with economic uncertainty and crime, in the country. Even so, he appeared hopeful that the banks and government agencies would soon be able to offer more support to small industries. In the end, he placed the main responsibility for continued poverty on Nicaraguan workers themselves, saying that what was lacking was an intense commitment to work, to seek opportunities, and to take risks. His characterization of Nicaraguans as insufficiently motivated was striking so soon after many of them had risked everything to defend their revolution. But the invocation in anti-Sandinista discourse of such views is often backed by charges that the state had been overly protective of workers and failed to develop competitive industries. When neoliberalism did not bring about a rapid improvement in the ability of small industries and commerce to compete successfully, the same analysts often fell back on the notion of a lingering legacy of dependency under the revolutionary government.

While this economist's view was widely shared at the INCAE and by other UNO supporters as well, a very different view was advanced by the social scientists at the UCA and in the majority of research institutes and NGOs I visited. The latter were generally sympathetic to the goals of the Nicaraguan revolution, in which many had participated, although they offered their assessments of mistakes of the FSLN as well as critiques of UNO policy and its consequences. Amalia Chamorro and other scholars in the School of Sociology at the UCA produced the most significant studies of small industries and commerce in the informal sector in Nicaragua (Chamorro, Chávez, and Membreño 1989, 1991). They used as their baseline the pioneering study of Managua's informal sector, a doctoral dissertation (De Franco 1979) completed just before the FSLN victory. The author of this landmark work, Silvio De Franco, offered a structural analysis of the expansion of the informal sector under conditions of underdevelopment, emphasizing external constraints on growth and identifying the particular difficulties experienced by the majority of women in the sector. De Franco later became minister of the economy and development and then president of the Central Bank under the UNO government, by which time his orientation had shifted significantly to the right (De Franco and Velázquez 1997).

In the neo-Marxist analysis of Chamorro and her colleagues, related to me in a number of conversations, the early years of the Sandinista government were represented as bringing support for the urban popular sectors and for small producers who were organized into state-regulated cooperatives. As a result, they argued, the growth of such areas as textile, leather, handicraft, food, and wood industries was promoted. However, a new pricing structure at that time resulted in lower earnings in the cooperatives and had the unintended consequence of encouraging informal (non-state-regulated) activity. In some cases, these analysts echoed the view of those less sympathetic to the revolutionary government, that state intervention in cooperatives had not benefited small industry in the long term.

Furthermore, these leftist academics contended, the Contra war and the U.S. economic blockade caused a series of social and economic dislocations in the country: scarcity of goods, restriction of imported items, high levels of inflation, and mass migration from the war zones to the cities. The Sandinista government turned its attention to the rural sector and agrarian reform to consolidate its base in the war zone and began cutting back on programs that had benefited popular sectors in the cities. The informal sector grew to the extent that a free market coexisted with the official market, and the war contributed to rural-urban migration. In Managua's sprawling Eastern Market, for example, the number of sellers was estimated at as many as ten thousand, mostly poor women, and rising in the early 1980s. A few became rich, but the majority barely got by. In an effort to control inflation the government held down wages, but this had the effect of encouraging formal sector workers to turn to the informal sector. The informal sector became the center of controversy in Nicaragua, and the government introduced policies restricting informal production and commerce that were clearly hostile to its workers, by then viewed as parasites and speculators—and as fodder for critics of state-led development. Some, like the UCA researchers, countered that in the context of war and economic hardship, informal workers were actually productive contributors to the economy (Chamorro, Chávez, and Membreño 1989). Not surprisingly, in contrast to the analyses offered at the INCAE, those at the UCA more frequently invoked the external constraints on development experienced during the Sandinista decade.

Two views of the postelectoral project of nation building follow from the two different readings of the decade of revolutionary government and its consequences for economic development exemplified by the INCAE and UCA analyses. The first corresponds to the dominant discourse of the Chamorro and Alemán governments, based on a neoliberal model of free market development, while the second is a discourse espoused by Sandinistas and other critics of government policies who call for a more gradual introduction of structural adjustment measures. Both were formulated during a transitional time when substantial change was being negotiated in the country, and both claim to have a primary commitment to a democratic process.

In March 1991, the maxi-devaluation that was intended to stabilize the currency meant a severe loss of real wages and buying power for most Nicaraguans. This was part of the IMF formula adopted by the government economic team that included massive privatization and cuts in state employment and social services, that is, the traditional "shock" program of economic adjustment. Later the same month, the Ministry of Finance announced the Occupational Conversion Plan, which, with USAID funding, offered state sector employees severance pay if they agreed to leave their jobs. Encouraged to establish small businesses, many who agreed to the plan purchased freezers to begin selling ice and ice cream from their homes— a dubious prospect as informal activities saturated the market.[6]

The ministry's director of budget planning and the author of the Occupational Conversion Plan, Fatima Reyes, described the plan in an interview as an integral part of the government's structural adjustment program. The stated objective, she said, was to "stimulate economic reactivation, motivating the voluntary transfer of employees from the public to the private sector, to set up small businesses or to work in private enterprises." An unstated objective appeared to be the removal of Sandinistas from the public sector, and in the process a disproportionate number of women also left their work. Interestingly, the emphasis was on moving people into commerce and the service sector rather than into production. When I asked if she thought that the entry of more people into small enterprises would further saturate that sector, Reyes minimized the concern by claiming that many who were adopting the plan were already involved in family businesses and the plan would simply assist them. Moreover, she described those electing the plan as mainly "housewives," evidently referring to female state employees. When asked what impact the plan would have on Nicaraguan families, she answered very positively that it would give women the opportunity to return home to their families. In so stating the objectives of the plan, she adopted the language of the UNO government's traditional family ideology (Fatima Reyes, interview, July 18, 1991).[7]

When I spoke with Amalia Chamorro of the UCA about the plan, she expressed the view that whereas the Sandinista government had attempted to formalize the informal economy by organizing urban cooperatives and, later, introducing sanctions against informal activity, the UNO government was doing just the opposite. By removing support for cooperatives, then cutting the number of formal sector employees and encouraging them to work on their own or in small businesses, the state was contributing to the proliferation of the informal sector. Moreover, she noted, it should have been obvious to the plan's creators that most of the new commercial enterprises would be doomed to failure. Her critical perspective suggested a more cynical reading of the UNO's "support" of small businesses, which might have served to mask its draconian cuts in the public sector and the implications for employment and the distribution of social services.

I interviewed a number of individuals in the Ministry of the Economy over the 1990s. María Hurtado de Vigil, director of the Office of Small Industries (i.e., businesses of up to thirty employees) and Microenterprises (i.e., up to five employees), has been a key player in government assistance to small business. On our first meeting, I inquired about the new emphasis on microenterprises at a time when the informal sector was still rapidly expanding. She responded that after the Sandinista government's early support for small industries and cooperatives, its economic adjustment of the late 1980s resulted in a high failure rate among these enterprises as well as a growing number of workers in the informal sector. As for the UNO government's free market policy favoring the entry of imported goods and increasing competition, she described this not in terms of the cost to Nicaraguan producers but in terms of consumers' right to better products. She told me that her office would support those small enterprises deemed "most likely to succeed" and acknowledged that those "most likely to fail" might include more businesses operated by women (María Hurtado de Vigil, interview, May 8, 1991).

My interview with Antonio Chávez of CONAPI offers a striking contrast. Head of the Managua region and, later, president of the national trade union organization, Chávez acknowledged that CONAPI is still identified with the FSLN, but he took pains to say that it has no "political color" and that the membership is politically diverse. Although CONAPI has recently had few resources and has offered only limited support to its membership, it remains the major organization representing the interests of workers in small industries. When I asked Chávez about recent government policies and their impact on women, he was quick to respond, telling me that women comprise over half of their membership, mainly in the textile and food industries, which have been especially vulnerable under the new policies. For example, he said, the lower tariffs on imported clothing as well as the recent entry of used clothing from the United States have severely undercut Nicaraguan women's production and sales. While he noted that the downturn in the sector began under the Sandinistas, he attributed this to the economic crisis that was in part due to U.S. intervention — and said that the UNO's shock treatment was far worse (Antonio Chávez, interview, May 8, 1991).[8]

Contention and Convergence

Clearly, the government, on the one hand, and CONAPI and workers in small industries and commerce, on the other — like the INCAE and UCA scholars — had very different assessments of the post-1990 situation in Nicaragua, especially of the economy. The language they used revealed some key differences, with the former advancing the position that microenterprises

30. *Antonio Chávez, then president of* CONAPI, *working in his office.*

could thrive under the new liberal market conditions if workers were given
the chance to become competitive and the latter emphasizing the failure of
small industries and informal sector workers to get by, let alone thrive, during a time of crisis. Although I have emphasized the differences between
the two dominant discourses, here I draw attention to the similar logic
underlying what appear on the surface to be distinct political-ideological
positions.

While Sandinistas and others critical of the government's economic policy could be said to be producing an alternative to the government's dominant discourse, or master narrative, of development, they have not produced
entirely different discourses. In fact, they share the underlying assumptions
that a measure of adjustment is necessary and that workers themselves embody the potential of the nation to forge ahead and "develop." Despite the
opposition to *neoliberalismo,* or the neoliberal model imposed by the government in response to IMF and USAID pressures, an alternative model has
not been offered. Instead, critics have pointed to the shortcomings and
high social costs of the neoliberal plan but have proposed a more gradual
introduction of measures to stabilize and adjust the economy, along with

programs to support small industries to become more competitive. At the turn of the twenty-first century, a viable alternative appears even less likely, although I suggest later that more hopeful prospects are embodied in the social movements emerging in civil society over the last decade.[9]

As the UNO government's promises to reactivate the economy grew more desperate in the face of worsening unemployment and deepening poverty, officials often invoked the errors of the Sandinistas and the inadequacies of Nicaraguan workers themselves to account for ongoing problems. That was the case in several meetings I had with Stefan Platteau, the Dutch head of PAMIC, created by the Ministry of the Economy in 1991. In his first year on the job, Platteau expressed the view that by offering credit and training to qualified microentrepreneurs, the problems of the past could be overcome. He shared the opinion held by many others that the revolutionary government had provided excessive support to workers without offering them badly needed training. He was intent on training highly motivated individuals to work in microenterprises, demonstrating their viability and making his program a success (Stefan Platteau, interview, February 24, 1992). Yet a year later Platteau revealed the tougher attitude and more cynical outlook becoming apparent among government officials. To overcome the problems of the Sandinista decade, he said, he must counter a "culture of distrust" with a "culture of management." The condescending language he used to describe workers' failings was resonant of the "culture of poverty" (or, in Nicaragua, sometimes termed "culture of subsidy") thinking of those in the development field who locate the obstacles to modernization in the people or in their state-directed economies rather than in problems stemming from globalization or the development process itself.[10] The reality is more complex, of course, but the ideological effect of holding workers responsible is to invite polemics and preclude the possibility of learning from the past (Stefan Platteau, interview, July 23, 1993).

Some members of government expressed an even deeper cynicism about the likelihood of economic recovery. As unemployment and underemployment rose in recent years, the growth of the informal sector continued unabated. A large number of people were selling items ranging from food and drink to TV antennas and exercise suits, as well as washing car windows at intersections in the city. In an acknowledgment of the severity of the problem, a joke was circulating: How can 30,000 new jobs be created? The answer: install 1,000 new traffic lights at urban intersections. Ironically, after the 1996 election of Arnoldo Alemán, huge traffic circles replaced lights at major intersections in the city, and some Nicaraguans quipped that the new president had gone that far to eliminate informal vendors from the streets.

During interviews over the last few years, Luis Carvajal, PAMIC's director of entrepreneurial development, called attention to the assistance offered to promising microenterprises to develop and market better products. The official presence of PAMIC in Managua as well as in national campaigns and fairs to promote products gives visibility to the government's apparent concern for small industry. Carvajal, like Platteau before him, believes that the Sandinista government was overly protective of workers in guaranteeing them a market and that quality suffered. In the neoliberal 1990s, some workers still expect the state to provide a safety net, but they are learning that they must "be competitive or die." This change is good, he said, and builds the self-esteem of those who manage to succeed (Luis Carvajal, interview, July 3, 1996).

In 1998, Carvajal stressed that the Alemán government had placed high priority on microenterprise development. He emphasized the importance of marketing techniques, finding niches, and having "vision." Pushing the point further, he told me that "natural selection" in this period of globalization would ensure that a "new type of entrepreneur who manages the tools of the market" will survive. Given that an estimated 60 percent of the economically active population works in small enterprises, this sector is bound to contract, he said, but there will be a positive outcome in terms of specialization and competition. Revealing the contradictions of the neoliberal era, he claimed that women are given special consideration as microentrepreneurs, even as he described the certain failure of many of their small industries (Luis Carvajal, interview, June 9, 1998).

Meanwhile, in recent years CONAPI has signaled its nonpolitical orientation and its concern to work effectively with — but sometimes in opposition to — the government. In 1996, when the organization challenged a proposed new law that would adversely affect cooperatives by eliminating their favored tax status, Antonio Chávez reported that it had helped to stem the decline of small industries. He pointed to some recovering enterprises and implied that CONAPI had played a role (while also acknowledging that a good coffee harvest that year had benefited the whole economy) (Antonio Chávez, interview, July 4, 1996). However, the CONAPI membership often complained that their organization's leaders served little purpose beyond maintaining their own positions and that small industries continued to suffer losses. Indeed, in a period of high unemployment and state sector layoffs, administrators in private and public offices such as CONAPI and PAMIC had a lot at stake in demonstrating their own worthiness and service to their constituencies. By 1998, CONAPI's image was tarnished: the former leadership was charged with corruption and a number of cooperatives elected to drop their membership. If an unstated objective of development programs is to support the apparatus established to promote development goals, this example from Nicaragua suggests that the apparatus of CONAPI may be in danger of foundering as that of PAMIC (now INPYME) gains ascendancy in the neoliberal era.

Working-Class Narratives: A Departure
from the Dominant Discourses

Until now, I have discussed two discursive practices in Nicaragua, that produced by neoliberals in government and the academy and that produced by Sandinista critics in CONAPI and other trade union organizations as well as the academy. Most of my research did not consist of interviews in offices, however, but rather talking with members of urban cooperatives and small industries around Managua and with residents of Barrio Monseñor Lezcano where many worked in the informal economy.[11] When I compared the dominant development discourses to what working-class Nicaraguans had to say, I expected that they would align themselves with one or the other discourse based on their life experience and political orientation. However, I discovered that the two dominant discourses were problematic and overlapping in themselves and that the discursive practices in urban cooperatives and barrios often departed from the dominant discourses. Here, I offer a sampling of the rich and diverse views of these working women and men — some of whom were introduced in earlier chapters — and what they expressed about the current situation in their country. Later, I argue that their persistent appeals to the body and personhood in relation to development offer, if not a well-formed political stance, a nascent alternative stemming from a consciousness that remains resistant and potentially revolutionary.

Some of the people I interviewed appeared to have adopted the neoliberal view that conditions were getting better, as evidenced by the increasing modernity of Managua and the introduction of new imported items, which they hoped one day to be able to obtain.[12] One example was the woman I spoke to in Barrio Monseñor Lezcano who was employed in the small but modern new supermarket, La Corona. Unlike the majority of those working as sales help, who were from better-off areas of Managua, the woman I met mopping the floor was from the barrio. She was no doubt satisfied to have a secure job, working forty-eight hours per week and earning about U.S. $100 per month. When I asked how she viewed the current situation, she glanced around at the fully stocked shelves of products, many of them luxury items: liquor, canned fruits, pastries, and other imported foods. She observed that things are better now and that before (under the Sandinistas) they were in decline. Before, they had to stand in line for goods, but now products are in ample supply. The policies are good, she said, expressing confidence that life would improve and that all would benefit from the greater availability of items on the market.

Others in the barrio shared the opinion that times had been particularly difficult under the Sandinistas. Although the barrio had strongly supported the insurrection that ended the Somoza dictatorship, a majority had voted for the UNO government in 1990. The widowed owner of a car parts workshop voiced her dissatisfaction with the current situation, saying that her business was down and she had to pay high taxes to the mayor's office. Like the majority of those I interviewed, she complained that "there are things to buy but no money to buy them." However, she went so far as to reminisce about the Somoza period, remembering it as a "royal time that we'll never return to," when you could buy cars and many desired products. She recalled the Sandinista period as "the dark part of Nicaragua's history, in every sense." In the end, she expressed the hope that the situation would improve in the future.

Another woman I spoke to had opened the front room of her house on the barrio's main square as a small shop where she offered soft drinks and occasional simple meals. She explained that the bottled drinks actually belong to a male acquaintance of hers who left his job under the Occupational Conversion Plan and began selling on his own, then asked her to sell for him. When asked what she thought of the present situation, she described herself as on neither side politically (neither Sandinista nor UNO) and as an active member of the evangelical church that owned the house she lived in. She said, "It's the same poverty," referring to conditions under the FSLN and UNO governments. Having lived in the barrio for twenty-five years and having observed the growing number of informal businesses, she complained that there are more sellers than buyers now and too many small shops and restaurants, so that everyone is suffering.

Despite their initial support for the UNO government, most of the people I talked to in the barrio were completely disillusioned a year or two after the elections. Without the expected level of U.S. support or the promised economic recovery, peace and the end of the economic blockade were insufficient to satisfy them. Most spoke up immediately about the failings of the government and its policies. While those in more privileged and powerful places debated about what measures would "start up" the economy, workers in the marginalized informal sector and the beleaguered cooperatives were quick to point to immediate problems such as unemployment, lack of credit, low wages, rising prices, and poor health. Whereas the former used the ideological maneuver of talking in abstract terms, the latter spoke directly to the effects on body and soul.

A number of women related their strategies for coping with the present economic situation. A seamstress from the small garment factory in the barrio that, like many small businesses, had fallen on hard times was the sole income earner for a household that included her two daughters and three grandchildren. When asked if her wages meet their needs, she said that she had to "stretch, stretch, stretch" her earnings. The household eats less and more simply; they wash their clothes only twice a week to conserve water and soap; and they do the ironing, considered essential by working-class Nicaraguans, just once a week. All this she refers to as "the struggle to survive." Difficult as this woman's life seemed when I spoke with her in 1992, it was far more difficult a year later when production at the factory came to a near-standstill and her income was greatly reduced.

One of the women who had worked for a decade in the garment cooperative, Obreras Unidas Textil, returned to her home when the group could not make the monthly payments on the building they used as a store. She continued to sew at home, but with sales of new clothing down, she had turned to selling cheaper used clothing imported from the United States. She complained that, unlike the Sandinista government, the UNO was not helping them, and she added that CONAPI was not helping much either. She was not hopeful about the future and did not see how any government could improve things. For now, she said, her family makes sacrifices, doing without basic foods, access to transportation, and other needs.

Don Nicolás, the retired carpenter and self-styled historian of Barrio Monseñor Lezcano, enjoyed talking, so I often sat with him to hear his recollections of the past and to listen to his strong views about the current situation. A longtime Sandinista, he compared the present unfavorably with the past. He said the Chamorro and Alemán governments have tried to stabilize the economy "on the backs of the people, making them suffer," and "the political cost is very high." He views the new orientation of the government as inevitable but expects that just as socialism failed in the country, so will capitalism and the neoliberal project. He pointed to a lack of national identity among Nicaraguan capitalists, who instead serve individual interests and international capital, making a successful national project unlikely.

Nicolás's neighbor, a retired man who used to work in a small enterprise making windows, talked to me about his family's situation. The ten family members living in his house depend mostly on his small pension and the salary of one daughter who works as a secretary. In the past, his wife took in washing for a neighbor, but now no one has money to pay for that service. They eat mainly beans, some cheese, but no meat. Telling me that his wife is a loyal Sandinista but that he is not, he sounded deeply resigned as he summed up the situation: "The working class is poor. The governments are alike. There is no work." The despair evident in his words suggests he has given up, although it also reveals a frank insistence on naming the material problems that poor and working people confront.

As should be clear, work and the lack thereof were at the center of most of my conversations in the barrio. A mother of two young children who worked as a schoolteacher told me that her husband had been without a job for nearly four years. He was suffering from "nerves" and had consulted a psychologist but found some relief when he became an evangelical. She later joined, too, and they have found a measure of peace, even as they continue to face economic hardship. Her invocation of faith as an alternative to medical healing and economic well-being, when those were unattainable, was striking.

Doña María, the older woman who was long active in the barrio and with the Mothers of Heroes and Martyrs, had much to say about the national situation during my visits with her. She acknowledged that there were economic problems under the FSLN government, but she attributed them largely to the war and the blockade. People at least had food to eat, because the government distributed cards that allowed everyone to get basic foods at reduced prices. Since 1990, she told me, small industry has been failing. There is no work, and people have no money to spend. With strong competition, small businesses like her front-room store fail while large businesses prosper. She also addressed the high toll the economic situation has taken on people's personal lives. People are not eating well, and they are suffering psychologically as well as physically. With eight people in her house dependent on her retired husband's pension and her small store income, she spoke passionately about the burden of neoliberal policies.

Clearly, economic policies have taken a heavy toll on both women and men. Taking a broader, historical view, we may observe that Nicaraguan experiences of revolution and counterrevolution as well as neoliberalism have been distinctly gendered. Masculine as well as feminine identities have been forged as men suffered from their disproportionate involvement in war and from rising unemployment, causing them to return home with a loss of dignity. For their part, women too participated in armed struggle at levels previously unheard of, they have experienced unemployment, *and* they have felt the impact of men's misfortunes within families and households. When men are present at home in greater numbers they may pitch in to help women or introduce new levels of stress, and when they abandon their families they may leave them feeling distraught or relieved; there are many different stories in the barrio.

Although some women felt that the burden of shouldering the economic crisis was shared equally by women and men, many articulated the ways in which women carry the heavier load. The situation is particularly acute for those in the high number of female-headed households, but even when men are present, women bear the main responsibility for feeding and clothing their children and performing housework. Circumstances are made more trying, some say, by husbands who, out of jealousy, do not want their wives to work even when their earnings are essential. As we have seen, several women in both the artisans' cooperative and the welders' cooperative had to abandon their work because their husbands' insisted they return home. The multiple demands placed on women as family members and as workers are rarely considered by government officials even as they express their commitment to making small enterprises succeed.

In general, the language used by workers in small industries and commerce to describe the current situation was far more direct and personal than the technical language of government bureaucrats and policy makers or of academics. Their descriptions of the effects of the economic adjustments on their lives were visceral — suggesting, in effect, how economic hardship was inscribed on their bodies and minds. One woman told me that her garment cooperative was "drowning" as a result of the policy that favored importing clothing and made materials more costly to purchase. A woman from another garment cooperative that was narrowly avoiding bankruptcy described the economic "blows" the co-op had experienced and the way that, since the elections, the free market policy was "killing" them. Tomás, the man who had served as head of the bakers' cooperative COOTPAM until the economic downturn drove the co op to sell its property, told me that the government is "asphyxiating" small industries and only helping large ones, even though the majority of workers in Nicaragua are employed in small industries. He concluded that between neoliberal politics and high unemployment, people are unable to get ahead and, more often, are losing ground.

In the last few years, people I have spoken with have used even stronger language to describe the effects of harsh economic conditions on body and soul. The owner of a small restaurant told me that the system is "killing them, massacring them." One baker I interviewed, Laura, gestured graphically as she described how competition from large industry-produced bread is "hanging them." A retired man, describing his family's increasingly meager meals, said they can no longer "endure." In keeping with the PAMIC official's prognosis that the neoliberal economy would mean the "survival of the fittest," people's stories made reference to small businesses expiring and, in a few cases, individuals committing suicide in desperation.

When even the activists among those I interviewed describe the Community Movement and the Mothers of Heroes and Martyrs working at the level of the barrio[13] as being "paralyzed," it is difficult to avoid representing these Nicaraguans as passive victims of circumstances beyond their control. However, while the people themselves often describe conditions as hopeless, they nonetheless speak about and act on their commitment to "struggle" and about the "hope" they hold onto as they "cope" with the economic situation. Some continue to participate in oppositional politics, whether at the barrio level or in the Sandinista Party, and others claim a victory in simply meeting their families' most basic daily needs.

Neoliberalism and Discourses of the Nation and the Body

For a brief time in the 1980s, Nicaragua stood as an international symbol of revolutionary hope or neocolonial anxiety, depending on one's political outlook. Now, in neoliberal times, Nicaragua stands variously for hopes deferred or capitalism's promise, again depending on one's perspective. But whatever view is held, there is agreement that the country is facing grave economic problems and that the body politic is ailing. Neoliberal policy analysts debate whether "gradual or shock therapy" is required to stabilize the pathologically ill economy, and leaders rationalize that "a gradual approach would mean the death of the 'patient'" (De Franco and Velázquez 1997: 104); ironically, by employing the metaphor of the economy or the body politic as a sick person, they rationalize harsher austerity measures and disregard the effects on physical bodies. Even Sandinistas and others critical of government policy work within the neoliberal system and call out for needed medicine, but what they have in mind is a palliative for "shock therapy"; Antonio Chávez made such an appeal when he complained that the government was not so much as providing "aspirin" for small industry's "migraine." The barrio residents and other low-income people I spoke with were the most explicit in saying that social and economic ills in the country are creating body ills in real, live individuals—a key point that is overlooked in the dominant discourses. In Nicaragua, as elsewhere, the political economic woes of a nation are often expressed and contested in terms of physical disorder and mental distress.

Certainly, body metaphors are employed across social classes to describe the nation's economy and its population. What appears notably different is the elite's notion of the harsh medicine that is needed to heal the nation and working-class and poor people's imagery of the bodily consequences of both the economic crisis and the medicine that is being administered to deal with it. As we have seen, the elite may blame workers for becoming "spoiled," "lazy," and "parasitical" under the Sandinistas and, now, for failing to take risks and become "competitive"; they may emphasize the physical price of "blood, sweat, and tears" that workers must pay to "survive." Poor and working people, of course, view things rather differently, as they describe the outcome of recent policy measures as ill health, depression, and sometimes even suicide.

While academics and policy makers advance discourses based on social and economic assessments (and, doubtless, their own personal and political interests), the physical and psychological welfare of working-class and poor people hangs in the balance. Their bodies function as a battleground in discussions that center on how quickly adjustment measures may be introduced and how much the population can withstand before irreversible damage is done — or before political protest grows stronger. Low-income workers and barrio residents offer their own critical, oppositional accounts as they describe their personal and family circumstances and suffering.

31. Among the especially destitute, men, women, and children scavenge in Managua's teeming garbage dump.

While these narratives are clearly marked by class, they are also deeply gendered as women's stories convey the extra burdens they carry in a society and economy that depends on them to perform increasing domestic responsibilities.

The brief personal narratives of hardship and struggle offered here may be unsurprising to those who have spent time in Latin America in periods of economic crisis and political transition. But I would agree with the geographer Patricia Price (1999) in calling for increased attention to the body, or what she terms "the very local," as a site (like the local, national, and global) where broad processes unfold. Indeed, there is some evidence that neoliberalism can produce health crises, as in the rapid spread of cholera in unprepared Latin American nations a few years ago (Petras and Morley 1992: 54). In Nicaragua, "natural" disasters such as Hurricane Mitch are followed by much more suffering because of the environmental devastation, poverty, and governmental disregard that stem from a free market orientation (*Envío* 1999b). And increasing reports of domestic violence in the country may be attributed to continued patterns of male dominance and to the women's movement's increasing support of women who report domestic abuse, but there appears to be a correlation with worsening economic conditions as well (*Envío* 1999a). Studies that have examined the psychosocial disruptions of the Contra war and economic adjustment in Nicaragua have found that the consequences are particularly acute for women and children (Fernández Poncela 1996; Quesada 1998). My research endorses the need to consider not only the materiality of subaltern lives but also the nondominant discourses of less powerful social sectors as they embrace "embodied" (often gendered) issues of national development.

In the project of nation building, the dominant discourses of Sandinista and neoliberal analysts and policy makers are not dichotomous and fixed frames of reference but rather constantly negotiated positions and practices. Sometimes they converge, and sometimes they contradict each other, based on changing circumstances and power struggles. Thus the Sandinistas have sometimes adopted a developmentalist discourse to promote a democratic process, without necessarily abandoning a more revolutionary project (Grosfoguel, Negrón-Muntaner, and Georas 1997: 9). Similarly, the Chamorro and Alemán governments have been characterized by differing degrees of willingness to compromise with the substantial political opposition. And in recent years, the disunity of the FSLN and the willingness of

Daniel Ortega as party leader to make a pact with the Alemán government have meant considerable divergence of interest within the party (*Envío* 1999d). Accordingly, shifting and contentious discourses have contributed to a complex political panorama in the country. In general, though, "workers" as a category are expected to build up the economy and society and "women" as a category are expected to maintain home and family in the new socially and politically conservative order.

The working-class Nicaraguans I interviewed in Managua reflected some of the views characteristic of the dominant political discourses, not surprising as they are citizens and voters who identify with national concerns. However, their narratives are often far more critical and oppositional, calling into question the efficacy and sincerity of the powerful social sectors in bringing about any change for the better. Although they sometimes express the antistatist view that all governments are alike and cannot be counted on, they also make an urgent appeal for action to alter the situation. While middle-class members of government and the political opposition debate how quickly economic adjustment should proceed and what social support should be offered to reduce its harsh effects, working-class and poor Nicaraguans name the problem as it is inscribed on their bodies as poverty, hunger, and despair.[14] A diverse group themselves, these women and men challenge notions of neoliberal development as inevitable and contribute to an understanding of the workings of power in society (Villarreal 1996). At the very least, they speak eloquently to the need for a living wage and social services, and at best, they offer searing critiques of discourses and practices that fail to address the unbearable burdens of adjustment policies. Their awareness of their economic vulnerability when the Sandinista safety net was removed is paralleled by an evident awareness of the vulnerability of their persons, their bodies. Finally, their refusal to accept silently the damaging effects of neoliberalism restores the memory of the revolution, which at its outset held out the hope of building an economic democracy, just when such a bold vision has been lost to many in the country.

Development or National Project?

Conversations and interviews with Nicaraguans from various social sectors have been at the center of my discussion in this chapter. A more extensive treatment would require the examination at greater length of the vast quantity of print media as well, including newspapers, journals, and reports. Nevertheless, the conversations I heard and participated in represent a broad cross section of issues that are currently debated in the country.[15] Moreover, my face-to-face encounters allowed me to hear the unofficial views of public figures as well as the views of working-class and poor Nicaraguans, who are frequently overlooked. By gathering professional accounts and personal narratives, I had the opportunity to consider the discursive strategies people deploy to give cultural meaning to their political and economic experiences.

María Rosa Renzi, an economist and the executive director of FIDEG, an NGO that studies the impact of neoliberal adjustment policies, offered an assessment of the situation in Nicaragua. Like many others, she emphasized that the cutbacks in state sector employment and the elimination of social services that had been provided under the Sandinistas brought inflation under control, but at great social cost. Renzi spoke of economic models, employment, and reactivating the economy, but she did not refer specifically to development. Indeed, when I questioned her about current development discourses she responded that Nicaraguans rarely speak of development, or *desarrollo* (María Rosa Renzi, interview, July 23, 1993). Elsewhere in Latin America and the third world, the term is frequently used among the general population, not just among specialists. In Nicaragua, *desarrollo* is employed in economic and political analysis but seldom in everyday conversation. In part, this may be because in the post-Sandinista government the Ministry of the Economy and Development had far less influence than the Ministry of Finance and the Central Bank. But the lack of engagement with "development" may also follow from the decade of Nicaraguan revolution and the popular resistance to received knowledge and imposed models from the North.

We might fruitfully turn, then, from discussions of "development" to the multiple ways in which Nicaraguans are constructing and struggling over a "national project" (Field 1998).[16] How likely is it, ten years after the defeat of the Sandinista government by an opposition bent on unmaking the revolution and remaking a neoliberal nation, that constructive action will emerge from the current expression of political differences? We might first question how different the articulated positions between the dominant ideologies and discourses really are, particularly at a time when the major party leaders—Alemán for the ruling Liberal Alliance and Ortega for the FSLN—have made a pact to gain personal advantage.[17] In both a national and a global sense, neoliberalism appears to be the only game in town.

Likewise, how different is CONAPI's recent campaign to encourage consumers to "Buy Nicaraguan" in order to benefit national producers and allow their products to become competitive with imported goods, from PAMIC's slogan to attract business directly to microentrepreneurs, "From the Entrepreneur to the Consumer, All Is Cheaper"? Both rely on nationalist rhetoric and call for national production and consumption to counter the harsh effects of neoliberalism and structural adjustment. One might argue, of course, that unlike CONAPI, which represents small producers themselves, PAMIC represents government interests trying to placate microentrepreneurs who are likely to be crushed under the neoliberal model. In this sense, CONAPI continues to make efforts, however compromised, on behalf of its constituency, while the PAMIC agenda may be not as much to assist small-scale producers as to serve the state by creating an administrative apparatus to contain dissent.

Raising these questions in the current context of Nicaragua and pointing to the convergence of formerly opposed political ideologies and discourses need not lead to entirely cynical conclusions, however. I have considered some alternative discursive practices in working-class Managua, particularly as they are inflected by concerns relating to gender and the body in connection with the economy and the nation. Whereas the discourses of dominant political interests are similar in their invocation of metaphors of illness and pathology—the economy "ailing"; the country "wounded" after Hurricane Mitch—working-class and poor Nicaraguans speak more directly of the effects of these force fields on their own bodies. Women, especially, recognize that their vulnerability to the consequences of low incomes, increasing violence, and uncertain access to basic needs is heightened. The frequent invocation of women as "mothers," whether by Sandinistas seeking their solidarity or by governments desiring to reinstate traditional family values (and, often enough, by women themselves), is understood by many to place additional responsibility on women to underwrite the social costs of development and nation building. Thus, in the midst of rising feminist concern that efforts to reestablish patriarchal authority and to curtail reproductive rights pose serious threats, a slogan of the women's movement, "My body is mine," resonates loudly.[18]

The same election that ushered in devastating economic policies and welcomed competition in the free market also opened the political and cultural space for social movements, independent of any single political party, to form and articulate alternative discourses. These emergent movements in civil society—the subject of the next chapter—including women, indigenous peoples, gay men and lesbians, environmentalists and others, have called for a new political culture.[19] Significantly, these groups share a concern for the integrity of the body, the right to live free of violence, hunger, and environmental threat, as well as the right to cultural, sexual, and political expression. Indeed, in relation to gender, race, and sexual orientation, there is some prospect of "changing Nicaragua's political economy of the body" (Lancaster 1992: 230). Attention to the relationship between discourse and power and to the construction of cultural meaning in the building of an oppositional politics is evident in these movements. Women and men in various social sectors, including workers in small and informal businesses, are questioning the conventional wisdom of government authorities and powerful economic interests as well as established political parties as they call for an extension of rights to all citizens. Without being overly sanguine, there is reason to agree with the claim that civil society embodies the best prospect of advancing a democratic alternative in the country.[20] What the new players will propose to put in place is uncertain, but let us not underestimate the creative spirit of a people who so recently waged revolution on the planet.

Chapter Eight

TOWARD A NEW
POLITICAL CULTURE

O N March 8, 1991, International Women's Day was celebrated in Managua. At the time, my research was still getting under way; my computer had been held up in transit from the United States to the American embassy in Managua because of heightened security imposed during the Gulf War. I was fortunate to have the use of a computer at the INCAE, where I had an office that year. And it was there that I attended a panel discussion and cocktail party in honor of women that day. I had been asked to be on the panel as the new resident feminist academic, but I declined, preferring the role of observer at the event.

While I worked at the INCAE that day, I noticed that we women were being congratulated by the men on the faculty and administration as if it were Mother's Day or Secretary's Day. Indeed, as we entered the lecture room for the afternoon panel, attended by a few government dignitaries as well as a handful of feminists from NGOs, each woman was given a long-stemmed red rose, a peculiarly gallant gesture to mark the occasion. This, then, was the tone of the event in that venue, which was to include panel participants representing the political Left, Right, and Center—an open forum for discussion, according to the organizers. Yet what followed was more antifeminist than feminist, and I began to wonder if this marked the neoliberal appropriation of the socialist feminist holiday celebrated worldwide.

The event began with welcoming remarks by Ninoska de Jarquín, head of the newly reestablished Nicaraguan Women's Institute (INIM) who brought greetings from Doña Violeta (Chamorro). She emphasized the defense of the family as the basic unit of society, suggesting that this would be the orientation of the INIM and marking a shift from the feminist direction of the past. Two more women spoke on the panel, a conservative member of the National Assembly who praised the UNO government and highlighted the new emphasis on the family, saying that if women were marginalized it was due to their "self-marginalization," and the feminist director of IXCHEN, a women's health center, who would not allow herself to be baited on the subject of women's access to abortion and reproductive rights. She instead focused on national reconciliation and referred to other celebrations of International Women's Day taking place in Managua that year, including the AMNLAE congress and the Festival of the 52 Percent, which signaled the diversity of the women's movement and the willingness of Nicaraguan women to "talk across differences."

I begin this chapter by describing this event because it captures one aspect of the changing political culture in Nicaragua of the 1990s. We may find in the INCAE's celebration the mix of a neoliberal openness to the free market of ideas and a conservative social agenda that has accompanied political transition in the country. A cynical reading of the mood in Nicaragua through this decade would take such reclamations of revolutionary practices and cultural meanings as definitive of the times. Often, I have been chastened by such developments in the country and by other scholars' admonitions against more hopeful readings of the present context. Yet, in all the time I spent in Nicaragua, I have been equally impressed by new initiatives that contribute to a political culture that is once again more inclusive, democratic, and innovative than what has gone before. Whether in the form of social movements, NGOs, or workers' associations, the changing currents in civil society in Nicaragua warrant attention. In this chapter, I may risk being called unduly optimistic in my assessment of the present situation, but I will be in the good company of Nicaraguans who are staking serious claims for a new way of doing politics.

Chapter 2 considered the tension between AMNLAE and autonomous feminist groups in Nicaragua—whose competing celebrations for International Women's Day I also attended in 1991. Here I want to provide a broader view of the transitional period when Sandinista sectoral organizations gained greater independence, when new identity-based movements emerged, and when nongovernmental organizations came on the scene as an important force for oppositional politics and change. I discuss the neighborhood, women's, workers', student, and youth movements, as well as the Christian base communities that were launched under the Sandinistas; the indigenous, peace, and environmental movements that have deep roots and now may be leading the way to a more comprehensive democratic politics of national reconciliation; and, finally, two less well known groups of activists I have followed over the years, in the workers' organization CONAPI organized under the Sandinistas and in the growing lesbian and gay movement, which began organizing clandestinely during the same period and more openly in the 1990s.

From Sectoral Organizations to New Social Movements

As civil society is charged with taking on the social responsibilities now eschewed by neoliberalism's shrinking state, its capacity as a crucial political domain for the exercise of democratic citizenship is increasingly being downplayed. Citizens, in this view, should pull themselves up by their own private bootstraps, and citizenship is increasingly equated with individual integration into the market. (Alvarez, Dagnino, and Escobar 1998: 1)

Writers, including those quoted above, have called attention to the prominent place in Latin America of civil society—most broadly defined as all that is not encompassed in the state and the market and significantly including what are sometimes termed "new" social movements. These social movements go beyond the rural peasant and urban labor movements of the past to embrace subaltern groups of women, racial minorities, low-income people, and other social "misfits" who have begun organizing in parts of the continent to claim their rights as full citizens. Without entering the debate over how "new" these social movements may be—for many indeed have historical antecedents—I draw insights from the rich discussion that has arisen over the cultural politics and democratic potential of these movements. Nicaragua presents a special case in many ways, as the Sandinista government encouraged the development of grassroots organizations, which only in the current context are finding an oppositional voice.

In discussions about the Sandinista period, it has been customary to direct attention to the major sectoral organizations that formed during that time. Much has been written about the Sandinista Defense Committees, the Rural Workers Association, the National Union of Farmers and Cattlemen, the Sandinista Workers' Confederation, the Nicaraguan Women's Association "Luisa Amanda Espinosa," and the Sandinista Youth movement.[1] These organized popular sectors were the FSLN's base of support in the rural and urban areas when the revolution triumphed, and they saw considerable growth during the Sandinista government's first five years. They helped to consolidate the revolutionary state and promote a democratic political system. Later in the decade, however, the mass organizations served mainly to implement party policy and were rife with sectarianism. Participation in the organizations fell off as resources directed to them were reduced and as their decision-making ability declined. With the exception of the UNAG, which maintained a more independent stance, the sectoral organizations found that their ability to address their own immediate problems diminished as the need for national defense increased (Polakoff and La Ramée 1997).

Although in a formal sense these popular organizations lost influence by the late 1980s, they were given greater latitude by the FSLN government. This allowed them more space to confront internal political questions, preparing them for the greater autonomy they would experience after the Sandinistas' electoral loss in 1990. In the case of AMNLAE, as we have seen, internal pressure came from feminists who were dissatisfied with the organization's compliance with party demands and lack of democratic process. The mass organization had been successful in drawing together women of varied backgrounds (but especially middle-aged and older women in neighborhood CDSs and Mothers of Heroes and Martyrs) in support of the revolution; but, ultimately, many feminists parted ways with AMNLAE in the early 1990s in order to embrace a broader and more radical political program for women—one they themselves would define.

The women's movement and feminism in Nicaragua are subjects that I have discussed already and that have received attention from many analysts and participants.[2] Here I want to emphasize the importance of the movement in charting a broader terrain for activism, for feminists and also as a model for other political constituencies. What is particularly striking about feminism in Nicaragua is its diversity: it ranges from a small but influential intellectual current and a strong NGO presence[3] to a popular base in a variety of women's organizations. This diversity has been both a strength and, at times, a cause for consternation as social class and other differences have been pronounced. Middle-class feminist collectives such as Partido de la Izquierda Erótica (PIE, Party of the Erotic Left) and later Las Malinches, along with such NGOs as CENZONTLE (named for a bird) and Mujer y Cambio (Women and Change), have taken the lead in theorizing women's position and formulating strategies for change. Women's health and legal clinics, including S.I. Mujer (Woman's Integral Services) and IXCHEN (named after a Mayan fertility goddess), have been established to meet immediate needs of the popular classes and also to enable women to become better informed on gender issues. In addition, the Central American University has offered one of the first gender studies programs in Central America, and Puntos de Encuentro offers courses to more diverse groups of women through what it calls "Universidad de la Mujer" (Women's University), focusing especially on gender and economic development. Such differences in the women's movement, typified by Las Malinches' vanguardist politics, on the one hand, and Puntos' strategy of appealing to a broad base of Nicaraguans (including men, youth, and people of different racial and class backgrounds), on the other, are still apparent at the beginning of the twenty-first century.

The Sandinista government gave more state support to women for research and action through INIM, which turned toward support of traditional families under Chamorro and was later joined in 1997 by Alemán's conservative Ministry of the Family. Recently, more progressive initiatives generally have been funded by private foreign foundations and governments and are decentralized, although a number of groups came together to form the Comité Nacional Feminista after the Nicaraguan women's conference held in 1992. The CNF experienced a rupture two years later over internal differences concerning orientation and leadership — marked also by differences of social class and educational privilege — but was reconstituted by a

32. *A woman addresses the crowd at an International Women's Day rally. The banner reads "Constructing our Lives without Oppression or Subordination."*

number of the former groups. Although there is sometimes competition for scarce resources, feminists continue to work together effectively through several *redes* (networks) on a range of issues, notably domestic violence, health, and other matters that concern women's fundamental rights to personhood and citizenship.

Nicaraguan women have become significant players in regional feminist politics. Following the January 1992 Nicaraguan Women's Conference in Managua, which drew more than eight hundred women, Nicaragua hosted the Central American Women's Conference, which was attended by some five hundred women from throughout the region at the Pacific Coast resort of Montelimar in March of that year.[4] There was later a strong "Nica" presence at the continental gathering of Latin American and Caribbean feminists, held for the first time in Central America, in El Salvador in 1993. Women's centers and offices in Managua publish national magazines and journals such as *La Boletina* and *La Feminista* and regional ones such as

Malabares: Revista Centroamericana de la Corriente (coming from the program office of La Corriente in Managua), giving them a wider reach. Best known was *Gente* (People), the weekly supplement of the Sandinista daily *Barricada*, which was edited by Sofía Montenegro and often covered feminist issues, which is no longer published. At present, feminists are making a difference by working in both women's organizations and mixed groups devoted to addressing the gamut of concerns in civil society.

Like the women's movement, the neighborhood movement underwent change with the political transition at the national level. As noted in chapter 4, the CDSs, or local neighborhood committees, were transformed into the Community Movement in the late 1980s and began to focus on local concerns in such areas as health and education more than on wider political concerns dictated by the FSLN. Even so, as I discovered in Barrio Monseñor Lezcano, there was frequent confusion among urban residents between the FSLN's activities and those of the MC, and often the same individuals were involved in both. Nevertheless, becoming a nonpartisan, nongovernmental organization was crucial for the neighborhood association's survival in a politically divided society. Differences in the neighborhood movement parallel differences on the Left at the national level, between those who continue to view the key struggle as that against capitalism and for socialism and those who maintain that there is now one world system, capitalism, and who try to work within it.

As sectoral organizations, the ATC, CST, and UNAG were notable for the large number of rural and urban workers who made up their ranks, about three hundred thousand collectively. They were viewed as key to the Sandinista government's success in developing agriculture and industry and in supporting the revolutionary project. They built up the nation's labor movement, although political differences later surfaced. Significantly, these organizations had active women's divisions that were sometimes critical of AMNLAE for not taking firmer positions to address women's concerns and that contributed to the formation of the autonomous women's movement. The workers' organizations were hit hard by the Sandinistas' electoral defeat in 1990, but a new organization, the National Workers' Front (FNT) formed during strikes that year and galvanized the union movement. An important victory of the newly configured labor movement, because it resisted the neoliberal privatization of state companies, was obtaining shares in many companies and full control in others.

Whatever the shortcomings of the Sandinista revolution, it made social subjects of those who before had little voice or political influence. It created popular organizations that continued to demand their rights under greatly changed circumstances in the 1990s. Whether or not the organizations declared their independence from the FSLN, they provided the basis for political opposition to neoliberalism. It may be argued that there were advantages to grassroots organizations of the FSLN being outside governmental leadership; the Chamorro administration spawned a revival of grassroots organizing because the movements were in a more comfortable, oppositional role. Put differently, we might say that the organizations found the social and political space within which to redefine their priorities and strategies, often in the face of government hostility or intransigence.

The Sandinista Youth movement drew together young Nicaraguans in solidarity with the revolution and later cultivated their continued activism through such cultural interests as music and dance. Students among them were a broad base within the FSLN, and since 1990 they have militantly demanded state universities' right to 6 percent of the national budget, as guaranteed under the constitution. No group has been better organized in recent years than students, whose annual protests over the budget receive popular support. Under neoliberalism, however, fifty thousand students in ten public universities compete with thirty thousand others in twenty-two new private institutions. The post-Sandinista governments have shown little commitment to the higher education of working-class and poor youth. Recently, a right-wing national youth organization was formed with U.S. support in an apparent effort to substitute conservative, Christian morality for that of the Sandinistas (Robinson 1997: 33). At the same time, some urban youth with few prospects for study or work are turning to violence and neighborhood gangs to gain a sense of identity (Rocha 1999).

In a significant development, mirroring other parts of Latin America, children and adolescents have recently organized to defend their right to work and their human rights more broadly (Liebel 1998: 28–33). Nicaragua's Movement of Child and Adolescent Workers (NATRAS) evolved from the Movement in Solidarity with the Rights of Street Children, which was organized by educators. As the movement has taken a political stance in favor of the right to work but against exploitation, it has lost the support of UNICEF, which seeks to eliminate child labor worldwide. The children and young teenagers have called for a cultural space in which to meet and sup-

33. Boys selling
newspapers in the
parks and streets.

port one another, and they have demanded that adults take them seriously as social and economic participants. Thus they have emerged as a significant sector in civil society.

Following the historic Latin American bishops' conference in Medellín, Colombia, in 1968 at which there was a call for ordinary people to make a "preferential option for the poor," Christian base communities (CEBs) were established as a popular organization in Nicaragua in the late 1960s and early 1970s. The CEBs were active in supporting the Nicaraguan revolution and the Sandinista government and are still committed to progressive, grassroots activity. Regarded as subversive and linked with liberation theology by the Somoza dictatorship, CEBs were often met with violence. This had the effect of persuading many devout Catholics (more than 80 percent of the population) that armed struggle was necessary to bring about justice

(Walker 1997: 6–7). Like other popular organizations that supported the revolution, this one became divided over political differences in the FSLN after 1990.

Nevertheless, the CEBs — particularly women members, who make up the great majority in the Nicaraguan popular church — continued to have an active presence in Managua. Along with other mass organizations, they have adopted an oppositional stance in relation to the state and have attempted to offer low-income Nicaraguans social services no longer provided by the government. A number of women involved in Managua's CEBs have organized neighborhood communal kitchens (*ollas comunales*) to provide meals and supplemental nutrition to pregnant and nursing women and young children — particularly important since Nicaragua led Central America in 1993 in the rate of infant mortality, 83 per 1,000 live births (Linkogle 1996: 140).

In short, the sectoral organizations formed under the Sandinistas underwent significant changes following the 1990 elections. Several, notably the neighborhood and women's organizations, achieved greater autonomy with the FSLN's defeat and turned their attention to their own, rather than party, priorities. In general, there were some advantages to building an identity in opposition to the post-Sandinista governments, as more aggressive political positions could be taken. Of course, the top-down organization of groups such as AMNLAE had led to a conformist orientation that did not offer the best prospect for developing a radical political agenda. For that reason and because the altered national context supported more pluralist approaches, new social movements and nonpartisan political groups emerged increasingly in the 1990s.

Indigenous, Environmental, and Peace Movements

In what follows, I consider a few of the best-organized social movements to have appeared in the 1990s. The indigenous movements in Nicaragua have a much longer history but have attained greater visibility and effectiveness in recent years. The environmental movement had its start as an organized force under the Sandinistas, but it too has grown in strength in the 1990s. The peace movement has its roots in efforts to demobilize the Contras and now has taken an institutionalized direction. These three movements are examples of autonomous organizing around cultural, economic, and political issues that are of prime importance in civil society. Along with the feminist and gay movements, discussed below, they address the concerns of a growing number of Nicaraguans and offer perspectives that are promoting renewed activism in the country.

Indigenous Peoples

The myth of "Nicaragua mestiza" has conveyed the mistaken notion that indigenous peoples have ceased to have a significant presence or independent cultural identity in the country.[5] When cultural diversity is acknowledged at all, it is most often the indigenous and Creole peoples of the Atlantic Coast region who are invoked. In recent years, however, somewhat more scholarly attention has gone to the cultural diversity of the Pacific and highland region, where indigenous people continue to live and to identify as ethnically distinct. While the subject is much too complex to discuss adequately here, I consider briefly what some historical and anthropological studies have contributed, as well as what indigenous Nicaraguans themselves have had to say about their political and cultural interests.

As Jeffrey L. Gould (1998) and others have shown, the official discourse in Nicaragua since the nineteenth century has celebrated the process of *mestizaje*, which, in that view, led to the triumph of a singular national cultural identity. The insistent nature of the discourse led many Indians to adopt the use of Spanish and the dominant dress style, but it did not lead them to break their identification with indigenous communities. Of course, the Miskito, Rama, and Sumo people of the Atlantic Coast are better known because of their continued use of traditional languages and cultural practices. In recent years, under the Sandinistas, they asserted a desire for political autonomy that received international attention and led to the Autonomy Law of 1987. But historically in the Pacific region, the barrios of Monimbó in Masaya and Sutiaba in León (and communities elsewhere) have had a vital political presence.

In contrast to the Atlantic Coast, known for its independent and often anti-Sandinista stance, Monimbó and Sutiaba are known as indigenous communities that contributed to the revolutionary movement. Monimbó was the first site of the general insurrection that began after the community independently rose up following the assassination of Pedro Joaquín Chamorro in 1978. And residents of Sutiaba, who had militantly resisted mestizaje and demanded the community's right to communal land when it was threatened with privatization in the 1950s, joined with other progressive artisans and workers in the struggle against Somoza. Traditional music and dance and the use of masks were integrated as oppositional cultural forms. When I visited these communities in the 1990s, I found that residents expressed considerable pride in their political participation as well as in their cultural identities as indigenous peoples — notwithstanding the power of the national ideology of mestizaje, which some accepted.

Sandinistas may have admired the rebel spirit and participation of indigenous populations, but when cultural differences and desires for autonomy interfered with plans for national unification, the central revolutionary government attempted to impose its authority. The resistance of Atlantic Coast peoples to the new authority, along with international concerns over human rights issues, led the government to move toward a policy of autonomy for the coastal region. Thousands of displaced Miskito Indians were allowed to return home and a measure of self-government was granted in an effort to pacify the coast. There were some setbacks, including the devastation of Hurricane Joan in 1988, but gradually the state gave up the assimilationist hope of controlling the region (Butler 1997).

Increasingly, indigenous groups are demanding recognition as peoples with a right to their own cultural and economic development. That the Atlantic Coast region contains the vast natural wealth of the country yet has only about one-twelfth of the national population, and that it actually has a majority of nonindigenous residents, has made the autonomy process more problematic. Different interests have needed to be accommodated, including those of indigenous women, who have fought for participation in all aspects of regional life. In 1987, the same year the Sandinistas passed the Law of Autonomy, they introduced a new constitution that recognized for the first time that "the Nicaraguan people are multiethnic."

Just three years later, the neoliberal government of Violeta Chamorro was elected, raising the question of how well the new rights of the region would be respected. Not surprisingly, her government did not abide by the agreement to accept regional heads of ministries and dismantled the promised bilingual-multicultural educational program. Other proposals were shelved, and autonomy was generally undermined. Over the course of the 1990s, under the Chamorro and Alemán governments, the autonomy law was on paper only, and economic interests have been allowed to despoil the forest and marine areas. The law should have protected cultural, linguistic, and land rights, but the absence of official property titles to land held for many generations has made it easier for outside interests to exploit the region. International activists have joined with Nicaraguans concerned about indigenous rights and the environment to bring greater attention to the loss of land rights and of indigenous knowledge. Both people and the environment are threatened by such initiatives as a "dry canal," or railroad that would span the country and disrupt the delicate biosphere.[6]

As noted earlier, there is an increasing recognition of cultural difference and identity in Nicaragua. Those Sandinistas and others who formerly looked to a unified project of nation building are persuaded now of the urgency to formulate a more inclusive and pluralist politics. Indigenous people, women, and other subaltern groups have helped to inspire such a rethinking of cultural politics. A key concern is to ensure that cultural and political spaces are opened to those whose participation in society has been limited both historically and in the current context of neoliberalism.

Environment

Environmental issues never received more attention than in the aftermath of Hurricane Mitch, which hit Nicaragua and its neighbors in late October 1998. The widespread devastation of human lives and land brought international aid and assistance to the region and generated a unified response by civil society in Nicaragua when the government failed to act promptly. More than three hundred groups, including NGOs and social movements, that identified with a host of concerns, came together to coordinate emergency relief and also to engage in sustained dialogue over civil society's response to the broader political economic crisis in the country.

The environmental movement itself may be traced to the Sandinista government's inauguration of a new natural resource policy in 1979. With a land base half covered with forests, one-third composed of lakes and rivers, and rich in minerals, Nicaragua is endowed with abundant resources, particularly on the Atlantic Coast. The Sandinistas nationalized many of the natural resources and mines that had been controlled by the Somoza family and canceled international forestry concessions. The Nicaraguan Institute of Natural Resources and the Environment (IRENA) was created to oversee the management and protection of the nation's resources. Unfortunately, other priorities, including agrarian reform, economic development, and, later, defense, displaced the government's commitment to the environment, and there was still no counterpart in civil society to insist on its urgency (Elizondo 1997).

Under the Chamorro government, the environment and a sustainable development policy received nonpartisan support. IRENA was granted more independence; it was taken out of the agricultural ministry and a couple of years later elevated to the status of Ministry of the Environment and Natural Resources (MARENA). International support, which began under the revolutionary government, continued to be directed to environmental programs. Nevertheless, once again economic development strategies, this time in the neoliberal framework, took center stage and displaced plans for environmental protection. The Ministry of the Economy and Development promoted foreign investment in forestry, fishing, and mining and to that end sought deregulation of the economy and other incentives for investors, often at odds with MARENA's environmental programs. By this time, NGOs and civil society more broadly were carrying out the most effective, local-level projects. As one analyst pointed out, the greatest knowledge of Nicaragua's biodiversity and ecology may reside in its indigenous peoples, although they were rarely consulted when development policy was formulated (Elizondo 1997: 137).

Major controversies arose in the early 1990s, particularly in relation to the use of several natural reserves that were the largest and most important in Central America. The government offered concessions to cattle ranching, agriculture, and mining industries on land that was to be protected. Vast forest lands were lost each year as a result, viewed as alarming in a country with more forested area than any other Latin American nation except Brazil. Public awareness of the situation grew, and concern was expressed that the future of the country was being mortgaged as the government pursued its economic development strategy.

The Chamorro government invited NGOs to submit proposals for environmental legislation, as part of a state-NGO initiative. However, even with the force of public opinion and emerging environmental organizations, protection of the environment continued to be viewed as standing in the way of private enterprise; the government rarely insisted on taking action that would jeopardize the pro-investment interests. In addition, the rural population's need for firewood and its practice of burning land in preparation for farming were taking a serious toll on the forests, accelerating the deterioration of the natural resource base. The NGOs and civil society have only begun the educational process that may lead to practices that are more environmentally sound (Elizondo 1997: 142).

The Alemán administration shows still less interest than the UNO government in confronting the now-disastrous environmental problems faced by the country. Indeed, a certain antagonism was shown by moving MARENA into the Ministry of Agriculture and Livestock and by building a road through a formerly protected tropical forest reserve. In 1998, a multitude of agricultural and forest fires erupted when traditional land clearing went out of control in the rural areas. Not only were over a half million hectares razed and land eroded, but the smoke made the air dangerously polluted even in Managua. Just before I traveled to Nicaragua that year, the city's international airport had to cancel flights for several days because of low visibility. Many urban residents told me of the difficulty they had breathing the air, something I experienced myself. A year later, civil society organizations met with the agriculture and forestry minister to propose initiatives to include environmental crime in the new penal code, to legislate indigenous lands, and approve a forestry law to prevent further massive damage (*Envío* 1999b).

Of course, Nicaragua's major ecological disaster occurred a few months later when Hurricane Mitch hit Central America. While the hurricane itself was uncontrollable, the damage was made worse by previous deforestation and environmental degradation in the affected area and by the government's slow response to the crisis. Agricultural support as well as the rebuilding of homes, schools, and health clinics in the region will be an urgent need for some time to come. Nicaraguan and international activists have called for land reform to halt the environmental decline that, in this recent case, made the disaster so very tragic.

The growing concern in the 1990s over the environment is seen in newer groups such as the Movimiento de Ambientalistas Nicaragüenses (MAN, or the Nicaraguan Environmental Movement), the Centro Alexander von Humboldt, and the Asociación Club de Jovenes Ambientalistas (CJA, or Young Environmentalist Association). When I visited their offices and read their publications, I was impressed by the range of their projects to raise environmental consciousness among the Nicaraguan public and to address such current issues as the impact of environmental degradation and tourism on natural resources, labor, and indigenous landholdings. While the Humboldt Center currently appears to have the highest profile, I was impressed by the activism of the young people involved with the CJA, which since 1994 has launched a social movement (now an NGO) that organizes youth around the country to address local, regional, and national environmental issues. The office staff showed a passionate commitment and a creative means of educating and mobilizing children and young adults to endorse environmentally sound practices and lifestyles. Other social movements, the women's movement in particular, have made the environment and sustainable development a key organizing issue. As the feminist intellectual Sofía Montenegro said in a recent interview, a priority is to "construct a discourse on development that integrates environment and gender as the central logic of the critique of the neoliberal model" (Quandt 1999: 5–6). While the politics she and other feminists are advocating have radical implications, the environment as a pivotal point has the advantage of appealing to a broad nonpartisan, multiclass base in Nicaragua.

Moreover, the environment appeals to a wide range of international supporters eager to make a difference in a country whose recent revolution they may or may not have admired. Not surprisingly, the environment and problems stemming from Hurricane Mitch are issues receiving the most attention from activists in the United States and elsewhere who may find Nicaragua's economic and political problems too intransigent to take on directly. To be sure, international support for preserving the nation's rain forest, protecting its water from mining pollution, and defending its diverse biosphere is often linked to more radical demands to cancel the national debt and allow the country to undertake the costly environmental projects that are necessary to bring degradation under control.

Peace

Nicaraguans' desire for peace can be traced historically in a country so often wracked by civil war. It resonates in the poem entitled "Paz" (Peace) by the country's premier poet, Rubén Darío, written in 1915 near the end of his life. As he queried, "Is there no one of a younger race who can shatter war's yoke"?[7] His plea for an end to bloodshed and his hope for peace were echoed in the 1980s when the Contra war divided members of society. A longing for peace and stability had a clear impact on the 1990 election, by all accounts, with a majority voting for the candidate whose election promised an end to the war and the economic embargo. But since then there has been further discussion of peace as a general objective for a society seeking reconciliation and sustainable human development. Inspiration came from the United Nations' emphasis on peace, human rights, environment, and development in recent years. Summarized as a "Culture of Peace," the objective is to promote humanistic ideals within a critical, reflective framework of analysis that will facilitate the transition into the twenty-first century. Not only in Nicaragua but throughout Central America, the Culture of Peace is being invoked as a new paradigm and plan of action (Tünnermann Bernheim 1996).

In Managua, the Martin Luther King Institute for Research and Social Action was founded with UNESCO support at the Universidad Politécnica de Nicaragua (UPOLI) in 1993. The director of the institute, Denis Alberto Torres, spoke to a group of internationalists at the Ben Linder House in 1996 about the goals of the program. He began by noting that many visitors came to Nicaragua in the 1980s out of a concern for the revolution and the Contra war but that far fewer were coming now, when the peace process was under way. He described the need not only to avoid further warfare but also to create an "irreversible peace" at both the macrostructural and the personal level in society. Torres praised feminists and environmentalists for their political work against forms of violence and for advocating new ways of interacting with mutual respect. The Martin Luther King Institute has begun to offer a master's degree in peace studies, the first in Central America. In addition to this initiative, a radio program is directed to youth. Torres serves as editor of the magazine *Cultura de Paz* (Culture of Peace), which raises questions of human rights, democracy, gender, environment, and conflict resolution; the publication has wide circulation in bookstores and supermarkets in Managua.

When I asked Torres about the possibility of creating a culture of peace in the context of what I termed a "culture of neoliberalism," he first agreed that the "savage capitalism" of neoliberalism presents an obstacle in the form of harsh economic conditions. But he went on to argue that human development—the "skin and bones" of people—is more important now than economic performance. Along with other Nicaraguan intellectuals, he appeared to be setting aside the economic, focusing instead on conflict resolution, reconciliation, and justice as the country's most urgent needs (Denis Alberto Torres, interview, June 27, 1996).

The concept of a culture of peace is intended to respond to the many forms of violence in the society, from warfare and armed conflict to domestic abuse. It is innovative in its attention to the social and psychological foundations of violence and to social class and gender differences in the experience of violence. Poverty and gender inequality are thus recognized both as forms of violence and as serving to reproduce violence. According to advocates, it is necessary to break the culture of violence and establish new forms of human interaction. If successful, a culture of peace would offer dignity, justice, and tolerance to a society weary from social conflict and factionalism. For women, it would offer democracy in the home as well as in the society. Clearly, Nicaragua is far from achieving such a social ideal, but what is striking is the level of seriousness and commitment in the discussion.

A similar perspective on the most fruitful directions for political organizing was offered by the historian Alejandro Bendaña, director of the Center for International Studies. Describing Nicaragua in the 1980s as a testing ground for cold war power politics, he said that the 1990s are a testing ground for postwar reconstruction. Now, he noted, social development and peace are key, and former Contra combatants must be brought into the process if it is to be successful. As he put it, the task is not only to eliminate weapons but also to eliminate the impulse to pick up weapons. NGOs and civil society have begun to respond by organizing a peace promoters' network and by training ex-combatants in conflict resolution and community building. Bendaña has observed instances of cultural affirmation in the country, particularly among indigenous people, women, and environmentalists. Like Torres, he noted that these groups have forced Nicaraguans to examine patterns of individual behavior, a part of the transformation process that generally has been neglected by the Left. He judges that a cultural ethic is the driving force for change in the country (Alejandro Bendaña, interviews, June 24 and July 3, 1996).

Time will tell if Nicaraguans will opt for a peaceful settlement of their differences. One man I interviewed in Barrio Monseñor Lezcano expressed the view that the only way that the new Somocismo (Somoza-style politics) under Alemán's government will end is through violence. He pointed to the brutal hunger of people today and the need for health care. When I asked what he thought of the idea of a culture of peace, he replied there are two kinds of Sandinistas, bourgeois and proletarian. While the former favor peace, he sides with the latter—who, he implied, would not view peace as a viable strategy.

In 1998, I attended the fifth anniversary celebration of the Martin Luther King Institute. Faculty, students, and invited guests were gathered for the festivities. Denis Torres spoke about the Culture of Peace and received an enthusiastic response. Whether or not it is only bourgeois society that looks to peace and reconciliation as viable alternatives, these are objectives that stand to benefit the multiclass nation.

The National Trade Union, CONAPI

The location of the CONAPI offices and meeting halls in the large recreational center known as La Piñata, across the street from the Central American University in the center of Managua, might suggest a high degree of visibility. Indeed, a large sign with the association's name can be seen from a distance along the heavily used Pista de la Resistencia (Resistance Road), also known as Pista de la Municipalidad (Municipality Road), depending on one's map and political orientation. But CONAPI rarely figures in the news of trade union activity or in scholarly analyses of sectoral organizations formed under the Sandinistas that have continued into the 1990s. The absence of wide recognition is more surprising in light of the prominent place of small industries in the Nicaraguan economy and in the lives of a majority of people in the city. However, it is less surprising given the low level of support from the FSLN that CONAPI received relative to other sectoral organizations both before and after the Sandinistas lost the 1990 elections and given that neoliberal governments began favoring large, competitive industries, on the one hand, and microenterprise development through their own ministries, on the other.

The brief history of CONAPI offers more clues to its low profile as a national trade organization.[8] The Sandinista government's early initiative to organize small industries into cooperatives led to the founding of CONAPI by the Office of Support to Small Industry in 1983, with 12,000 workshops and 50,000 individual members from around the country. As the Contra war began to have adverse effects on the economy, it was hoped that the organization would facilitate the distribution of lower-cost materials to enterprises at the regional and national levels. Four areas of production were identified as most important in the sector—food, garment, leather and shoes, and wood—and likewise in CONAPI. Despite the founding date of 1983 and the fact that the tenth anniversary of the organization was celebrated in 1993, CONAPI was not established as a legal entity until 1989, when it held its first national congress. About 250 production and service cooperatives and 10,000 workshops were affiliated with CONAPI at that time, for a total of 28,000 members — numbers that would fall off sharply a few years later. At first, cooperatives alone were drawn into membership, but soon individual small producers also joined (but not those in commerce and services). CONAPI had its beginnings as a state organization but became a nonprofit private organization that receives support from a number of international sources including about ten NGOs based in Managua, funded by countries that include Norway, the Netherlands, and Canada (Santamaría 1990).

A bronze plaque outside the CONAPI offices identifies both dates, 1983 and 1989, in the organization's history and lists the names of the members of the Consejo Directivo Nacional (National Leadership Council) whose terms began in 1989. Ana Lorena Rondon, appointed by the Sandinista government, was the first president, and she was succeeded by the vice president, Gustavo Hernández. Antonio Chávez was secretary of the Third Region (Managua) and then president during much of the period of my research. A total of four women and eleven men made up the council at the time it was formed. CONAPI's mandate is stated on its plaque: "For the economic, political, and social development of medium and small industries and artisans of Nicaragua." The inscription goes on to read, "We are a force confronting the future ahead and serving the people through the creative work produced by our hands." Many small producers and members of cooperatives who joined CONAPI would say that the plaque's promise could not be fulfilled, as the organization was only getting under way when the national elections brought about a political sea change just a year later and eroded the organization's ability to serve its constituency.

At the outset, CONAPI's mission was to support a large yet marginalized economic sector that was viewed as having the potential to play a much more prominent role in production and employment in the country. The organization's principal objectives were to assume a strong position vis-à-vis the state and other institutions in order to promote the interests of small industry; to offer services to develop quality production in the sector; to assist in supplying materials and marketing products; to offer training and to help organize cooperatives and enterprises; to assist in obtaining credit and offer legal aid; to create a program specifically for women; to promote the sector at the national and international levels; and to seek national and international funding.

Because CONAPI became active just when the Sandinistas were introducing economic adjustment measures, the organization needed to adapt its expectations to fit the new, more austere conditions. Further adaptation was needed when neoliberalism ushered in still more crushing adjustments. Since CONAPI became an independent, nonpartisan organization, there has been more open criticism of the failure of the Sandinistas to set controls on quality, resulting in poor standards of production in the small-industry sector and little ability to compete successfully in the Central American region. This has aggravated the present situation, when many small industries are not competitive and are struggling to improve the quality and marketing of their goods. Most criticism, however, goes to the post-Sandinista governments for offering even less assistance and for creating a national economy that is hostile to the sector.

Like other sectoral organizations formed under the revolutionary government, CONAPI traded state support for autonomy, and while the organization lost the FSLN's limited assistance, it gained the right to represent its own interests in negotiations with Chamorro's and Alemán's governments. CONAPI is positioned now to take an oppositional stance with the government, as it has done recently in protesting the elimination of protective tariffs, low-interest credit, and favored status to cooperatives. Nevertheless, it lacks the strength to be effective and must sometimes accommodate to more moderate interests in its constituency. The leadership takes pains to present itself as free of ideological or party commitments to attract support and membership and to appeal to the government on behalf of a broad base of Nicaraguan workers.

CONAPI has taken a stand in recent years when small industry has been threatened by changing national policy. When the UNO government announced the maxi-devaluation of currency in March 1991, the organization was among the first to make a public call to resist the "economic shock plan," claiming that the drastic measure would attract foreign investment and exploit Nicaraguans (*Barricada*, March 2, 1991). Spokespersons for CONAPI argued that the plan was in violation of agreements made in a concertación between government and representatives of sectoral organizations five months earlier. One point agreed on was that the small and medium business sector would be a priority for improving the economy, yet no support was forthcoming from the UNO government. Moreover, it was anticipated that the Occupational Conversion Plan would drive former public employees into small businesses, adding to current problems. Along with other sectoral organizations, CONAPI urged its affiliates to be ready for the struggle ahead — although of course the policies went into effect and workers needed to adapt as well as possible.

A year later, in 1992, CONAPI held meetings to discuss the devastating effects of neoliberal policy on small industries. On February 16, the leadership drew several hundred members as well as a representative of the FSLN, Gladys Baez, and a representative of the UNO, María Hurtado, to a special assembly, which was followed by a march to the president's house to demand a meeting with Violeta Chamorro. I joined members of the artisans' Cooperativa Francisco Estrada at the assembly where we heard CONAPI's president, Ana Lorena Rondon, address the large gathering. She argued that the free market would mean the end of small businesses in the country, calling attention to the UNO government's failure to provide protection to small industry as promised under the terms of the concertación, and said that CONAPI would not accept the "development plan" being set in place. Rondon compared Nicaragua's new policies unfavorably with those in other Central American nations, where protection of small industries enabled them to become competitive. Furthermore, she referred to the unemployment rate of about 60 percent, noting that much of the buying public that small producers depend on are among those who are out of work.

Then, María Hurtado, head of the UNO's Office of Small Enterprise, addressed the group. She began by offering to hear CONAPI's concerns but quickly turned to a defense of UNO policies. Invoking the mistakes of the Sandinista government, she suggested that the current government had inherited economic problems that were being resolved through the structural adjustment program of 1991 and the reactivation plan of 1992. She highlighted the UNO's role in bringing about peace and an end of the military draft, as well as the concertación dialogue. Now, she maintained, small industry needed to improve the quality of its products as well as find new markets. Those assembled were growing noisy and restless by this point, although she continued, saying that the Central Bank, headed by Silvio De Franco, was offering credit on more favorable terms and that there was already some protection for small industry. The impatience in the meeting room was apparent, but polite applause followed when she concluded. Before the group broke up, Rondon read the letter that would be presented to President Chamorro in the afternoon, which stated that the current policy was a severe blow to the Nicaraguan people and that, as the nation was largely made up of small producers, protection of their sector through a policy of gradualism was critical.

On March 31, Rondon completed her term as president and Gustavo Hernández took over the post. Having built up CONAPI from 1983 through 1992 as a sectoral organization of the FSLN, Rondon was viewed by this time as an asset but also a liability in negotiating with the UNO government, since her appointment by the FSLN government was perceived as political (particularly because she was married to Comandante Victor Tirado, a member of the FSLN's National Directorate).[9] Soon after, on April 9, representatives from CONAPI met with Antonio Lacayo, minister of the presidency, and members of the National Assembly to present their proposals, including a call for technical support and a lowering of taxes, and their demand for clarification of how much U.S. aid to Nicaragua would be allocated to small industry.

CONAPI had little satisfaction in the months after the meeting when the government failed to respond to most points raised, although the deadline for payment of taxes was extended. By the end of the year, CONAPI's publication, El Pequeño Industrial (December 1992–January 1993), called the government's free trade agreements with Mexico and other nations a "death blow" (tiro de gracia) to small industry. In an editorial a couple of months later, Antonio Chávez (March–April 1993: 1) wrote: "We can't continue to carry the weight on our backs of the structural adjustment program that has created an external opening, a savage and disloyal competition for the sector, and that has put it in grave crisis." Moreover, there was growing concern about the government's evident desire to steer small producers away from the trade union organization, still perceived as Sandinista, and toward PAMIC's organization of microenterprises (although in later years there were some coordinated activities between CONAPI and PAMIC, as reported in El Pequeño Industrial, no. 16 [1995]: 17).

At the time, CONAPI was seeking more sources of nongovernmental support for the small industry sector. Antonio Chávez, then vice president of CONAPI, asked me several times if I had information regarding any possibilities, and I told him what little I knew. He spoke of the long-term objective of achieving self-sufficiency after receiving international support during that difficult period. In one effort to raise needed funds for the administration of CONAPI, the organization was developing a "carnival" in the recreational area of La Piñata. A new roller-skating rink, a train ride for children, a "castle of terror," and games of chance were in operation, and new shops and small restaurants had opened in surrounding pavilions. Chávez told me that this was a way to generate income and promote their products, but he acknowledged that with high unemployment reducing people's resources for spending on leisure activities, attendance at the carnival was very low.

Under Hernández's leadership, CONAPI lost the confidence of many members, both because of his personal qualities and because of the national situation, and in 1993 Chávez tried to restore a degree of trust as the new president — although, a few years later, he too was charged with mismanagement of the virtually bankrupt organization. CONAPI acknowledged a loss of membership as a result of the decline of small businesses but often counted cooperatives and individuals who in the past were active members whether they remained active or not, thereby inflating its membership (payment of dues of $2 per month was a poor indicator, since only about 10 percent of members paid regularly). Efforts were made to refashion the organization and appeal to consumers' nationalist sentiment to "buy Nicaraguan" with catchy new slogans, such as "Clothes, shoes, nacatamal, buy national" and "Nicaraguans, by consuming national products you will generate employment." Other efforts aimed to demonstrate to the government small industry's efficiency and potential. Contests were held to recognize quality products. Some forty women and men in small industry were selected to travel to the United States for a two-year technical training course funded by USAID. And ten production cooperatives and twenty service cooperatives that were considered among the most "efficient" were selected as subjects of a study to demonstrate positive results to USAID, but this did not result in more financial support. In general, CONAPI was viewed by its membership and the government alike as unable to lend much support to the scores of workers in small enterprises who were experiencing crisis conditions. Officials in CONAPI stated that they did not want a return to the paternalism of the Sandinista period, but they did desire the opportunity to succeed; Chávez expressed his view that the government had offered "no transfusion of blood or even vitamins" to assuage the harsh effects of neoliberal policy.

The organization recommended an "entrepreneurial mentality" and an "injection" of training to improve quality in small industry.

CONAPI was undergoing a change with the political economic transition in the country. The leadership and those members who joined when the organization was just forming in the early to mid-1980s tended to have a more loyal commitment to the ideals that brought them together in the first place and a personal commitment to the FSLN, whereas those who joined at the end of the decade or later tended to reflect more ambivalence, or even disdain, for CONAPI's inability to make good on its promises. These differences were evident in the four cooperatives I studied: the seamstresses and artisans (organized in 1983 and 1987 respectively) demonstrated strong loyalty to their cooperatives and somewhat less commitment to CONAPI, the bakers' cooperative (organized in 1979) gave up on the trade organization a few years later to work as independent businesses (some of which nonetheless retained individual membership in CONAPI). The welders (organized in 1991) never made the commitment to join CONAPI, divided as they were between identifying as an independent women's collective and a workers' cooperative affiliated with a trade federation; that they disbanded as a collective a couple of years later may be due in part to their lack of support from a broader organization, although many affiliated small producers failed during the same period. In 1992, Chávez told me that those who voluntarily left CONAPI were lacking in consciousness and were not standing by the trade union movement. By 1994, however, he reported that due to national economic conditions only 6,000 of the 40,000 small businesses that existed in the country ten years before were still operating (Close 1999: 140).

A study of women's participation commissioned by CONAPI (Pérez Alemán et al. 1991) indicated that women joined the organization earlier in some parts of the country, such as Managua, than in others. On average, a woman member of the organization was thirty-eight years old, had four children, had a primary school education, and provided the main economic support of her household. More than half of the women performed at least four hours of work per day in the household beyond the hours spent in small-industry employment. Furthermore, the study found that women's representation in the leadership of the organization had held steady at about 27 percent of council members and that women were fully 53 percent (closely proportionate to their number in CONAPI) of heads of cooperatives belonging to CONAPI. Pérez Alemán found, as I have, that the double duty of work and family responsibilities kept women from making further commitments to the organization, whether in terms of participating in training programs or assuming leadership positions. This was true for Carmen, who was elected to the position of vice-secretary of the Third Region (Managua) only to give it up when she found that between the artisans' cooperative and her family, she did not have time to serve as a CONAPI official. Besides, the co-op considered that the other artisans would be essentially subsidizing CONAPI if Carmen contributed her unpaid time as an official — something they could ill afford to do.

The organization's Women's Office was intended to encourage the participation of women at every level, but CONAPI members commented that the office lacked stable and effective direction and had made little difference to women. CONAPI's intentions were generally good and went beyond those of government offices, but the recommendations of Pérez Alemán for further action on behalf of women appeared to go unheeded.[10] For example, it was suggested that additional programs be directed to areas in which women are active and are experiencing great difficulties in the neoliberal economy, such as garment and food production, but the leadership failed to respond; as we have seen, the seamstresses' cooperative Obreras Unidas Textil felt abandoned by the CONAPI leadership when it offered no assistance during a time of crisis for small-scale garment producers.

By 1996, one of CONAPI's key concerns was the government's plan to reform the Law of Cooperatives, which would mean the loss of small industries' exoneration from payment of some taxes, so that their taxation would double. As president, Antonio Chávez was worried that this change, motivated as he saw it by the IMF and the World Bank, would hurt small industries just when they needed support and lead to the liquidation of a number of businesses. He indicated that small industries had recently made some gains, in part due to the nation's agricultural harvest that year, which had bolstered the economy, but the planned government legislation would mean a substantial setback. Meetings with other sectors and a transportation strike were planned to protest the likely consequences of the government action.

When I returned to Nicaragua in 1998, I found that CONAPI was still less empowered to be of assistance to cooperatives and small industries. The Cooperativa Francisco Estrada, for example, had broken relations with

CONAPI in part because the co-op had a debt to the organization (as well as to an NGO) that it could not repay and so lost its right to affiliation, and also because members felt that CONAPI had little more to offer them. There was a perception that the trade union had become corrupt and that the leadership alone benefited from the outside support it received. At that time the position of president passed, as had been customary, to the vice president, a woman named Flora Vargas. When I visited her office, a staff member told me that CONAPI's current membership numbered 405 men and 233 women, which, if accurate, is extremely low. According to the figures on women small producers, 121 were in garments, 55 in crafts, 46 in food, 6 in wood and furniture, and 5 in leather and shoes.

Like other sectoral organizations formed under the Sandinistas, CONAPI has gained autonomy since the 1990 elections and has sometimes benefited from taking an oppositional stance in relation to the Chamorro and Alemán governments. Where it has suffered more adverse effects than other organizations, however, is in the crushing consequences of neoliberal policy for cooperatives and small industries in the country. Women have been particularly disadvantaged insofar as they are overrepresented in areas such as garment and food production, which have experienced the most competition from larger and foreign industry. Thus efforts to refashion CONAPI in accordance with neoliberal times and to appeal to the government to slow the process of opening Nicaragua to the global market have been insufficient to protect or support individuals working in small industries. At the present time it is hard to foresee recovery for an organization that earlier had a vision of working with other sectors and with civil society to build a more productive and democratic society.

Lesbian and Gay Organizing

A decade ago, there was almost no public visibility of gay Nicaraguans organizing to identify common interests and concerns. Lesbians and gay men[11] located one another by informal means, but there were no established channels, centers, or associations for doing so. Indeed, the sociologist Barry Adam (1989) wrote of "homosexuality without a gay world" among men in Nicaragua. Similarly, Roger Lancaster's (1988a, 1992) ethnographic research in Managua described the traditional category of the *cochón*, a Nicaraguan man who engaged in sex with other men, but distinct from the

Western notion of the homosexual. While same-sex sexual practices may have been widespread for some time among Nicaraguans who do not identify as gay, the 1990s have made visible a growing number of others who do identify — politically and culturally — with the transnational movement of lesbians and gay men. I want to suggest that any consideration of the cultural politics of this decade must consider this notable development.

Lancaster and Adam were more aware of men's same-sex practices than of women's, and both brought attention to the large number of Nicaraguan men who had sex with other men without necessarily considering themselves "gay." In general, the "passive" partner is stigmatized as homosexual (the cochón) while the "active" (penetrating) partner is regarded as macho, masculine — enjoying sex with men as well as women. Adam (1989: 76) suggested that the absence of a developed urban culture in Managua, the lack of privacy in most homes, the economic hardship and political unrest during the 1980s — along with the conservative institutions of the family and the Catholic Church, and machismo — conspired to "inhibit the growth of a public gay life beyond the current scene of homosexual men 'hanging out,' keeping their eyes open in the most populated bars, streets, and cinemas." Thus, he concluded, "there is no publicly recognized gay identity" (77).

Lancaster (1988a) went further to argue that while Nicaraguan male sexuality may have something in common with that of the ancient Greeks and some contemporary non-Western societies, it should be understood as fundamentally different from that of modern, Western societies in which gay identities have emerged. His insistence on examining local traditions of same-sex practices is a corrective to those views that assume that universal sexual identities accompany similar sexual practices. To be sure, he shows that Nicaraguan men's practices are frequently different from those common among gay men in the United States and Europe, but even when they are alike, the meanings given by the men and their societies vary. Lancaster's culturally sensitive approach contributes much to an understanding of the dynamics of sexuality and power among Nicaraguan men through the period of the Sandinista revolution.

Nevertheless, from the vantage point of the late 1990s and the turn of the twenty-first century, it is apparent that earlier writers did not anticipate the development of a gay social movement and identity politics that were already in the making. Lancaster's work did in fact offer a brief historical context for attitudes about homosexual practices, linking a negative stance during the Sandinista years to the lingering association with a more sordid, tourist-oriented nightlife in the prerevolutionary period. But the fact that there was a publicly recognized, if small, gay culture that was condoned by Somoza and a bar that catered to gay men in the 1960s (*El País* 1992: 7) was less well known to researchers. In contrast to the years of the dictatorship, the revolution's social subjects were expected to exhibit moral rectitude and self-sacrifice, with CDS neighborhood organizations enforcing proper behavior. The popular perception was that the homosexually inclined bourgeois had left for Miami after 1979 and any continued gay presence was more likely to be found among internationalists entering the country. Lancaster (1988a: 119) noted that some Nicaraguan youth referred to themselves as gay, but he maintained that given the different cultural context, "what a Nicaraguan means when he calls himself 'gay' is very different from what a North American has in mind when he uses the same term." While I am mindful of the admonition to beware of imposing transnational meanings on local practices, I want to suggest that with the benefit of my own more recent observations as well as other reports—particularly accounts by and about women—a somewhat different picture comes into focus (Ferguson 1991; Randall 1993; Thayer 1997).[12]

By the late 1980s, there was awareness in and outside Nicaragua that the Sandinista government was offering some support for AIDS education and prevention (Schreiber and Stephen 1989). What was not generally known, however, was that the government was also clamping down on organizing by lesbians and gay men on their own behalf during this time. Only in the early 1990s, after the electoral loss, did some begin to share their story. In Margaret Randall's (1994) interviews with Nicaraguan women in the early 1990s, Rita Arauz spoke out as a lesbian who returned to the country in the mid-1980s after living in the United States for a decade. On her return, she participated with other Sandinista lesbians and gay men who, by 1986, were meeting to talk about gay rights politics. Sometimes, more than sixty lesbians and gay men met together, even though the government prohibited organizing outside formal political structures. In March 1987, about a year after the meetings began, Sandinista State Security became aware of them and responded by calling in some thirty participants for questioning, fingerprinting, videotaping, and, in some cases, including that of Arauz, arrest (although they were released the same day).

At first, the government was effective in silencing those gay Sandinistas who had begun organizing, as they agreed not to go public about their meetings or their experience with State Security. As Arauz described the incident, those called in defended themselves with dignity, and when they left, the Sandinista State Security officers were embarrassed about the intervention. The activists' support for the Sandinista revolution led them to shield the government from the international response that was sure to come if the media spread word of the effort to suppress human rights organizing.[13] Soon, however, a much more open movement of gay Nicaraguans began to emerge.[14]

Despite the repression of outright political organizing and the denial of FSLN Party membership to several activists, AIDS education began about a year later, after a San Francisco–based health colloquium addressed the issue in Managua in 1988. To its credit, the Ministry of Health (significantly, headed by sympathizer Comandante Dora María Téllez) supported the Popular AIDS Education Collective (CEPSIDA), a grassroots program at the community level, at a time when AIDS had barely surfaced as a problem in the country. Condoms were distributed in gay men's cruising areas and were made available to students, sex workers, and others. This paved the way for more activity in the gay community, and over the next few years a number of lesbian and gay groups emerged from the small cadre of AIDS activists. In general, the public space the groups claimed as well as their (non-separatist) politics reflected the fact that they grew out of a revolutionary movement that called for greater inclusion in society — even if much of the society was not ready to accept their sexual difference as legitimate.

A decision was made by a group of about fifty gay and lesbian Sandinistas to come out publicly for the first time during the celebration of the tenth anniversary of the revolution. On July 19, 1989, they wore black T-shirts with pink triangles and marched together to the annual gathering in the Plaza de la Revolución. As reported by the activist Hazel Fonseca (Randall 1993), their act did not go unnoticed by the party leadership and empowered them for additional public activity. This collective "coming out" was just a couple of weeks before my first trip to Nicaragua, and by the time I began traveling regularly to Nicaragua, there were clear signs of gay political and social activity in Managua. Nimehuatzín, a visible and active AIDS education NGO founded in 1990 and headed by Rita Arauz (whose years in the United States, notably, were spent in San Francisco), was located adjacent to the Central American University; its logo of dancing condoms was proudly displayed on a large sign outside as well as on its T-shirts, which were seen around the city. The gay-friendly office space was clearly a magnet for more than just AIDS work and allowed lesbians and gay men to locate one another. Other centers and groups were forming during this time as well.

Lesbians in Nicaragua had a public and well-received "coming out" at the Festival of the 52 Percent at Managua's recreational center, La Piñata, which I attended in March 1991. Along with other women's groups, lesbian organizations had an information booth at the event. At the gala conclusion of the weekend, the women at the booth had a lively business as people lined up to purchase slices of lemon meringue pie. I recall the evident pride of one woman there, who wore a pin declaring, "Mi amor tiene nombre de mujer" (My love has a woman's name). It was a memorable evening; some of Nicaragua's favorite musicians performed, and people danced, men with women, women with women, all together.

A major step forward in building a public presence was taken in June 1991, when Gay Pride was celebrated publicly for the first time in Nicaragua. Announcements for the landmark event were circulated widely, and several hundred people attended a showing of the subtitled North American film, *Torch Song Trilogy*, along with music and a panel discussion on the experiences of gay men and lesbians. I attended the event, which attracted a diverse group of Nicaraguans and some internationalists to the Coro de Angeles, a cultural center that frequently hosted musical and literary events as well as films. The open-air space was filled with anticipation, and the importance of the occasion was marked by the presence of a number of well-known Nicaraguans. During the same week, a lesbian poet read her work for a university audience and several lesbians and gay men were interviewed by the Sandinista radio station. A month later, the feminist center Puntos de Encuentro began publishing *La Boletina*, which also gave public attention to gay pride and politics. Around this time, lesbian and gay Nicaraguans traveled to Mexico for an international gathering on gay politics, which contributed to further mobilization.

Certainly, gay activists in Nicaragua were aware of, and some had been part of, gay organizing in other countries. A number of them said that their nascent movement was inspired in part by the accomplishments of movements in the United States and Europe. Yet they also maintained that their principal motivation for organizing was their specifically Nicaraguan, or

Latin American, experience. Out of the Mexican gathering came a Latin American network to link those with related experience, and Nicaragua held the delegate seat for Central America (Randall 1992). The tension between international influence and the local (sometimes called "authentic") politics of the region is evident in remarks made by the activist Lupita Sequeira, interviewed in *Sex and the Sandinistas* (1991), a documentary made for British television.[15] One of two Nicaraguans interviewed who spoke in English (the other was Rita Arauz), she insisted that their movement was not imported from outside the country—although she also acknowledged the connection between the Nicaraguan struggle and that of people everywhere. Just as feminists are often charged with adopting "bourgeois" ideas from the West, so are gay Nicaraguans susceptible to charges of being corrupted by outsiders. Significantly, this activist is shown painting indigenous designs in a mural outside the Xochiquetzal Foundation, an NGO offering medical and psychological services and AIDS education, particularly to the gay community. In the early 1990s, it may have been most important to assert an independent politics, even if that meant a certain degree of mythmaking (referencing indigenous roots) characteristic of gay movements elsewhere. By later in the decade, however, the links between Nicaraguan and other movements were generally acknowledged in a climate of more open discussion.

The post-Sandinista context of neoliberalism, with its evident support for individualism in the market economy, contrasts with the social conservatism of the period, which emphasizes the traditional family as the foundation of society.[16] In that context, the fledgling lesbian and gay movement was galvanized in 1992 by the reactivation of Nicaragua's sodomy law. Known as "Article 204," this part of the penal code criminalizes sodomy that is conducted "between persons of the same sex" in a "scandalous way." Calling for the repeal of the article, more than twenty-five groups came together in June that year to launch the Campaign for a Sexuality Free of Prejudice with panels, protests, and celebrations of Gay Pride. The Xochiquetzal Foundation, codirected by the lesbian feminists Hazel Fonseca and Mary Bolt González, played a leadership role in generating support for the campaign (and continues to organize yearly Pride events). With funding from Norway, the foundation was able to distribute published information about Article 204, with documentation from the Center for Constitutional Rights regarding the law's breach of human rights guaranteed in the 1987

34. In a public park,
graffiti written
in English reads
"Danger, Keep Out
Gays."

Constitution. Notwithstanding its imprecision, the law targeted both lesbians and gay men and was soon regarded as one of the most unjust in the Americas. Despite strong opposition to it, in Nicaragua and beyond, the law remained on the books.[17]

Gay activism was becoming well established in Nicaragua, principally in Managua and to a lesser degree in the city of Matagalpa. The mainstream publication *El País* (1992) featured an article that announced, "[T]he gay world has come to Nicaragua." It traced the roots of the gay movement and listed various cultural venues for gay men and lesbians. The article signaled a degree of public acceptance and recognition of gay culture and human rights in Nicaragua.

To celebrate Gay Pride in June 1993, the Xochiquetzal Foundation published the first issue of *Fuera del Closet* (Out of the Closet), a magazine that contained poetry and articles concerning the right to pleasure, other rights of gay men and lesbians, homophobia, sexual violence, and AIDS. Its editorial noted that gay Nicaraguans had chosen to join with many other countries in celebrating Gay Pride annually on June 28, the date when, in 1969, gay patrons at the Stonewall bar in New York City fought back against a police raid. Well known for sparking the gay liberation movement in the United States, the event is honored by those seeking to identify with the transnational gay movement. Rita Arauz made the salient point that another date more appropriate to Nicaragua's history (perhaps marking the resistance to State Security) could have been selected (Randall 1994). However, it is clear that for many gay Nicaraguans, there is much to be gained by identifying with other movements across national borders. The discourse of gay politics reflects that view, for example, frequent invocations of the 1974 decision of the American Psychiatric Association to remove homosexuality from the list of mental illnesses in efforts to counter homophobia.

Women, generally feminists, have been the most visible spokespersons and leaders in the lesbian and gay movement.[18] Not surprisingly, AMNLAE has shied away from the issue of sexual orientation and gay rights, but the feminist center Puntos de Encuentro and women's health centers like S.I. Mujer and IXCHEN have offered workshops on women's sexuality and supported gay rights. In March 1999, a new lesbian magazine, *Female Humans [Humanas]: For the Visibility of Lesbians and Their Human Rights*, began publication. The magazine's editorial group of independent (nonpartisan) lesbians declared their desire to provide a new and open space for cultural expression and for sharing national and international news of interest to Nicaraguan lesbians.

The distance that lesbians have come in gaining visibility in the last few years could be observed during the Gay Pride main event in June 1996. Held once again at Coro de Angeles, the event was planned to honor the publication that month of Mary Bolt González's book, *Sencillamente Diferentes . . .* (Simply Different . . .) (1996). The author, trained in psychology, based her study of lesbian self-esteem on interviews she conducted in urban areas of Nicaragua. The work was published by Xochiquetzal, the NGO for which she serves as codirector, and was welcomed in the Managua community with considerable fanfare. Bolt González shared a panel with respondents to the book, including Hazel Fonseca (codirector of Xochiquetzal) and

Dora María Téllez (the highly respected Sandinista comandante who had joined with the renovationist MRS a year before), who made laudatory remarks about its importance. As in previous Gay Pride celebrations, there was a large and appreciative audience, and many joined in affirming the need to support the gay movement. The evening concluded with music by the popular singer Norma Elena Gadea.[19]

Claims for space and visibility have had an impact in Managua, as lesbians have carried out social and political projects and received media attention (particularly in the now-defunct Sandinista daily *Barricada* and its weekly supplement *Gente*). Yet women and, especially, lesbians can still go unnoticed in a machista society in which even gay men may fail to see their growing presence in the public sector. When a new bar opened and *Barricada* announced that it would provide a welcome space for all who are "different," apparently signaling an openness to all sexual minorities, I went one night with a small group of women.[20] All others present at the middle-class venue were men, who later enjoyed a rather raucous transvestite performance at the bar. When I passed by the bar the next morning, I spoke briefly with the earnest young man, a journalism student, who had performed in drag. I commented that there had been few women the night before, and he said with surprise, "That's because it's a gay bar." Lesbians may be out in front in gay politics, but they are often still overlooked in popular culture.[21]

Efforts at inclusion are evident at the level of political organizing, where, instead of the LGBT (lesbian-gay-bisexual-transgender) formulation commonly invoked in the United States, LGBTT is used to include transvestites as another category of difference or identity found in Nicaragua as elsewhere in Latin America.[22] Less attention has gone to social class differences in the LGBTT community, as a clear majority of those who find a public forum for expression, cultural venues, and other social privileges continue to be from the middle class or the elite. Lesbians, in general, have benefited from international feminist delegations to Nicaragua. As Rita Arauz told Margaret Randall, "[W]e'd always tell our foreign sisters, 'Ask about the lesbians. Ask for us by name — my name, the names of the others. Remind them that we exist, that we're here and we're not going away'" (Randall 1994: 277). Thus sexual orientation was identified as a feminist issue, making the Sandinista leadership and other Nicaraguans better aware of lesbians' existence in the country. This was furthered by the formation of such lesbian organizations as Nosotras (We Women), Entre Amigas (Among Women Friends), the Lesbian Feminist Collective, and the Group for Lesbian Visibility.

Perhaps a sign of the growing visibility of lesbians in Nicaragua is the backlash that is occasionally expressed, even by self-identified Sandinistas and feminists.[23] During my trip to Managua in June 1998, a great focus of discussion and media attention was the allegation by Zoilamérica Narvaez, daughter of Rosario Murillo and stepdaughter of Daniel Ortega, of her stepfather's long-term sexual abuse and harassment. While Ortega remained silent and hid behind his parliamentary immunity, Murillo spoke frequently and publicly against her daughter's allegation, even looking to the conservative cardinal Obando y Bravo for support. Appealing to religion and the nuclear family, she was quoted as charging that Zoilamérica's supporters were motivated by their "uncertain sexual identity" to try to influence her daughter, "projecting known patterns of hatred for the opposite sex, rejecting marriage and traditional family, rejecting motherhood, and in general the values and culture of heterosexual relations" (*La Prensa*, June 5, 1998, 1).[24]

During that time, I visited with the head of the Women's Program of CONAPI and asked her about links between her office and the women's movement, and she felt free to tell me that the feminist and lesbian "aspect" of the movement had alienated a number of women in CONAPI. She added that she did not believe Zoilamérica's account and that those women supporting Zoilamérica were lesbians. She could not say what the motivation might be, but she clearly felt that such support would discredit Zoilamérica.[25] Indeed, feminists in Nicaragua and internationalists in general were supportive of Zoilamérica's right to speak out and be heard and of the need for justice to be served — no matter what the outcome. Sex and politics are greatly fraught in this case, and there is much at stake in the ongoing claims that are being played out for public consumption.[26]

In their final years in power, the Sandinistas opened a space for more open discussion of sexuality, personal life, and politics, and now, *after* the revolution, their leadership faces its own deep crisis in precisely these areas. Perhaps it is not so surprising that just as the sensitive issues of sexuality and domestic violence were getting public exposure in Nicaragua, the cultural anxieties still prevalent in the machista culture again are rising to the surface. Now, however, independent social movements (both feminist and gay) and a discourse of human rights lend support to those who have been silenced in the past.

In this period of globalization, the transnational flow of ideas, information, people, and technologies is increasing. As news of Nicaragua's scandal received full-page coverage in *Newsweek* and other international media, more positive developments have also occurred. Social movements—with local histories and transnational politics—have emerged that are not inclined to give uncritical support to any party or individual and are insisting on social justice and democracy. For the first time, the call for justice and equality includes the private sphere as well as the public sphere, the integrity of the body and the person as well as the society.[27] In that sense, "body" politics and "place" politics are coming together in the making of a new political culture.

Chapter Nine

CONCLUSION

Remembering Nicaragua

T HE close of the twentieth century and the millennium has prompted us to look back and to look forward, to take stock of global changes during our lifetimes and to imagine what future may already be in the making. Recent retrospectives have considered the dismantling of the Soviet Union and the Berlin Wall a decade later to see what hopes were fulfilled and what disappointments have followed in the postsocialist era. Far fewer reflections have been offered concerning changes of the last several decades in Latin America, where the demise of socialist governments in a few nations and persistent repression in others have been deeply dismaying to many on the Left. Cuba remains a contentious area and still receives critical attention from the United States, yet as the Special Period of the 1990s has led the Cuban government to seek economic development through tourism and partnerships with other countries, the island has experienced something of a cultural renaissance.[1] The Dirty War of the 1970s in Argentina remains present in the silent marching of the mothers and grandmothers of the Plaza de Mayo, reminding the world that justice has not been served as long as there is no accounting for their family members' disappearances.[2] In the Central American region, analysts have questioned what is remembered and what is forgotten in republics that experienced the brutal force of wars and repression in recent decades.[3] While the politics of memory allows some to rehabilitate history and justify the past, others oppose such cynical rereadings, question their own continued suffering, and recall another past of revolutionary hopes deferred. The challenging task ahead for these societies and nations is to pursue both justice and reconciliation in the interest of a lasting peace.

How is Nicaragua remembered more than twenty years after the revolution's victory and ten years after the Sandinistas turned over government control to a coalition of opposition parties? How do Nicaraguans themselves reflect on their collective past, and how is that past imagined in the rest of the world? To a great extent, global amnesia has set in as international attention has turned to new hot spots, influencing even the way Nicaraguans view themselves and their history. It may take catastrophic events or further political unrest to bring media interest back to the country, as we saw recently with Hurricane Mitch. One thing, however, is clear: the past is contested just as the present is contested, and Nicaragua — as a particular location at a particular time — is invoked in manifold ways to support claims that are at once political and cultural.[4] Not surprisingly, these claims differ dramatically depending on gender and class distinctions, elite and nonelite status, and whether they are made at the local, national, or international level.

To draw together the various threads of ethnographic analysis presented here, I want to conclude by suggesting that Nicaragua presents a kind of palimpsest that shows traces of the past, layer upon layer, from prerevolutionary days to the Sandinista period to the neoliberal era. In what follows, I refer to interpretations of these past traces and current overlays as I have discovered them within Nicaragua and beyond its borders. Just as the figure of Sandino stands in silent rebuke on a Managua hillside overlooking the newly built and heavily financed national cathedral and city center, many other aspects of the present clash mightily with the revolutionary past, which often lies just beneath the surface. At the same time, as this study shows, we find evidence of more recent traces of oppositional culture and politics in the neoliberal present. These latest traces signal hopes and prospects for a more democratic future.

In this final chapter, I argue that the evident triumph of neoliberalism on the continent has had significant implications for Nicaragua and those who have come to identify with and embrace the country. Then I discuss my research findings in light of the particular consequences that the recent political economic transition has had for low-income women and other subaltern sectors in society. This is followed by an assessment of the narratives employed to shore up one position or another, honoring the revolutionary past or justifying the neoliberal present, and the cultural and political practices that correspond to these narratives. I return to underscore a point made at the outset of this study, that history and the politics of location are key in the remembering and forgetting of Nicaragua and in the way that the nation's experience is invoked by its citizens and others throughout the world. *After Revolution* concludes with a postscript written after my latest visit to Nicaragua in June 2000.

The Triumph of Neoliberalism

As we have seen, neoliberalism appears victorious in Nicaragua as in much of the world at century's end. Writing of the Nicaraguan revolution and other progressive initiatives in Central America, the literary and cultural critic Ileana Rodríguez states:

> Admittedly, the constitution of the revolutionary state was beyond the pale. The revolutionaries undertook its construction when the formation of the global paradigm defining the nature of productive capital was already, it seems, well under way. The forces of entropy straining the social fabric presided over the State's final collapse. Furthermore, during their brief life cycle, the revolutionary states discussed the necessity of forming part of larger marketing structures, capitalist or socialist. (1996: xviii)

With the benefit of hindsight, we may agree that the likelihood of a socialist-oriented project succeeding in Nicaragua in the 1980s was slight, particularly with Reagan's politics dominating the region and socialism crumbling worldwide. In the 1990s, some sectors of the Left appear to have joined forces with the Right in making a claim to the spoils of capitalism, although mobilizing for economic and social justice continues to find expression in civil society.

The post-Sandinista period has seen the rapid introduction of harsh measures designed to adjust and stabilize the economy while downsizing and divesting the state of its former responsibilities. When this has eliminated protection of vulnerable social sectors the popular reaction has been alarm at the outcome, but the FSLN has only weakly called for a more gradual application of these measures. Sectoral and trade union organizations, including CONAPI, take issue with the rolling back of the gains of the revolution but find it necessary to negotiate on the government's terms to slow the opening of the market to foreign competition. Members of surviving cooperatives and workers in the informal sector describe viscerally how new policies and conditions are inscribed on their bodies and minds, but their words are frequently eclipsed by the dominant discourses of development.

The changes brought about with neoliberalism in Nicaragua are most striking in the remaking of Managua as a city emulating developments in other urban centers, even if the result is a pale reflection of that in better-endowed global cities. Most revolutionary murals have been painted over and other symbols of the Sandinista decade have been removed, while new monuments are being erected. Streets, plazas, and barrios have been renamed in an effort to erase the memory of the previous decade, while grandiose traffic circles use precious water for fountains and make use of colored lights and music to hail the modern city under construction. Restaurants and shopping malls give Managua the appearance of a modernizing place in the social landscape and offer the urban elite safe destinations when they venture from closely guarded homes. All these changes in Nicaragua's capital signal efforts to construct a new national identity centered on consumption, for those who can afford it, in the market economy.

The Displacement of Subalterns

As the physical space of Managua is altered, it has become more welcoming to the wealthy elite but more hostile to those in the majority who are unable to benefit from neoliberal modernity. The Alemán government's beautification projects emphasize "progress" and "development" in the form of a new presidential palace, commercial centers, and other monu-

35. *One of Managua's new traffic circles, with fountains and colored lights, at Metrocentro.*

ments to modernity. To accomplish these projects, one hundred poor families were driven from their homes to make way for a private presidential park by the new palace and another two hundred families were forced to move to make way for a monumental obelisk in the new plaza honoring Pope John Paul II. One of the affected residents was quoted as saying, "Poverty is not being cured in Nicaragua, it's just being relocated." Another stated, "The government wants to 'beautify' Managua (to appear 'more developed'). Our poverty offends them. Their works accomplish nothing for us, the poor. All we are is an obstacle. So they relocate us" (*Nicaragua Alert!* November 1999: 5).

Thus low-income people's right to urban space is contested at the same time that their opportunities for employment are shrinking and their ability to participate as consumers in the urban economy is ever more tenuous. As we have seen, the downsizing of the state sector meant the loss of many jobs held (disproportionately) by Sandinistas and women, a large number of whom entered the informal sector to try to make a livelihood under ad-

verse conditions. Street vendors have found it impossible to continue working at major intersections that were converted into traffic circles, and those
selling at home meet growing competition from neighbors who have employed the same strategy to deal with poverty and unemployment.

The rising crime rate and gang activity in Managua, which clearly are
related to the economic crisis and social disaffection, have made the city still
less hospitable, especially for women and children. Those women and girls
(and, sometimes, young men) who have turned to such precarious means
of gaining a livelihood as prostitution take significant personal risks. Marginal employment and unemployment contribute to physical and mental
health problems, as revealed in interviews in Barrio Monseñor Lezcano
with residents who could not afford privatized care. Economic uncertainty
may also add to existing problems of sexism and domestic violence, as studies have indicated. The well-being of children is at stake as state support of
preschool care and education is diminished and many need to work under
dangerous conditions to help support their families. Starting at a very young
age, children wait in streets and parking lots to beg for tips for guarding
parked cars — including at the modern new malls, where patrons often fear
turning the children down and risking vandalism to their expensive cars.

36. Many in Managua live in conditions of deep poverty.

37. *The elite in the city often choose to reside in high-security gated communities.*

These developments in the neoliberal era prompt us to ask once again, following Saskia Sassen, whose city is it?

Narratives of Nationhood

In this post-Sandinista period of political economic transition, the terms of national inclusion and identity are being negotiated on a daily basis. The widespread erasures of revolutionary traces have been accompanied by the installation of nationalist and religious monuments intended to evoke nostalgia for a more distant and shared cultural history, on the one hand, and yearnings for modernity in the making, on the other. School books financed by USAID offer a sanitized version of Nicaraguan history and society, at the same time that they reintroduce conservative middle-class values regarding gender relations and the family. As we have seen, high-level officials who set economic policy hail the return home of women cast out of state employment, suggesting that women's economic well-being would be sacrificed to the project of constructing the neoliberal nation. As president, Violeta Chamorro managed to present herself first and foremost as "mother" of the country, and with some success as she mobilized national sentiments for healing and reconciliation.

The neoliberal ideological shift has privileged those who can compete successfully under new conditions in the market economy, while those who lack the resources to succeed in microenterprises or larger industries are a casualty of the national project of developing and marketing better-quality products. Although in many instances subsidized production under the Sandinistas did not lead to higher-quality goods or sustainable development, it has become all too easy to scapegoat cooperatives and their poor production for the failure of small industries in the country. Workers, once regarded as "heroic," are now viewed as "dependent" on the support of NGOs as they were formerly dependent on the state for their survival. Now, microenterprises are championed as a sort of neoliberal cause célèbre, but these refashioned small industries appear to be failing much as the cooperatives have failed in recent years, as policy initiatives work to their disadvantage.

While most Nicaraguans agree that the nation is "ailing," they are less certain of "the cure." The shock therapy of structural adjustment is frequently invoked as the only remedy available, and public debate hinges on the best way to apply it. As we have seen, however, those most in need of economic and social assistance (the poor, women, children) offer alternative accounts of the bodily effects of inadequate jobs, food, housing, and other basic needs. At the very least, their narratives of personal pain and collective suffering should sound a national alarm for the government and political parties. The everyday woes of those living in poor and working-class neighborhoods, expressed in oppositional narratives, could provide the staging ground for productive discussion of what is fundamentally at stake in neoliberal development.

At the present time, however, the two most powerful political figures in the country, former opponents Arnoldo Alemán and Daniel Ortega, have made a pact to protect their personal and political interests, stalling open debate and national reconciliation. The charges of corruption and sexual abuse that the two seek to shield from public scrutiny have brought dishonor to them as individuals but have done little as yet to lessen the power they wield in the Liberal Party government and in the FSLN. Even so, the tarnished image of the nation and the severity of the problems faced by the majority of its citizens have galvanized civil society to organize and protest current conditions.

Civil Society and Oppositional Culture

My research has suggested that a new political culture is in the making as autonomous social movements and nongovernmental organizations take up where the Sandinista Party left off following the presidential elections a decade ago. The FSLN Piñata (the giveaway of state property before turning over government control to the UNO) and a loss of confidence in the party leadership's willingness to move toward transparent and democratic politics led to the party's split a few years later. Many Sandinistas turned their activism toward a growing number of NGOs and non-party-based movements that promised to be less hierarchical and more inclusive and to take up issues that before were deemed risky or unimportant. I have followed Nicaraguan politics long enough to refrain from making any judgments about the direction in which the country is moving, as surprising turns abound, but I think it fair to say that important changes in political organizing are under way.

Some of these changes were evident by the late 1980s, when the Sandinistas relaxed control of sectoral organizations. After the electoral loss, increasing autonomy was projected, notably for the neighborhood organizations and AMNLAE. However, a particularly significant development in the 1990s has been the emergence of feminist and women's groups along with indigenous and environmental groups unconstrained by the FSLN or other political parties. Moreover, as the state has been cut back and political parties have taken a secondary role in leading innovative change, NGOs have often benefited from the involvement of progressive sectors of the population. There is indeed some concern that a new form of dependency may result, with international funding agencies taking the place of the revolutionary state, but for the time being the NGOs serve as an important location of social research and action on behalf of those affected adversely by the neoliberal agenda.

Immediately after the crisis brought about by Hurricane Mitch, Nicaragua saw the positive response of many civil society groups that formed a coalition to offer emergency assistance and also to plan for a more sustainable development in the country. Observers in and out of the country were reminded of the period in the 1970s following the earthquake that destroyed much of Managua, when political activism grew in strength. Both of these disasters drew attention to the callous response of governments;

38. At a march, a woman's placard suggests countering machismo with "Feminist Intelligence."

they responded too slowly to emergency conditions and failed to undertake reconstruction with the seriousness the situations demanded. It is too soon to say if the recent social mobilization will build into a more coherent national project or if political fragmentation will occur. The most vibrant feature of the current political culture, however, is the diversity of forms of expression in civil society, with groups as distinct as CONAPI and feminist and gay activists calling for an extension of democratic rights to everyone in the society.

Mapping Nicaragua

If Nicaragua two decades ago was a place of hopes and dreams for many residents and a destination of "tourists of revolution," to use Lawrence Ferlinghetti's wry turn of phrase, what does the nation now represent for Nicaraguan and global citizens? How is Nicaragua mobilized in the thoughts of those whose lives are played out on its terrain and of those more distant from its shores? I want to reiterate here what I noted in the introduction, that place and time figure as critical factors in memory and discourse — or the absence thereof — concerning Nicaragua in the world. That is, I want to bring attention to the way that Nicaragua, in both its revolutionary past and its neoliberal present incarnations, is remembered and forgotten, imagined and reimagined, in the postsocialist period of capitalist globalization. Moreover, I want to emphasize the significant place of gender, as well as social class and other differences, in this work of memory and in the process of change that is under way.[5]

Beneath the veneer of increasing modernity in Managua and elsewhere in post-Sandinista Nicaragua, a dispirited people express dismay at the failure of political economic change to bring relief to their families and communities. A year after the devastation of Hurricane Mitch, more torrential rains caused serious damage to vulnerable areas and reminded residents once again of the precarious situation in which they live. Meanwhile, such influential institutions as the IMF, the World Bank, and the World Trade Organization seem to have forgotten already the severe setback that previous disasters meant for the region as they predicted continued growth under the neoliberal development model. Such assessments mask the economic, physical, and emotional hardship that many women, men, and children are experiencing in the present context of modernizing Nicaragua.

While international lenders and policy makers have often only perpetuated problems in Nicaragua and many international analysts and activists have turned from Nicaragua to other sites, some individuals and organizations have continued to offer vital assistance through material reconstruction and moral support. Those who have stayed or returned have become aware of the ways in which poverty, stress, and painful memories have been inscribed on the minds and bodies of many Nicaraguans. Apparent, too, is the particular way that women have been affected, as they not only maintain families under harsh conditions but also suffer rising domestic and sexual abuse. The country has confronted these problems from the neighborhood level to the national level, as in the case of charges against the former president and celebrated FSLN leader, Daniel Ortega, and the issues have become part of everyday discourse. In response to the public outcry over family violence as well as post–Hurricane Mitch suffering, assistance in emotional healing has come from the women's movement in Nicaragua and from feminist and progressive organizations based in the United States and elsewhere.[6] In addition, the long-term and engaged commitment of some international scholars conducting research in Nicaragua has countered the cultural amnesia that has otherwise followed in the postrevolutionary era.[7]

Nicaraguans' memories include the crises of the earthquake in 1972, Hurricane Joan in 1988, and Hurricane Mitch in 1998, as well as the repression of the Somoza dictatorship, the Contra war, and now the harsh economic effects of neoliberalism; for women, there are added memories of gender inequalities and abuse—layers of trauma experienced in their lifetimes. Yet, for many, the Sandinista period is remembered as a time of hopeful participation in a process of political and social transformation that ultimately went awry for reasons that are still being debated. Ileana Rodríguez, now based in the United States, offers this lyrical, melancholy evocation of her country as she situates herself as a writer "after the Sandinista electoral defeat, away from the conflicts of the revolutionary transition taking place in that remote geographical area":

The public plazas inflamed with the tumult of the masses became but a memory. The indigenous voices identifying the towns where the struggle had taken place, now printed in texts, joined the process of political reversal as they changed into poetry and rhetoric. (1994: xiii)

Nicaraguans are now experiencing contentious political and cultural negotiations over their history. National icons Rubén Darío and Augusto César Sandino are appropriated by those wishing to support the neoliberal status quo through a process of universalizing and thus neutralizing the cultural figures' radical appeals for social justice (Whisnant 1995: 444). Likewise, gains made by women under the Sandinista government are being recast as destructive of the family so that traditional Christian values opposing women's reproductive rights, employment, and even sex education may be reestablished. Just as I found Managua undergoing a refashioning in the 1990s, David E. Whisnant (ibid.: 448) writes of the way the "Miami boys" have "transformed the Managua night: neon-lit bars and exclusive clubs, designer clothing, Nicaragua's first surf shop, one-hour photo processing, expensive cars cruising the scene, and pervasive preening, posturing, and dalliance shaped by the old gender roles and rules." He concludes:

It was as if the revolution had never been, as if the 1972 earthquake had unhappened and the Avenida Roosevelt had reassembled itself from the rubble, as if the gaudy movie of the cotton-rich days of the 1960s were rolling again, as if the ghost of old Somoza García walked again, charming the *norteamericanos* with his colloquial English — as if indeed the Miami boys were not (as they fancied) gyrating to Madonna under the neon, but swaying to "Managua, Nicaragua" by Kay Kyser and His Orchestra. (448)

Commenting on the Nicaraguan practice of identifying locations by landmarks that may no longer exist, Whisnant identifies the layers of memory that can be traced from William Walker to the U.S. Marines and the Somoza dynasty, Ronald Reagan and the Contras to the Miami boys — emphasizing the extent of U.S. intervention in the last two centuries of Nicaraguan history. He suggests with some irony that "it is the landscape of the mind that matters most — not things as they are, but things as they have been" (448–49).

If the world has to a large degree forgotten this Central American nation — or simply consigned it to the broad category of the poor, needy, and underdeveloped — in the midst of global political restructuring that is centered elsewhere, it is at our peril and to our significant loss. The new society that the Sandinista revolution began to construct, for all its shortcomings, and civil society's present efforts to build on a democratic foundation even under grim national conditions, should continue to inspire our admiration and our imagination as world citizens embarking on the twenty-first century.

Postscript 2000

June 5, arriving at Managua's International Airport (formerly named for Augusto César Sandino). We do not descend from the plane directly onto the steaming hot tarmac as in my past trips to Nicaragua but rather pass through a cool jetway to a recently remodeled and modernized airport terminal. There, we are greeted by bold signs for Victoria beer and Flor de Caña rum, among Nicaragua's best-known commercial products, and then quickly whisked away to taxis. This welcome to turn-of-the-millennium Nicaragua is a sign of more to come in its capital city. After two years away, I expect to find evidence of Hurricane Mitch's impact throughout the country, yet the effects are concentrated in the disaster area and are less visible in Managua than I anticipated.[8] Instead, I find change of a far different order than I could have imagined. Although I had seen the neoliberal remaking of the city a couple of years before, I am stunned by the pace of urban development, as new roads, hotels, and shopping malls appear to have sprung up magically. Driving on a familiar road, I am shocked to find a new traffic circle with a towering Christ figure at its center. During the three-week period I am in the country, I watch as the immense Juan Pablo II Plaza, with phallic obelisk looming large, nears completion; I am startled to discover just before leaving the country that a new middle-class colonia (neighborhood) is rapidly going up as a backdrop to the plaza, where poor families' housing so recently has been razed. Even those living in Managua for years tell me that the changes seem to have occurred overnight.

The opening of a McDonald's restaurant two years before in the renamed Plaza Güegüense drew wide attention and now attracts middle-class Nicaraguan families who arrive in their luxury vehicles, particularly on Sunday afternoons, and order McPollo (McChicken) sandwiches and Big Macs at prices on a par with the United States. More spectacularly, two malls now compete in downtown Managua, though the gleaming Metrocentro Plaza, which I described earlier as it was under construction, has a more upscale clientele shopping at the pricey Eclipse department store and enjoying espresso at the city's second Casa del Café. Plaza Inter brings more working-class people, who can rarely afford to shop there but learn to ride the escalators and buy something to eat in the sprawling food court. Both malls have movie complexes that charge admission of about U.S. $2, allowing some entry across classes, but the theaters are still prohibitively expensive for many. These commercial centers cater principally to higher-income populations, but those with more modest resources nevertheless come to them as places of recreation, even if they consume little more than the malls' physical space.[9]

Gated communities (urbanizaciones) are in greater evidence around the city, while poor settlements are less visible, at least on the major streets. But the poor themselves are perceived as a problem insofar as children demand coins for washing car windows at every major traffic light, and crime is rising in the city. High walls and guards at attention protect elite residents in exclusive neighborhoods, similar to the close surveillance I observe in and

39. *The new mall at Metrocentro.*

outside the new malls where the elite shop. I am hurried away more than once by uniformed guards as I take photographs of these new establishments, as if I am stealing something precious from them. The new roads, plazas, government buildings, and commercial centers are heavily financed by international donors, yet Alemán's ubiquitous billboards announce "Works, Not Words" (Obras No Palabras), suggesting his own beneficence.

At the national level, tourism has grown to become the second most important industry, after coffee production. Cruise ships stop at San Juan del Sur on the Pacific Coast and ecotourism is becoming more popular in the mountains to the north. The five-star all-inclusive beach resort, Montelimar, advertises such features as a casino and airport pick-up service from Managua. In the capital city, hotels, car rental agencies, and tourist services are expanding. Catering to international tourists as well as meeting a national demand, prostitution is on the rise, and for the first time I become aware of *travestis* (transvestites) as sex workers on downtown streets near the Intercontinental Hotel.

The Nicaraguan government is by now notorious for a level of corruption rivaling that of the Somoza dictatorship. While Alemán grows richer, Daniel Ortega also benefits from the pact the two have made, as the Sandinista leader continues to have parliamentary immunity that protects him from Zoilamérica Narvaez's charges of sexual abuse. The powerful may escape scrutiny for their moral failings and criminal behavior, but the less powerful still experience a harsh and repressive political climate. Article 204, the antisodomy law, remains on the books but for the most part is not enforced, although a young working-class lesbian, Aura Rosa Pavón, recently was arrested and, after her release, murdered in what many regard as a hate crime.[10] As the government engages in discussion of a revised penal code, moral intolerance is manifesting itself in the fast erosion of women's reproductive rights as well as in the slow pace of removing the sodomy law.

The neoliberal economy continues to favor larger industry and the few smaller enterprises that are competitive under the new conditions, IMPYME (formerly PAMIC) still organizes highly visible fairs in which to promote local production of crafts, furniture, and other items, and artisans now set up outside the Metrocentro Plaza once a month, a study in contrasts with the modern shops inside the mall. But most small industries and microenterprises suffer losses and CONAPI appears even weaker in the harsh economic climate. When I visit the trade organization's offices, I find them virtually abandoned. Instead, an NGO funded by Norway, FUNDEPYME, has occupied an office and taken on the responsibility, formerly held by CONAPI, of supplying credit to small industries.

I spend time visiting members of all four of the cooperatives I have followed in the past. The artisans and bakers are still in operation, though not as members of CONAPI; the seamstresses continue working at home and the welders have never resumed working together. The jewelry makers have seen changes in their workshop since Marlene sold some of her land and her house, which stood adjacent to the shop until it was torn down; she has taken up residence in half the space of the workshop, while the artisans work in a more compact area. As they reported two years before, they are determined to work independently as jewelers sharing a work space. They have only a small amount of jewelry for sale, though they are constructing a small exhibition space outside the workshop in order to draw more customers. Marlene tells me that she is continuing to look for new markets, including in Panama, with the help of an enterprising friend. Although the jewelers have expressed their national pride in using indigenous materials of the region in their craft, it is notable that Marlene's friend is encouraging the artisans to adopt designs found in her Christie's catalogue from New York.

The mother and daughter bakers, Luz and Laura, are still struggling to remain in business. Their shops look somehow sadder, without the commercial innovations and visual appeal of earlier years. The seamstresses still encounter tough competition from mass-produced clothing and from the Zona Franca, but they carry on. Teresa actually appears to be better off than two years before, as her health has improved, but she is the exception rather than the rule; she continues to volunteer her time to the CONAPI office of the Managua region, although the low level of activity there often makes her efforts seem pointless. Finally, visiting the home of one of the former coordinators of the welders' collective, I discover that Doris is still employed in her office job at the women's hospital, although her mother expresses the wish, as she has frequently in the past, that I take Doris back with me to the United States so that she can improve her situation.

In Barrio Monseñor Lezcano, I find none of the dramatic physical change that is so striking in the downtown area. In fact, talking to Don Nicolás and others, I hear numerous complaints about all the money that is being poured into developing the center of the city while outlying barrios go without street repair and basic improvements. Doña Monica's restaurant, which she had opened enthusiastically with three other women a few years ago, had to "close" officially because they could not pay the required fees — although they still welcome customers for lunch and scrape by selling items to neighbors who come to their door. I learn that Doña María is still in the United States and that she was heartbroken when her husband died in the past year and she could not afford to return for his funeral. Patricia has had a third baby, and her vast extended family is even more crowded in their home around the corner from Casa Ave María. On my last day in the country, she offers to take me on a walk around the barrio, which turns into an insider's tour of local gangs and prostitutes, all young people of her acquaintance. I don't have to venture far to see and hear about the grown daughters of the woman across the street, well depicted by Grant Gallup:

A bevy of enterprising women live with their Momma in a humble house across the street from the Casa Ave María and try to hump out a living as sex workers in this restored capitalist democracy. Their clients call for

them in luxurious vehicles—great diesel four-wheel drives with shad-
owed windows—and off they go to the No Tell Motel. Some of these
drive-ins have canvas curtains to hide the license plates in their garages.
Many of these johns refuse the use of condoms, and pay extra for the
thrills—putting all the women at risk of their lives in our HIV era. In the
brave socialist eighties, the Sandinistas shut down the *prostíbulos* and
took the *rameras* [prostitutes] and *tamarindos* [tamarind fruit] off to the
campo [countryside], where they learned how to make marmalade from
pineapples, and earned a sticky meager living. But capitalism has different notions of what is a salable sweet commodity—and the chief one in
its market is the human person. The *mermelada* of the mercado. (Gallup,
e-mail com., January 29, 2000)

Despite the hard living of so many, the gains of civil society remain apparent in Nicaragua, particularly in the form of highly visible and active
NGOs. A directory of nongovernmental organizations that is updated on a
regular basis has grown thick and serves to link groups and individuals working on related projects (Liehl 1999). Several of the most prominent NGOs
are truly extensions of social movements, and in a number of cases are
flourishing. Puntos de Encuentro, the feminist center, has experienced significant expansion, including a documentation center, more classes, research projects, and an innovative venture into producing a novela, a TV series that promises to be a sort of progressive "Friends," introducing gay and
other unconventional characters. Meeting with several staff members, I am
impressed by the attention given to youth, racial minorities, gay men and
lesbians, those with disabilities, and others regarded as "different" (a T-shirt
I purchased there reads "Somos diferentes, somos iguales"—We're different, we're equal). Likewise, the CJA, the young environmentalist group, is
buzzing with activity when I visit; they are hosting children and youth from
around the country who are the winners in competitions to represent environmental concerns through artwork and other forms of creative expression. When I visit Nimehuatzín, I am shown a valuable research library
that has outgrown the available space, and Rita Arauz is busy preparing to
leave in a few days for a world conference on AIDS to be held in South Africa.
At Xochiquetzal, Hazel Fonseca talks with me about the Gay Pride events
that are under way, including a presentation on sexual practices and safer
sex, which I attend. The directors of these last two NGOs are equivocal when

I ask whether there is an identifiable lesbian and gay movement in Nicaragua, telling me that there are communities, groups, and processes of change that may or may not constitute a movement. More energy is going to the local projects of smaller groups, but the high level of activity I observe in all these organizations convinces me that they are indeed participating in a vital political culture with transformative potential.

The attention to body politics is evident in the current concerns of both the Left and the Right in Nicaragua. On the one hand, organizations like those just mentioned are addressing such issues as violence against women, reproductive rights, racial inequality, the right to sexual expression, and the right to live and work in safe environments. Cultural openings are apparent, for example, as the North American film concerning transgender issues, *Boys Don't Cry*, is shown and talked about and as intellectuals and activists find space in which to discuss a host of concerns ranging from the rights of indigenous peoples to the right of everyone to health and well-being. On the other hand, the government is at present threatening to end women's right even to therapeutic abortion in the case of rape or incest and is challenging the legal right to practice professionally (and sometimes even the citizenship rights) of several prominent activists. Thus the integrity of the body and the right to defend it is very much at stake, and the political climate is ripe for oppositional movements to grow.

June 25, Leaving Managua for Miami. As I leave Nicaragua this time I am in a reflective mood, thinking over what I have seen and heard during this trip to the country. Along with my field notes recording the many conversations I have had with people, I am bringing back books that offer retrospectives of the Nicaraguan revolution and its meaning for those who participated in it (Ramírez 1999) as well as for those who admired and supported it as internationalists (Brentlinger 1995; Kruckewitt 1999). I also have acquired and watched a video, *Managua en mi corazón* (Managua in My Heart), produced by the Alemán government's Institute of Culture, which nostalgically recalls a very different city and nation. Idealizing the glory years of Somoza when Managua's elite enjoyed urban pleasures in the venerable old city, the video moves so quickly past the cataclysmic earthquake in 1972 that it entirely overlooks the revolution. The radical revision, and excision, of history that the video achieves is clear in its final moments, as images of the new Managua under development in the last few years celebrate the

40. *One of many signs with Alemán's slogan, "Works, Not Words," here signaling a road construction project.*

neoliberal present—linking it directly to the prerevolutionary past, with no hint of irony or self-consciousness.

As always, I am both sad and relieved to be leaving, trying to sort through the clash of images and ideas I have encountered. The night before, I was awakened by sounds outside and feared it might be a street fight. After a day of touring barrio gang sites and having heard of a recent shooting in front of Casa Ave María, I summon my courage to go to the front of the house and see for myself. What I thought were gunshots turned out to be drums, and I heard the faint traces of musicians passing through the barrio—a fitting reminder to me of the way that everyday violence and gaiety coexist in Nicaragua, in the streets as well as in the imagination.

Now, at dawn in the airport, I wonder at the modern technology of security, the new Coke machines that accept córdoba coins, the cart offering specialty coffees, and, on the floor above, the colorful artesanía for sale to departing tourists. I finally settle into my seat in the plane and sleepily begin reading John Brentlinger's book, based on his experiences in Nicaragua during and after the revolution. A seat away, an African American man of

about forty dressed in jeans and T-shirt looks tired, too. Although I am cu-
rious about what he might have been doing in Nicaragua, I hold back from
talking, worrying that it will be a long flight if I am engaged in conversation with a zealous missionary or right-winger (increasingly common in
the country). Eventually, out of boredom perhaps, we begin talking and it
turns out he is from Mississippi, a career officer with the U.S. military on
his way back from a humanitarian mission involving construction projects
in Nicaragua. When he asks about my profession and I tell him, he says
that I look like a schoolteacher all right, then apologizes rather too much.
I tell him I would not have picked him out for an army man, which I cal-
culate to be more flattering to a man who is off duty. I try not to reveal too
much about my views of U.S.-Nicaragua relations, although I finally ask
him what his group heard about the country before going there. While he
seems to have little familiarity with the history and politics of the region he
has just visited, he volunteers that "we" messed over the Nicaraguans pretty
badly in the past. Surprised, I agree, figuring his knowledge on that score
likely does not come from the military. He goes on to say that because of
language differences, the North Americans were not able to communicate
much with the Nicaraguans who worked alongside them during a few long
weeks of heavy work, yet they felt camaraderie. When he later inquires why
I am marking the book I am reading, I confess that I too am writing a book
on Nicaragua and want to remember some things. He seems impressed, to
the point that I think he is mocking me, but he is sincere. By the end of the
flight, we have talked about our teenage sons and families, and we joke as
we go through customs.

Back home, a few weeks later, I read a short news article reporting that
the Nicaraguan and U.S. armies have begun joint maneuvers to work on
humanitarian and community projects. Called New Horizons, the initiative includes projects to build health centers and a school in Matagalpa
over a four-month period with two hundred reserve troops from the United
States. Along with the two countries' joint military efforts to combat drug
trafficking, this is viewed as a way of improving relations between the formerly hostile nations.[11]

Living with contradictions and uncertainty is nothing new in Nicaragua, where the social and political landscape has long been complex. While
the U.S. military warms up to the country, U.S. and other international
lenders are threatening to cut off support if the government does not deal

with its rampant corruption. Meanwhile, reports mount of multinational corporations dismissing hundreds of women garment workers in Nicaragua's Zona Franca who have dared to organize for better conditions.[12] Soon the nation will hold its next presidential election and the two leading parties, the Liberals and the Sandinistas, are expected to face off once again. The Nicaraguan people wait to see which way the wind will blow and what the future will bring, but they are not sitting still as they wait. Rather, they are taking the measure of their time, remembering the past, imagining the future, and cautiously building on the gains that have gone before.

NOTES

Chapter One

1. Some of the works consulted in the historical summary that follows are Burns 1991; Hoyt 1997; Walker 1997; Gordon 1998; Gould 1998; LeoGrande 1998.
2. Throughout this work, I use the convention of describing "first world" regions and cultures as "Western" to differentiate them from the "non-Western" or "third world" regions and cultures, although the terminology is problematic. "Northern" might in some cases be preferable; however, the geographic imprecision and analytic limitations remain. In any event, it must be recognized that Nicaragua is located in the Western Hemisphere and shares many attributes with the West.
3. Deborah A. Gordon (1995: 433) comments on the way that ideas of social revolution as well as travel to such countries as Cuba and Vietnam have figured in the desires of Western feminists and leftists, including anthropologists who were becoming aware of imperial practices.
4. For an appraisal of Rich's contribution to current studies of the politics of location, see Kaplan 1994.
5. See also, for example, the poet Lawrence Ferlinghetti's *Seven Days in Nicaragua Libre* (1984), the report of Peter Davis (1987) based on a short visit to Nicaragua, and the letters from Nicaragua written by Rebecca Gordon (1986) who spent six months with Witness for Peace. Other writers who have traveled elsewhere in Central America have written memoirs of their experiences (e.g., Joan Didion [1983], writing on El Salvador).

   Travel to Nicaragua also deeply affected the lives of anthropologists who worked there during the Sandinista revolutionary decade. Michael James Higgins and Tanya Leigh Coen (1992: 7), wrote, "We see the hopes and dreams of the people of Nicaragua and the people in the Barrio William Diaz Romero as a search for a form of radical democracy." Roger N. Lancaster (1992: 9) wrote, "And I can say—like George Orwell writing of Catalonia—that for the first time in my life, I really believed in socialism." Charles R. Hale (1994: vii) hoped that his book would convey "a sense of the best principles and ideals of the Sandinista revolution, which provided much of the inspiration for what I did, and which have left an indelible influence on my thinking about the relationship between political activism and academic anthropology." Edmund T. Gordon

(1998: 2), who spent almost ten years living on Nicaragua's Atlantic coast, asks, "How does one write about the defining period in one's adult life without nostalgia?" And Les W. Field (1999: 13) notes, "[T]he Nicaraguan Revolution was from my perspective the most interesting event in the world."

A recent newsletter of the Nicaragua Network, established twenty years ago in Washington, D.C., captures well the sentiments of many who identified with the struggles of Nicaragua:

[The] dream lives on in the lives that were transformed by the Revolution. It lives on in the collective response by so many communities to the ravages of Hurricane Mitch. It lives on in the determination of sweatshop workers (many of whom weren't even born in 1979) to organize to defend their rights. It lives on in the environmental and the women's movements and in so many other organizations struggling for social justice.

In many ways the dream also lives on in our own country. Of the 100,000 or so U.S. citizens who visited Nicaragua in the 1980s, thousands were transformed and remain active today in human rights and social movements in this country. (Chuck Kaufman, National Co-Coordinator, April 1999)

6. See Rosset and Vandermeer 1983 and Diskin 1983 for critical analyses of U.S. policy and news coverage of Nicaragua in the 1980s.

7. For discussion of the U.S. propaganda campaign against Nicaragua, see Walker 1997: 11–12.

8. That trip, led by Margaret Randall, examined the impact of the Special Period on women workers, artists, writers, and family members.

9. See Marcus 1998 for further discussion of multisited ethnography.

10. For a short description of the INCAE, founded after President John F. Kennedy's request in 1963 that the Harvard Business School and the U.S. government help to establish a high-quality graduate school of management in Central America, see Colburn 1991: 50–54.

11. Arjun Appadurai and Carol A. Breckenridge (1992) find that in discussing "heritage" in India, museums are "good to think." Thomas Abercrombie (1999: 150) has described a recent collection of Andeanist essays as "good to think" about contemporary anthropology and Latin America.

12. For assessments of the Nicaraguan revolution, see Booth 1985; Walker 1986, 1991; Spalding 1987; Martínez Cuenca 1992. For discussion of the post-Sandinista period, see Spalding 1994; Prevost and Vanden 1997; Walker 1997.

13. Further discussion of the suitability of postmodern critique to Central American revolutions may be found in Beverley and Zimmerman 1990: ix–xvi. As the authors point out, there may be a problem in extending a concept developed in advanced capitalist consumer societies to the Central American region,

which in some instances still awaits "modernity." Yet, they argue, the forms of cultural resistance in evidence in Nicaragua and elsewhere "rise up on a postmodern terrain, understood in a broad sense" (xii). They point to two definitive problematics of postmodern culture that are pertinent to the region: the collapse of the distinction between elite and popular cultures and the collapse of the "grand narratives" of "Western" progress. Marxist in origin (see Jameson 1984), postmodernism goes on to critique the European Marxist tradition, making it particularly relevant to the analysis of third world societies and histories.

Chapter Two

1. Many scholars have written on the Nicaraguan revolution and the social transformation brought about by the Sandinista government (e.g., Booth 1985; Walker 1986; Spalding 1987). For discussion of women in these processes, see Padilla, Murguialday, and Criquillon 1987; Collinson 1990; Randall 1994.
2. Volunteer grassroots organizations were formed by the Sandinistas and eventually comprised about half the adult population. They were formed by sector and included the CDSs, AMNLAE, the Sandinista Youth (JS), the Rural Workers Association (ATC), the Sandinista Workers Confederation (CST), and the National Union of Small Farmers and Cattlemen (UNAC) (Walker 1986: 107).
3. In chapter 5, I discuss in more depth the gendered impact of structural adjustment in Nicaragua. For feminist assessments of the consequences of structural adjustment for women in various parts of the world, see Elson 1991 and Benería and Feldman 1992.
4. As I argue in this chapter, however, this coincidence of economic crisis and emergent social movements is less surprising when we consider the widespread development of feminism in Latin America during the "lost decade" of the 1980s (Sternbach et al. 1992). See also Quandt (1993), who has discussed the postelectoral rise of popular organizations in Nicaragua.
5. I discuss this question of public and private spheres and productive and reproductive work in Babb 1986.
6. For discussion of these collective struggles among Latin American women, see Fisher 1993; Radcliffe and Westwood 1993; Mujica 1994.
7. See Kampwirth 1996b for a discussion of Violeta Chamorro's maternal politics and the UNO's gender agenda. Deeply gendered political campaigns, with "Daniel" represented as a proudly strutting rooster and "Doña Violeta," symbolically dressed in white with outstretched arms, the image of the holy mother, contributed to a gender gap in the vote. Women may have been motivated more than men to support the candidate who embodied the hope for an end to war and economic hardship. Lancaster (1992: 290–93) also discusses the gender dimension

of the 1990 election and its outcome; he particularly notes women's response to the unbridled machismo of Daniel Ortega and the motherly, peacemaking image of Chamorro. Interestingly, a political poll in 1999 found Violeta Chamorro the most popular political figure (Grant Gallup pers. com.).

8. Here I have turned from a discussion of postmodernism as a mode of analysis to a consideration of postmodernity as an objective set of historical conditions. As discussed in note 13, chapter 1, some might question extending the concept of postmodernity developed in capitalist consumer societies to a Central American nation that is not yet fully "modern." Later chapters elaborate on Nicaragua's uneven development.

9. I discuss the emerging lesbian and gay movement in more detail in chapter 8.

10. I do not mean to underestimate the importance of political economy at a time when postmodern anthropologists often overlook the theoretical contribution of Marxism; see di Leonardo 1993 for a useful discussion of the significance of political economy to feminist and postmodern anthropology. For a far-reaching examination of cultural politics in Latin America that draws on Marxism, feminism, and postmodernism, see Alvarez, Dagnino, and Escobar 1998.

Chapter Three

1. LeoGrande (1999: 21) has recently made this point.

2. An article in the monthly newsletter *Envío* (1999d: 11) commented on the excessive attention given to Managua, stating, "As we all know, Managua isn't Nicaragua."

3. See Massey 1987 for further critique of the view of Managua workers and service providers, including the informal sector, as unproductive and parasitic in Nicaragua.

4. Few authors have described the city of Managua in much detail as it was either before or after the earthquake. Two exceptions are the Nicaraguan author Juan Aburto (1989), who writes affectionately and nostalgically of Managua in the earlier part of the twentieth century, and the U.S. political scientist Forrest D. Colburn (1991), who relates his everyday, often amusing, experiences while residing in the city.

5. Like many place-names, these names of roads were changed after the 1990 election, to Municipalidad and Portezuelo. Maps that are in circulation show both old and new names. I knew the roads by the names given by the Sandinistas.

6. In 1998, Daniel Ortega was publicly charged by his adoptive stepdaughter, Zoilamérica Narvaéz, with long-term sexual abuse and harassment. The case is under consideration by the Inter-American Commission on Human Rights (*Envío* 1999b: 30). I discuss this matter further in chapter 8.

7. Interestingly, some new murals are making use of indigenous motifs, perhaps looking to a more distant and less contentious past to represent continuities and strengths in regional traditions. Of course, urban popular culture has not been entirely eclipsed but rather altered in the current context. Relatively few studies have examined urban culture and cultural politics in Nicaragua, but for useful contributions see Borland 1994; Martin 1994; Whisnant 1995; Field 1999.

8. Rocha (1999) writes on the recent growth of youth gangs in Managua, which now number about sixty of the ninety in the country. Armed and disillusioned, they have occasionally joined with other groups including university students and transport workers in violent conflicts in the city. Made up almost exclusively by young men, the gangs purport to be defending their turf in Managua's neighborhoods.

9. See Lancaster's book, *Life Is Hard: Machismo, Danger, and the Intimacy of Power in Nicaragua* (1992), for a rich discussion of a Managua barrio through the early 1990s.

10. Lancaster (1992: 293) comments on the contradictory discourses of women themselves as the 1990 elections approached, publicly supporting the revolution while privately revealing concern about the draft, the war, shortages, and so on. He also notes Chamorro's retrograde politics of gender, which promised to restore dignity to women as mothers but at the price of lost opportunities in the public sector.

11. The Nicaraguan government's 1998 Demography and Health Survey, which included interviews with more than 13,600 Nicaraguan women, found that one in three women had experienced sexual abuse or physical mistreatment (*Envío* 1999b: 31).

12. This was not the first McDonald's restaurant in Managua, however. McDonald's Managua was established in 1975 in a commercial center, but during the revolutionary decade shortages meant declining standards, so in 1988 the restaurant's name was changed to Donald's and it gave up the franchise (Colburn 1991: 20–23).

13. See Borland 1994 for a discussion of a very different beauty pageant in Nicaragua, that was held in the indigenous neighborhood of Monimbó, Masaya, to honor the India Bonita.

14. Lancaster (1988b: 38–43) describes the Fiesta of Santo Domingo as an annual expression of popular religion and revelry in Managua. He notes that it is largely male dominated, yet there are exceptions when women become involved in the lively procession of dancing "cows," "Devils," and "Indians."

15. See Yúdice 1998: 357 for a discussion of the ways in which neoliberalism and globalization have changed the material and social spaces of cities. He notes that while new spatial arrangements often position the poor majority in the pe-

riphery surrounding pockets of wealth, civil society has often responded to the situation by opening up new forms of progressive cultural struggle.

16. In my research in Managua, I was also keenly aware of the ongoing erasures of the revolutionary period. I spent time photographing some of the remaining murals, with the knowledge that they might vanish at any time. Gathering oral histories also had a sense of urgency, as memories of the previous decade were fading.

17. Such measures are taken by middle- and lower-income people as well, insofar as they can afford to protect their homes with bars on windows and doors and with other forms of security. Where I lived, we hired someone to stay in the house when we were absent. Even so, robberies occurred occasionally at night, as when someone managed to scale the wall and abscond with laundry and other items accessible outdoors. One of the women's cooperatives I followed during my research, the welders, depended in large measure on the demand for protective iron bars for homes.

Chapter Four

1. While I also refer to "neighborhoods," I frequently use the local term "barrio" because of the stronger sense of place that it conveys.

2. The few anthropological studies based in Managua have generally focused on the level of the barrio. For example, see Higgins and Coen 1992; Lancaster 1992.

3. See Hoyt 1997: 57–62 and Polakoff and La Ramée 1997: 186–91 for useful discussions of the transition from Sandinista Defense Committees to the Community Movement. Although I point out that barrio activism has declined in some cases, this study also shows that other forms of political activism have increased precisely because the state is less responsive to social needs.

4. During that first visit, I recall that the home I stayed in had the collected works of Lenin, although there were few other books on view. And a neighbor's young children were named Vladimir and Lenin.

5. The prevalence of small front-room stores, or pulperías, was so widespread that a FLACSO study of gender and the informal sector with which I was briefly affiliated also focused its interviews in this barrio.

6. In 1992, the mayor's office offered conflicting information on the number of households and the population in the barrio. One source reported 3,115 households and 18,690 residents, while another gave figures of 2,500 households and 30,000 inhabitants (the latter suggesting about 12 residents per household, or double that of the first source). Residents in the barrio tend to estimate somewhere between the two figures, but some estimate that as many as 45,000 live in Monseñor Lezcano.

7. This would add another fifteen or so city blocks to the barrio. In addition, the cemetery takes up the equivalent of another thirty-six city blocks. See Traña Galeano 1991 for a short description of the General Cemetery's history.

8. This hospital, dating back to the Somoza years, still appears as "Leprocomio" (leper colony) on some maps of the barrio. Although it was first directed to those with leprosy, the hospital now treats a range of diseases.

9. I am grateful to Grant Gallup for conversations about this street and its residents, which provide some of the material in these paragraphs.

10. See Kunzle 1995: 122–23 concerning the mural *The Visitation,* or *Under the Volcano.*

11. The ruralization of Managua concerned the Sandinista government enough that cows were officially banned from the city in 1986 (Massey 1987: 102).

12. Casa Ave María is located near the boundary of Barrio Monseñor Lezcano and Barrio Javier Cuadra, which is named for the Sandinista martyr. With the change of boundaries, the Casa may technically be in Javier Cuadra, but they are still paying the lower taxes of Monseñor Lezcano and people consider the street to be part of the latter barrio.

13. Often, stores closed during the Sandinista years when shelves could not be stocked because of shortages and lack of financing.

14. As noted earlier, many place-names in Managua are undergoing changes since 1990. Although the Mercado Roberto Huembes, the second-largest market in the city (after Mercado Oriental, the Eastern Market) has been renamed Mercado Central (Central Market), it is still popularly known by its Sandinista name.

15. By 1996, I found that the company had been sold and was then called Industria Agrosa. It employed only about 80 workers and was producing oil, soap, and flour. The workers I spoke to said that in the heyday of the Aceitera Corona, 3,000 workers were employed in day and night shifts.

16. I was assisted in my interviewing by Alexandra Shutze and María del Socorro (Coco) Miranda Blanco, students at the Central American University, and particularly by Ana Patricia Moreno, a Nicaraguan graduate student from the University of Iowa.

17. Throughout this book, I use fictitious names for those individuals from the barrio, urban cooperatives, and so on, whom I discuss at some length. I mean no disrespect when I refer to them in the text by using fictitious first names only. In some cases, I knew only their first names but referred to them using Don or Doña as a courtesy. This way they had a measure of privacy, and, at the same time, we were able to adopt the conversational informality that is common in Nicaragua. In the case of well-known individuals whose identities would be known in Nicaragua and who would want to have their real names used, full names are given.

18. Such racialized discourse is fairly common in Nicaragua, including among some who are more conscious of class and gender. See Lancaster 1992 for a discussion of race in Managua and Gordon 1998 for an extended analysis of race on the Atlantic coast and in Nicaragua more generally.

19. More reflections on previous and more recent activism in the barrio are found in a *diagnostico* of Barrio Monseñor Lezcano prepared by the FSLN in the months leading up to the 1990 elections.

Chapter Five

1. For discussion of the impact of structural adjustment on women in Nicaragua since 1990, see Fernández Poncela 1996; Metoyer 1997.

2. A number of writers have offered extensive analyses of this decade of revolutionary government in Nicaragua (e.g., Booth 1985; Walker 1986, 1991; Spalding 1987; Martínez Cuenca 1992). A few have considered the situation of women in the revolutionary process (Randall 1981; Molyneux 1986; Padilla, Murguialday, and Criquillon 1987; Collinson 1990).

3. For example, the writers for *Envío*, the monthly magazine of political analysis, published in Managua, Nicaragua.

4. A summary of the effects of neoliberalism is offered by Nicholson in the newsletter *Nicaraguan Developments*, 7, no. 1 (1999): 4–5.

5. Lacayo's extensive televised introduction of the plan was widely viewed as masterful in avoiding widespread panic and opposition to the plan. Lacayo, Chamorro's son-in-law, emerged as the major spokesperson for the UNO government.

6. For a more extensive discussion of structural adjustment programs under the Sandinistas and the UNO government, see Stahler-Sholk (1997). He indicates that while the UNO government made some attempt to soften the adjustment by offering limited support for employment, this barely offset the growing rate of unemployment.

7. See Montoya 1996 for a useful discussion of women's involvement in two rural cooperatives organized during the Sandinista period and the mixed success they had due to difficulties faced by many cooperatives as well as persistent male bias against women's participation in the economy and society beyond the household. Montoya's work also discusses the general problems women faced as they made claims to public space usually controlled by men. See also Pérez Alemán 1990 for a discussion of women's participation in rural cooperatives in the Sandinista period and the difficulty of carrying the burden of housework and child care as they performed more agricultural work.

8. For further discussion of women in cooperatives and small industries in Nicaragua, see Pérez Alemán, Martínez, and Widmair 1989; Montoya 1996; Field 1999.

9. It is possible that Marlene's status as a foreigner gave her a somewhat privileged position within the cooperative and in its relations with CONAPI. However, as a long-term resident who was the most senior co-op member in age and who had no intention of returning to Germany, her foreign status alone did not account for the respect she enjoyed. As the co-op explored international markets, she was able to call on German resources in a limited way, with little success.

10. CONAPI formed in 1983 and was officially founded in 1989. The first president was a Sandinista appointee, Ana Lorena Rondon. The association is discussed at much greater length in chapter 8.

11. I later learned that, before returning home, Blanca worked briefly selling meat at Mercado Huembes.

12. In addition, Paola later told me that any earnings she brings home her husband is likely to spend at the cockfights, his weekend addiction. Another reason she has not sought to work outside the home is that there have been robberies nearby and she worries about leaving her house unattended.

13. Several women from the Atlantic Coast came for about a month at a time to train at the cooperative, whose members wanted to support women of the region from which much of their material came (with, perhaps, the added advantage of keeping up personal connections in that region to facilitate economic exchanges).

14. Some women told me that the store had been sold and the money divided among the members. Teresa, however, said that some money from rent had been distributed but the store was not yet sold; she felt certain it would be soon. I was unable to discover why such radically different versions of the story were related to me. Quite clearly, once the store was gone, the women had less frequent communication and information was unevenly shared.

15. Another sewing cooperative that I visited several times over the years, the Julia Pomares Cooperative, had an interesting history that suggests that even with a central work space, hard work, and international solidarity, current conditions are destructive to small industry. This co-op, named in honor of the wife of the martyr German Pomares, was founded in 1984 by thirty seamstresses who received support from CONAPI in the form of materials. In 1988, they suffered under the Sandinista adjustment, but with the help of a German activist who joined them that year they continued to find markets, especially from international support groups. After 1990, neoliberalism eroded their ability to sustain the co-op and finally, in 1998, they decided to close.

16. The office building remained on the market for at least a year, and I do not know whether the membership ever benefited from the sale, as they should have distributed proceeds from the sale of the property.

17. Women had acquired work in nontraditional areas in part because of men's greater involvement in the Contra war. The head of the women's division of INATEC told me that as men demobilized and sought to return to work, women were threatened with loss of their jobs. Her office prepared women to challenge the traditional division of labor and find stable employment.

18. I have written more about the politics of the informal sector elsewhere (Babb 1997a). For a brief consideration of gender and the urban informal sector in Central America, see Pérez Sáinz and Menjívar Larín 1994; the authors consider the growth of the informal sector to be related to the degree to which structural adjustment measures were implemented and also, in the case of Nicaragua, to external interventions by the United States.

Chapter Six

1. Field's (1999) ethnographic research on artisans in western Nicaragua may be cited for its attention to small-scale manufacturers of pottery during the Sandinista period.

2. In some cases, the line between working independently and in microenterprises was blurred, as in the case of the mother of Doris, one of the welders discussed in the last chapter. Doris told me that her mother, who had a pulpería for many years, had formed a microenterprise with other women operating pulperías in order to receive assistance from the NGO known as FAMA. Her mother, however, did not appear to identify as a *microempresaria*.

3. This is revealed in De Franco's (1979) doctoral dissertation on the informal sector in Nicaragua before 1979.

4. While most programs supporting microenterprises did not direct special support to women, a few did, including the national technical institute SINACAP (later INATEC). The Instituto Nicaragüense de la Mujer (INIM), or Nicaraguan Women's Institute, and the INCAE's Women's Program also directed attention to women in microenterprises. The NGO MEDA conducted a study of women microentrepreneurs and access to credit and then directed assistance to women; a Dutch couple who staffed MEDA until 1992 deliberately targeted support to women because they knew that women were more likely than men to direct their incomes to family needs rather than their personal needs.

5. This document defines microenterprises as having up to five individuals and a maximum capital of U.S. $5,000, although the average work unit is found to have an investment of just U.S. $638.

6. Social movements since the 1990 national election are taken up in more detail in chapter 8.

Chapter Seven

1. The woman at the meeting, held July 21–23, 1993, identified herself as an organizer, and she later led the other women in a consciousness-raising session. Her reference to neoliberalism (spoken of often in present-day Nicaragua) and, especially, postmodernism (rarely mentioned except among intellectuals) set her apart as more highly educated than most of the women present. Nevertheless, it was unclear why she referred to postmodernism except to allude to theorizing as oppressive to nonelites. Her comment has remained in my mind as I have explored how postmodernism may contribute to critiques of neoliberalism.

2. I occasionally use quotation marks to call into question the meaning of particular terms.

3. To a certain degree, this rethinking stems from my previous work, in which I have taken a critical view of Western-defined development, resisting any notion that such development would free third world societies from poverty and underdevelopment (Babb 1989, 1997a). That work has built on the critical writings of Marxist, feminist, and other scholars, a number of them from non-Western societies.

4. See Mohanty 1988 for a key discussion of representations of "third world" women in feminist scholarship and colonial discourses.

5. For a discussion of Latin American social and cultural movements that call for the fundamental "right to have rights" and that include the body, gender, and sexuality in their purview, see Balderston and Guy 1997; Alvarez, Dagnino, and Escobar 1998. A fuller treatment of the subject in the Nicaraguan context would need to examine the sexual politics of reproductive rights and of the emergent lesbian and gay movement (see chap. 8).

6. See Spalding 1994 and Walker 1997 for further discussion of these policies.

7. For further discussion of the UNO's conservative gender agenda, see Kampwirth 1996b.

8. This interview with Antonio Chávez of CONAPI was conducted on May 8, 1991, the same day as the preceding interview with María Hurtado de Vigil in the Ministry of the Economy, presenting an interesting contrast. CONAPI has received very little attention from writers assessing organizations formed under the Sandinistas. My personal communication with the political scientists Tom Walker and Rose Spalding confirms my sense that because the association has had few resources and thus has been weak in comparison with other sectoral

and trade organizations, it has gone largely unnoticed. In my own research I had many occasions to visit CONAPI, which I discuss further in chapter 8.

9. We should not be surprised, however, that the Left in Nicaragua has not come up with concrete proposals for alternatives to neoliberalism. Throughout Latin America, the Left has produced an ideological critique and has called for mechanisms to protect those social sectors in the most precarious positions, but few have clung to "the purity of revolutionary struggle and of socialism" or suggested a new alternative (Zamora 1995: 11).

10. For more discussion of the cultural politics of economic development and the free market model, see contributions to Rosen and McFadyen (1995) and Alvarez, Dagnino, and Escobar (1998).

11. In chapters 4 and 5, I describe the four cooperatives I followed most closely over the years as well as this barrio in the western part of Managua where I lived for some time and interviewed in several city blocks.

12. See chapter 3 for a discussion of the changing face of Managua.

13. A number of writers have discussed popular organizations that formed under the Sandinistas, including the Community Movement and Mothers of Heroes and Martyrs. For a recent review from the vantage point of the mid-1990s, see Walker 1997. I discuss the organizations at greater length in chapter 8.

14. In making this argument I do not wish to overlook the fact that working-class people are also capable of political analysis and that middle-class people somatize their politics as much as workers, as shown elsewhere in this chapter.

15. A more extensive discussion of economic development and nationhood would also go beyond gender and class to include attention to issues of race and ethnicity. The notion of "Nicaragua mestiza" masks significant cultural differences in the country that continue to limit the prospects of a national project. For historical and anthropological examinations of these questions, see Lancaster 1992; Gordon 1998; Gould 1998; Field 1999.

16. For a useful discussion of gender, race, and nation building in Latin America, see Radcliffe and Westwood 1996.

17. Alemán seeks to avoid charges of corruption and Ortega seeks continued immunity from charges of long-term sexual abuse made by his adoptive stepdaughter (Envío 1999b).

18. During the last few years, the feminist NGO Puntos de Encuentro has made this slogan well known though its publication La Boletina, bumper stickers, and so on.

19. For more discussion of popular organizations and social movements in the 1990s, see Walker 1997.

20. For a recent discussion by Nicaraguan analysts of the prospects for the emergence of a political alternative in the country and a case for civil society as the likely source, having the visionary capacity and the ability to put pressure on

political parties and the government, see *Envío* 1999e. A similar point is made for Latin America in general by Petras and Morley (1992: 193), who view the growth of social movements as "the most formidable force for transforming society."

Chapter Eight

1. For assessments of these sectoral organizations, see Polakoff and La Ramée 1997.
2. For discussion of women's participation in the Sandinista revolution, see Collinson 1990; Murguialday 1990; Rodríguez 1990. For more recent assessments of the development of the women's movement and feminism into the 1990s, see Randall 1992; Chinchilla 1994; *Barricada Internacional* 1995a; Criquillon 1995; Kampwirth 1996a; Montenegro 1997; and contributions by María Teresa Blandón and Sofia Montenegro in Küppers 1994. The proceedings from the women's conferences that I mention are also excellent resources. In Babb 1997a, I discuss the Nicaraguan women's movement in relation to feminism in Latin America.
3. Ewig (1999) offers a useful analysis of the democratic potential of the NGO-based women's movement in Nicaragua from the vantage point of the mid-1990s. Her work points toward the important question of whether, now that the women's movement is no longer solely identified with AMNLAE and controlled by the FSLN, dependence on and competition for international support may limit prospects for self-sufficiency and dictate new agendas. As Ewig notes, most of the fifty-nine NGOs currently identified with the women's movement are headed by middle-class professional women who speak the language of transnational feminism; working-class women activists seeking support for their programs may be disfavored.
4. I attended the national women's conference in January 1992, but I was out of the country during the Montelimar conference of Central American feminists two months later. However, I did attend AMNLAE's fifth national assembly held outside Managua in El Crucero just a few days later. About four hundred delegates participated and were welcomed by coordinator Gladys Báez, who addressed the achievements of AMNLAE's forty-eight *casas de la mujer* (women's houses) in offering medical and legal services, technical training, and consciousness-raising workshops. The opening plenary was interrupted by chants of "Without the participation of women, there is no revolution" and "Not one step back," familiar Sandinista slogans. Daniel Ortega entered to wild applause by the largely working-class and popular-sector women in attendance. Later, commissions and working groups met to discuss a range of issues.
5. Adams (1957) contributed to this notion with his cultural survey of Central America. After spending a brief time in Nicaragua, he found little to distinguish "In-

dian" populations from the rest of society. That those in the indigenous barrio of Sutiaba in León spoke Spanish and dressed like mestizos led him to a view of the "deculturation" of Indians in the region. More recently, scholars have countered the notion of indigenous cultural extinction (Whisnant 1995: 179–80; Gould 1998: 7; Field 1999: 29–31). Nicaraguan intellectuals have also engaged in the discussion, with Jaime Wheelock holding the view that the indigenous population was extinguished in the nineteenth century and Marcos Membreño calling for more attention to the still-indigenous cultures in the Pacific region.

6. There may be a danger of equating "the indigenous" with "resources," or of idealizing indigenous peoples who are actually quite diverse, culturally and politically. This may be seen in the discourses of some international activists as well as scholars. I do not mean to commit the same error in my discussion of indigenous people, the environment, and peace. Obviously, indigenous people are social subjects and the environment and peace are social issues (although raised by environmentalists and peace activists as social subjects). My grouping of these three stems from their impact on independent social movements.

7. From the poem "Paz" by Rubén Darío (1988), translated by Lysander Kemp.

8. In addition to my interviews with members of CONAPI, I have consulted the few written sources that describe the organization. Among these are Santamaría 1990 and Pérez Alemán et al. 1991. The principal author of the latter, Paola Pérez Alemán, was commissioned by CONAPI to conduct an analysis of the situation of women in small and micro industry in Nicaragua. I am indebted to her for introducing me to CONAPI and two of the cooperatives that became central to my research. Since 1992, CONAPI has published a bimonthly magazine, *El Pequeño Industrial*, presenting news and opinions for distribution to the membership, which I have consulted as well.

9. When I interviewed Rondon in 1993, she was no longer active in CONAPI. She was not a worker in small industry at the time of her political appointment, and in 1993 she was just launching a business in the sale of leather to artisans making shoes, handbags, and so on. In general, she described CONAPI as having lost ground and "space" since the time the organization was founded under the Sandinistas. She also commented on the founding of PAMIC by Minister of the Economy Silvio De Franco and said that now "everything is microenterprise" (Ana Lorena Rondon, interview, July 8, 1993).

10. This study is exceptional in calling for women's programs to accommodate their domestic responsibilities. Pérez Alemán urged that women members of CONAPI be brought into the planning process and that programs be held in convenient locations near women's homes with attention to the need for transportation and child care. Moreover, she recommended attention to gender issues in all of CONAPI's programming, not just in courses and meetings directed specifically to women.

11. I use the terms "lesbian" and "gay" to signal the self-conscious political organizing of women and men who so identify in Nicaragua. Most often, the words *lesbiana* and *homosexual* are used, but occasionally *gay* is used. As I indicate in this chapter, some Nicaraguans are inclusive enough to employ the terminology LGBTT (lesbian-gay-bisexual-transgender-transvestite), but those who have played a public role in the movement generally identify as lesbian or gay.

12. See also the work of Howe (1999), who is particularly attentive to how gender and sexuality figure in questions of nationhood and how the global articulates with the local in the making of social movements at the turn of the twenty-first century. I am grateful to Cymene Howe for her useful comments on my discussion of lesbian and gay organizing.

13. A few years ago, I might have hesitated to relate this incident, but now it has been discussed in print by a number of Nicaraguans in the more open discussion about the Sandinista period. In the published interviews by Randall that I cite, no one suggests the sort of harsh repression of gay politics found in some other countries. Moreover, no one compares the treatment of lesbians and gay men to the better-known suppression of human rights of indigenous peoples of the Atlantic Coast during the Sandinista years.

14. Memories of the details of political organizing among lesbians and gay men vary slightly but are in broad agreement.

15. *Sex and the Sandinistas* is a video directed by Lucinda Broadbent (England, 1991). Interestingly, the video has been shown widely internationally but could not be shown in Managua because some gay Nicaraguans who appeared in it voiced their desire not to be "outed" publicly (*El País* 1992: 9).

16. This was noted by the feminist philosopher Ann Ferguson (1992) soon after the UNO victory in 1990.

17. At the international level, opposition was strong as well. A letter from the International Commission for Gay and Lesbian Human Rights (based in San Francisco) protesting Article 204 appeared in *Barricada*, June 21, 1992. Amnesty International also protested.

18. There may be several reasons for this greater participation by women, including the longer-term activism of feminists, among them lesbians (many of whom participated in the National Feminist Committee), and also gay men's greater involvement with the specific issue of AIDS in Nicaragua. One well-known collective of gay men was SHomos, which along with the lesbian group Nosotras was under the wing of Xochiquetzal.

19. I noted that the following day newspapers did not report the event. Instead, *Barricada* ran the front-page headline, "Women in the Ring!" about women in a boxing match in Managua.

20. There were more gay bars under the Somoza government, but they generally closed during the Sandinista government. Public spaces for gay men were few,

and many used the area near Lake Managua and in the old cathedral, until it was boarded up, for cruising. For lesbians, public space was virtually nonexistent. New bars, mainly directed to men, began opening after 1990, particularly with the return of the "Miami boys." Still, obtaining a permit was sometimes difficult, as in the case of a bar that was denied permission to open in 1991 in Las Palmas, a middle-class neighborhood near President Chamorro's home (*Times of the Americas*, December 11, 1991, 10–11).

21. The terminology may be confusing here, as a "gay" bar in Nicaragua would indeed attract mainly men. What was interesting in this case was the inclusiveness of the announcement of the new bar, which nonetheless drew men almost exclusively. In talking to this young man, it was my impression that lesbians were simply not on his "radar screen."

22. Transvestism may also be observed in Nicaraguan culture among men not generally identified as either "gay" or "cochones." See Lancaster 1997 for a discussion of one young man's spontaneous performance in a Managua barrio. See also Codina 1992 for a view of the historical and cultural participation of "travestis" in Nicaragua and elsewhere in Central America, for example, among market sellers and in traditional fiestas.

23. A case of lesbian-baiting occurred in 1995 when a well-known Sandinista and the first woman to be considered seriously for the party's National Directorate (DN) was publicly rumored — on the Sandinista station Radio Yá — to be having an affair with the daughter of the former FSLN vice president and leader of the MRS. She stepped down from consideration for the DN, evidently in part due to the scandal.

24. On June 10, 1998, Murillo took out a paid half-page in *La Prensa* to publish her letter to the representatives of the National Commission on Human Rights, in which she made precisely the same claim. The next day, the same paper reported that she had sought benediction and affirmed her "return to God," showing her with clasped hands in prayer alongside Cardinal Obando y Bravo.

25. This same woman, the head of CONAPI's Women's Program, revealed a keen interest in gay culture and said that she had been "pursued" by lesbians. She had once visited a gay bar and also reported on that year's Ms. Gay pageant, held the same week as the Miss Nicaragua pageant, and admired the drag queens' elegant dress.

26. Laura Kipnis (1999) offers a particularly cynical reading of the Nicaraguan sex scandal. She draws some interesting parallels with the Clinton scandal in the United States that was unfolding at the same time but suggests that Narvaez's decision to go public with her allegation was motivated largely by the cultural politics of Western feminism and "abuse narratives" pitched to an international audience. The analysis is provocative but underestimates Nicaraguan

women's ongoing (local) struggles over domestic violence as well as the complicated set of circumstances surrounding the allegation.

27. Of course, we can trace the beginnings of this concern to the Sandinista period, when political attention and legislation was directed to what Kampwirth (1998) describes as personal politics and power dynamics in the family. She identifies emergent concerns over reproduction, contraception, abortion, prostitution, legitimacy, and the rights of sexual minorities. Although she would not refer to these concerns, as I do, in terms of "body politics" (Kampwirth pers. com.), it is striking that all embrace rights to personhood and the body. In the post-Sandinista 1990s, social movements addressed these issues more forcefully, although they often met greater resistance from the government.

Chapter Nine

1. At the 1999 meetings of the American Anthropological Association, Ruth Behar referred to the "rediscovery" of Cuba and the "Buena Vista Socialization" of Cuban culture in the United States.
2. See Bouvard 1994 and Arditti 1999 for discussion of the mothers and grandmothers of the Plaza de Mayo who continue to call attention to two generations of "disappeared" family members and relatives in Argentina.
3. This was the topic of a panel at the 1999 meetings of the American Anthropological Association (AAA) in Chicago, "Between Remembering and Forgetting at the Close of the 20th Century: Truth, Reconciliation and Social Justice in Latin America." I co-organized (with Rosario Montoya) a session for the 2000 meetings of the AAA titled "Remembering Nicaragua and Cuba." The recent controversy over Rigoberta Menchú's Guatemalan testimony reveals how fraught is the process of remembering and interpreting personal and collective histories in Latin America.
4. The Central American region as a whole lost strategic importance to the United States in the 1990s and in that sense has been forgotten — something that may be beneficial or harmful depending on the circumstances (Puig 2000: 33).
5. See Massey 1994 for an important feminist theorization of the cultural geography of gender.
6. For example, the Wisconsin Coordinating Council on Nicaragua (WCCN) has sponsored tours to Nicaragua of health care workers who offer training in "emotional reconstruction" to local women leaders. See *Sister City Update* 15, no. 2 (Fall 1999). Paula J. Ford (2000) also describes the process of "social healing" by Nicaraguan women confronting problems of domestic violence and maternal mortality.

7. For example, the political scientist Tom Walker, whose work is cited in several chapters, may have conducted the longest ongoing research in the country. Cynthia Chávez Metoyer (2000) has written a book that considers economic policy change and the women's movement in Nicaragua during the post-Sandinista decade. Rosario Montoya and James Quesada are two more scholars whose important work on Nicaragua is appearing in print and who are continuing to do research in the country.

8. While earlier predictions were that the devastation of Hurricane Mitch would cause a large number of people from the affected area to migrate to Managua, most relocation to the city appears to have been temporary. In the view of some who have followed the consequences of Mitch, residents of the region have come to regard the hurricane as one more setback among many they have experienced in their lifetimes.

9. I am grateful to Nadine Jubb (e-mail com., July 25, 2000) and also to those at the Ben Linder House who discussed with me the social class implications of Managua's urban development of the last few years. Jubb points out that there are really two new centers of Managua. Alemán has rebuilt the old center with new government buildings, notably the new presidential palace (largely with support from Taiwan), along with fountains and plazas. The Metrocentro commercial center and hotels under construction along the Masaya highway offer competition as another downtown focal point.

10. Several human rights organizations, including the Group for Lesbian Visibility, have publicized the case through leaflets protesting the legal system's failure to bring those accused of committing the murder to justice and to protect the rights of lesbians and gay men.

11. For discussion of these maneuvers, see *Nicaragua Alert!* (July 2000: 7).

12. As I write this postscript, National Public Radio is featuring a lengthy report on the firing of women workers at the Chentex factory, a Taiwanese multinational located in Managua (NPR, August 18, 2000).

BIBLIOGRAPHY

Abercrombie, Thomas. 1998. "Commentary." *Journal of Latin American Anthropology* 3(2): 150–67.

Aburto, Juan. 1989. *Managua en la memoria*. Managua, Nicaragua: Editorial Vanguardia.

Adam, Barry. 1989. "Pasivos y Activos en Nicaragua: Homosexuality Without a Gay World." *Out/Look* (Winter): 74–82.

Adams, Richard. 1957. *Cultural Surveys of Panama-Nicaragua-Guatemala-El Salvador-Honduras*. Washington, DC: Pan American Sanitary Bureau, Regional Office of the World Health Organization.

Afshar, Haleh, and Carolyne Dennis, eds. 1992. *Women and Adjustment Policies in the Third World*. New York: St. Martin's Press.

Aguiar, Neuma, ed. 1990. *Mujer y crisis: Respuestas ante la recesión*. Caracas, Venezuela· Editorial Nueva Sociedad.

Alemán, Verónica. 1993. Sexist Laws Scorched. *Barricada Internacional* XIII(359): 19–20.

Alemán, Verónica, and Carla Miranda. 1993. Networking to Solve Their Problems. *Barricada Internacional* XIII(362): 23–25.

Alvarez, Sonia E. 1990. *Engendering Democracy in Brazil: Women's Movements in Transition Politics*. Princeton, NJ: Princeton University Press.

Alvarez, Sonia E., Evelina Dagnino, and Arturo Escobar, eds. 1998. *Cultures of Politics, Politics of Cultures: Re-visioning Latin American Social Movements*. Boulder, CO: Westview Press.

Appadurai, Arjun. 1996. *Modernity at Large: Cultural Dimensions of Globalization*. Minneapolis: University of Minnesota Press.

Appadurai, Arjun, and Carol A. Breckenridge. 1992. "Museums Are Good to Think." In *Museums and Communities: The Politics of Public Culture*. Ivan Karp, Christine Mullen Kreamer, and Steven D. Lavine, eds. Pp. 34–55. Washington, DC: Smithsonian Institution Press.

Arana, Mario. 1997. "General Economic Policy." In *Nicaragua without Illusions: Regime Transition and Structural Adjustment in the 1990s*. Thomas W. Walker, ed. Pp. 81–96. Wilmington, DE: SR Books.

282   AFTER REVOLUTION

Arditti, Rita. 1999. *Searching for Life: The Grandmothers of the Plaza de Mayo and the Disappeared Children of Argentina.* Berkeley: University of California Press.

Babb, Florence E. 1986. "Producers and Reproducers: Andean Marketwomen in the Economy." In *Women and Change in Latin America.* June Nash and Helen I. Safa, eds. Pp. 53–64. South Hadley, MA: Bergin and Garvey.

———. 1989. *Between Field and Cooking Pot: The Political Economy of Market-women in Peru.* Austin: University of Texas Press.

———. 1997a. "Women, Informal Economies, and the State in Peru and Nicaragua." In *Women and Economic Change: Andean Perspectives.* Ann Miles and Hans Buechler, eds. Pp. 89–100. Washington, DC: American Anthropological Association.

———. 1997b. "Women's Movements and Feminism." In *Cross-Cultural Research for Social Science.* Carol R. Ember and Melvin Ember, eds. Pp. 23–40. Englewood Cliffs, NJ: Prentice Hall.

Balderston, Daniel, and Donna J. Guy, eds. 1997. *Sex and Sexuality in Latin America.* New York: New York University Press.

Barricada Internacional. 1993. "Recession Decimates Small Businesses." January: 7.

———. 1995a. "Separation Time." January: 4–5.

———. 1995b. "Divided Forces: The Nicaraguan Feminist Movement." March: 17–24.

Benería, Lourdes, and Shelley Feldman, eds. 1992. *Unequal Burden: Economic Crises, Persistent Poverty, and Women's Work.* Boulder, CO: Westview Press.

Beverley, John, and José Oviedo. 1993. "Introduction." In *The Postmodernism Debate in Latin America.* John Beverley and José Oviedo, eds. *Boundary* 2, 20(3): 1–17.

Beverley, John, and Marc Zimmerman. 1990. *Literature and Politics in the Central American Revolutions.* Austin: University of Texas Press.

Blumberg, Rae Lesser. 1991. "Income under Female versus Male Control: Hypotheses from a Theory of Gender Stratification and Data from the Third World." In *Gender, Family, and Economy: The Triple Overlap.* Rae Lesser Blumberg, ed. Pp. 97–127. Newbury Park, CA: Sage.

Bolt González, Mary. 1996. *Sencillamente diferentes . . . : La autoestima de las mujeres lesbianas en los sectores urbanos de Nicaragua.* Managua, Nicaragua: Centro Editorial de la Mujer (CEM).

Booth, John A. 1985. *The End and the Beginning: The Nicaraguan Revolution.* Boulder, CO: Westview Press.

Borland, Katherine. 1994. "The India Bonita of Monimbó: The Politics of Ethnic Identity in the New Nicaragua." In *Beauty Queens on the Global Stage: Gender, Contexts, and Power.* C. Ballerino Cohen, R. Wilk, and B. Stoeltje, eds. Pp. 75–88. New York: Routledge.

Bouvard, Marguerite Guzman. 1994. *Revolutionizing Motherhood: The Mothers of the Plaza de Mayo*. Wilmington, DE: SR Books.

Brenes, Ada Julia, Ivania Lovo, Olga Luz Restrepo, and Sylvia Saakes. 1991a. "La reforma económica y su impacto en las mujeres del sector popular urbano de Managua." In *La mujer nicaragüense en los años 80*. Ada Julia Brenes, Ivania Lovo, Olga Luz Restrepo, Sylvia Saakes, and Flor de María Zúniga, eds. Pp. 207–44. Managua, Nicaragua: Nicarao.

Brenes, Ada Julia, Ivania Lovo, Olga Luz Restrepo, Sylvia Saakes, and Flor de María Zúniga. 1991b. *La mujer nicaragüense en los años 80*. Managua, Nicaragua: Nicarao.

Brentlinger, John. 1995. *The Best of What We Are: Reflections on the Nicaraguan Revolution*. Amherst: University of Massachusetts Press.

Broadbent, Lucinda. 1991. *Sex and the Sandinistas*. Video. England.

Burawoy, Michael. 1999. "Afterword." In *Uncertain Transition: Ethnographies of Change in the Postsocialist World*. Michael Burawoy and Katherine Verdery, eds. Pp 301–11. Lanham, MD: Rowman and Littlefield.

Burawoy, Michael, and Katherine Verdery. 1999. "Introduction." In *Uncertain Transition: Ethnographies of Change in the Postsociulist World*. Michael Burawoy and Katherine Verdery, eds. Pp. 1–17. Lanham, MD: Rowman and Littlefield.

Burns, E. Bradford. 1991. *Patriarch and Folk: The Emergence of Nicaragua, 1798– 1858*. Cambridge, MA: Harvard University Press.

Butler, Judy. 1997. "The Peoples of the Atlantic Coast." In *Nicaragua without Illusions: Regime Transition and Structural Adjustment in the 1990s*. Thomas W. Walker, ed. Pp. 219–34. Wilmington, DE: SR Books.

Caldeira, Teresa P. R. 1999. "Fortified Enclaves: The New Urban Segregation." In *Cities and Citizenship*. James Holston, ed. Pp. 114–38. Durham, NC: Duke University Press.

Carvajal, Luis. 1996. Interview with author. Managua, Nicaragua, July 3.

———. 1998. Interview with author. Managua, Nicaragua, June 9.

Centro de Investigación y Estudios de la Reforma Agraria (CIERA). 1984. "Managua es Nicaragua." Unpublished manuscript. Managua, Nicaragua.

Chamorro, Amalia, Mario Chávez, and Marcos Membreño. 1989. "El debate sobre el sector informal urbano en Nicaragua (1979–1989)." In *Informalidad urbana en Centroamérica: Evidencias e interrogantes*. R. Menjívar Larín and J. P. Pérez Sáinz, eds. Pp. 153–86. Guatemala City: Fundación Friedrich Ebert.

———. 1991. "El sector informal en Nicaragua." In *Informalidad urbana en Centroamérica: Entre la acumulación y la subsistencia*. J. P. Pérez Sáinz and R. Menjívar Larín, eds. Pp. 217–57. Caracas, Venezuela: Editorial Nueva Sociedad.

Chávez, Antonio. 1991. Interview with author. Managua, Nicaragua, May 8.

Chinchilla, Norma. 1994. "Feminism, Revolution and Democratic Transitions in

Nicaragua." In *The Women's Movement in Latin America,* 2d ed. Jane Jaquette, ed. Pp. 177–97. Boulder, CO: Westview Press.

Close, David. 1999. *Nicaragua: The Chamorro Years.* Boulder, CO: Lynne Rienner.

Codina, Teresa. 1992. "Lesbos en el Nuevo Mundo." *Pensamiento Propio* 10(94): 2–4.

Colburn, Forrest D. 1991. *My Car in Managua.* Austin: University of Texas Press.

Collinson, Helen, ed. 1990. *Women and Revolution in Nicaragua.* London: Zed Books.

Cornia, Giovanni Andrea, Richard Jolly, and Frances Stewart, eds. 1987. *Adjustment with a Human Face.* New York: Oxford University Press.

Criquillon, Ana. 1995. "The Nicaraguan Women's Movement: Feminist Reflections from Within." In *The New Politics of Survival: Grassroots Movements in Central America.* Minor Sinclair, ed. Pp. 209–37. New York: Monthly Review Press.

Cuadra, Pablo Antonio. 1993. *El nicaragüense.* Managua, Nicaragua: Hispamer.

Darío, Rubén. 1988. *Selected Poems of Rubén Darío.* Translated by Lysander Kemp. Austin: University of Texas Press.

Davis, Peter. 1987. *Where Is Nicaragua?* New York: Simon and Schuster.

De Franco, Silvio. 1979. "Employment and the Urban Informal Sector: The Case of Managua." Ph.D. dissertation, University of Wisconsin. University Microfilms.

De Franco, Silvio, and José Luis Velázquez. 1997. "Democratic Transitions in Nicaragua." In *Democratic Transitions in Central America.* Jorge I. Domínguez and Marc Lindenberg, eds. Pp. 85–110. Gainesville: University Press of Florida.

di Leonardo, Micaela. 1993. "What Difference Political Economy Makes: Feminist Anthropology in the Postmodern Era." *Anthropological Quarterly* 66(2): 76–80.

Didion, Joan. 1983. *Salvador.* New York: Simon and Schuster.

Diskin, Martin. 1983. *Trouble in Our Backyard.* New York: Pantheon Books.

DuBois, Marc. 1991. "The Governance of the Third World: A Foucauldian Perspective on Power Relations in Development." *Alternatives* 16(1): 1–30.

Einhorn, Barbara. 1993. *Cinderella Goes to the Market: Citizenship, Gender and Women's Movements in East Central Europe.* London: Verso.

Elizondo, Desirée. 1997. "The Environment." In *Nicaragua without Illusions: Regime Transition and Structural Adjustment in the 1990s.* Thomas W. Walker, ed. Pp. 131–45. Wilmington, DE: SR Books.

Elson, Diane. 1992. "From Survival Strategies to Transformation Strategies: Women's Needs and Structural Adjustment." In *Unequal Burden: Economic Crises, Persistent Poverty, and Women's Work.* Lourdes Benería and Shelley Feldman, eds. Pp. 26–48. Boulder, CO: Westview Press.

Elson, Diane, ed. 1991. *Male Bias in the Development Process.* Manchester, England: Manchester University Press.

Enríquez, Laura J. 1991. *Harvesting Change: Labor and Agrarian Reform in Nicaragua, 1979–90*. Chapel Hill: University of North Carolina Press.

Envío. 1991. "Women in Nicaragua: The Revolution on Hold." 10(119): 30–41.

———. 1992a. "Economic Takeoff: The Little Train That Couldn't." 11(135): 18–20.

———. 1992b. "A National Project." 11(137): 31–40.

———. 1993. "The Far Right: 10 Months on the Offensive; and USAID's Strategy in Nicaragua." 12(142): 3–10.

———. 1994. "Happy New Year from the IMF." 12(150): 3–9.

———. 1998a. "Nicaragua: A Country Still in the Making." 17(207): 3–8.

———. 1998b. "A Time for Opportunities and Opportunists." 17(209): 3–13.

———. 1999a. "Nicaragua Briefs." 18(210–11): 28–31.

———. 1999b. "Domestic Violence on the Rise." 18(212): 25.

———. 1999c. "The Zoilamérica Case." 18(215): 30.

———. 1999d. "The Pact's Roots Go Deep and Its Fruits Are Rotten." 18(216): 3–11.

———. 1999e. "Is the Game All Sewn Up? Questions and Contradictions." 18(218): 3–11.

Escobar, Arturo. 1984–85. "Discourse and Power in Development: Michel Foucault and the Relevance of His Work to the Third World." *Alternatives* 10(3): 377–400.

———. 1992. "Culture, Economics, and Politics in Latin American Social Movements." In *The Making of Social Movements in Latin America: Identity, Strategy, and Democracy*. Arturo Escobar and Sonia E. Alvarez, eds. Pp. 62–85. Boulder, CO: Westview Press.

———. 1995. *Encountering Development: The Making and Unmaking of the Third World*. Princeton, NJ: Princeton University Press.

Escobar, Arturo, and Sonia E. Alvarez, eds. 1992. *The Making of Social Movements in Latin America: Identity, Strategy, and Democracy*. Boulder, CO: Westview Press.

Evans, Trevor. 1995. *La transformación neoliberal del sector público*. Managua, Nicaragua: CRIES (Coordinadora Regional de Investigaciones Económicas y Sociales).

Ewig, Christina. 1999. "The Strengths and Limits of the NGO Women's Movement Model: Shaping Nicaragua's Democratic Institutions." *Latin American Research Review* 34(3): 75–102.

Fagen, Richard R., Carmen Diana Deere, and José Luis Coraggio, eds. 1986. *Transition and Development: Problems of Third World Socialism*. New York: Monthly Review Press.

Feijóo, María del Carmen. 1989. "The Challenge of Constructing Civilian Peace: Women and Democracy in Argentina." In *The Women's Movement in Latin America*. Jane S. Jaquette, ed. Pp. 72–94. Boston: Unwin Hyman.

Ferguson, Ann. 1991. "Lesbianism, Feminism, and Empowerment in Nicaragua." *Socialist Review* 21(3–4): 75–97.

Ferguson, James. 1990. *The Anti-Politics Machine: "Development," Depoliticization, and Bureaucratic Power in Lesotho.* New York: Cambridge University Press.

Ferlinghetti, Lawrence. 1984. *Seven Days in Nicaragua Libre.* San Francisco: City Lights Books.

Fernández Poncela, Anna M. 1996. "The Disruptions of Adjustment: Women in Nicaragua." *Latin American Perspectives* 23(1): 49–66.

FIDEG (Fundación Internacional para el Desafío Económico Global). 1991a. *Seminario regional: El impacto de las políticas de ajuste sobre la mujer en centroamérica y Panama.* Managua, Nicaragua.

———. 1991b. *Situación del sector informal en la ciudad de Managua.* Managua, Nicaragua.

Field, Les W. 1998. "Post-Sandinista Ethnic Identities in Western Nicaragua." *American Anthropologist* 100(2): 431–43.

———. 1999. *The Grimace of Macho Ratón: Artisans, Identity, and Nation in Late-Twentieth-Century Western Nicaragua.* Durham, NC: Duke University Press.

Fincher, Ruth, and Jane M. Jacobs, eds. 1998. *Cities of Difference.* New York: Guilford Press.

Fisher, Jo. 1993. *Out of the Shadows: Women, Resistance and Politics in South America.* London: Latin America Bureau.

Ford, Paula J. 2000. "Narratives of Social Healing: Cultural Politics and the Nicaraguan Women's Movement." Ph.D. dissertation, University of Iowa.

Foucault, Michel. 1984. *The History of Sexuality.* Vol. 1. Hammondsworth, England: Penguin.

Fox, Richard G. 1972. "Rationale and Romance in Urban Anthropology." *Urban Anthropology* 1(2): 205–33.

Fundación Internacional "Rubén Darío." 1995. "Memorias." *Simposio: Identidad y crisis: Influencia del intelectual en la sociedad nicaragüense.* Managua, Nicaragua: Fundación Internacional "Rubén Darío."

Gal, Susan, and Gail Kligman. 2000. *The Politics of Gender after Socialism.* Princeton, NJ: Princeton University Press.

Gibson, Bill. 1987. "A Structural Overview of the Nicaraguan Economy." In *The Political Economy of Revolutionary Nicaragua.* Rose J. Spalding, ed. Pp. 5–41. London: Allen and Unwin.

Gilbert, Dennis. 1988. *Sandinistas: The Party and the Revolution.* Cambridge, MA: Basil Blackwell.

Gladwin, Christina, ed. 1991. *Structural Adjustment and African Women Farmers.* Gainesville: University of Florida Press.

Gordon, Deborah A. 1995. "Conclusion: Culture Writing Women: Inscribing

Feminist Anthropology." In *Women Writing Culture*. Ruth Behar and Deborah A. Gordon, eds. Pp. 429–41. Berkeley: University of California Press.

Gordon, Edmund T. 1998. *Disparate Diasporas: Identity and Politics in an African-Nicaraguan Community*. Austin: University of Texas Press.

Gordon, Rebecca. 1986. *Letters from Nicaragua*. San Francisco: Spinsters/Aunt Lute.

Gould, Jeffrey L. 1998. *To Die in This Way: Nicaraguan Indians and the Myth of Mestizaje, 1880–1965*. Durham, NC: Duke University Press.

Grosfoguel, Ramón, Frances Negrón-Muntaner, and Chloé S. Georas. 1997. "Introduction: Beyond Nationalist and Colonialist Discourses: The *Jaiba* Politics of the Puerto Rican Ethno-Nation." In *Puerto Rican Jam: Rethinking Colonialism and Nationalism*. Frances Negrón-Muntaner and Ramón Grosfoguel, eds. Pp. 1–36. Minneapolis: University of Minnesota Press.

Guillermoprieto, Alma. 1995. "Managua, 1990." In *The Heart That Bleeds: Latin America Now*. Pp. 23–46. New York: Vintage Books.

Hale, Charles R. 1994. *Resistance and Contradiction: Miskitu Indians and the Nicaraguan State, 1894–1987*. Stanford, CA: Stanford University Press.

Higgins, Michael James, and Tanya Leigh Coen. 1992. *Oigame! Oigame! Struggle and Social Change in a Nicaraguan Urban Community*. Boulder, CO: Westview Press.

Holston, James, ed. 1999. *Cities and Citizenship*. Durham, NC: Duke University Press.

Holston, James, and Arjun Appadurai. 1999. "Introduction: Cities and Citizenship." In *Cities and Citizenship*. James Holston, ed. Pp. 1–18. Durham, NC: Duke University Press.

Hostetler, Sharon, Jo Ann Lynen, and Leia Raphaelidis. 1996. *A High Price to Pay: Structural Adjustment and Women in Nicaragua*. Washington, DC: Witness for Peace.

Howe, Alyssa Cymene. 1999. "Re-Engendering Revolution: Nicaraguan Feminism and the Sexualities of Post-Sandinismo." Paper presented at the meeting of the American Anthropological Association, Chicago, IL.

Hoyt, Katherine. 1997. *The Many Faces of Sandinista Democracy*. Athens: Ohio University Press.

Hurtado de Vigil, María. 1991. Interview with author. Managua, Nicaragua, May 8.

Jacobs, Jane M., and Ruth Fincher. 1998. "Introduction." In *Cities of Difference*. Ruth Fincher and Jane M. Jacobs, eds. Pp. 1–25. New York: Guilford Press.

Jameson, Fredric. 1984. "Postmodernism, or the Cultural Logic of Late Capitalism." *New Left Review* 146: 53–92.

Jaquette, Jane, ed. 1989. *The Women's Movement in Latin America: Feminism and the Transition to Democracy*. Boston: Unwin-Hyman.

———. 1994. *The Women's Movement in Latin America: Participation and Democracy.* 2d ed. Boulder, CO: Westview Press.

Kampwirth, Karen. 1996a. "Confronting Adversity with Experience: The Emergence of Feminism in Nicaragua." *Social Politics* (Summer–Fall): 136–58.

———. 1996b. "The Mother of the Nicaraguans: Doña Violeta and the UNO's Gender Agenda." *Latin American Perspectives* 23(1): 67–86.

———. 1998. "Legislating Personal Politics in Sandinista Nicaragua, 1979–1992." *Women's Studies International Forum* 21(1): 53–64.

Kaplan, Caren. 1994. "The Politics of Location as Transnational Feminist Critical Practice." In *Scattered Hegemonies: Postmodernity and Transnational Feminist Practices.* Inderpal Grewal and Caren Kaplan, eds. Pp. 137–52. Minneapolis: University of Minnesota Press.

Keith, Michael, and Steve Pile. 1993. "Introduction, Part 1, The Politics of Place . . ." In *Place and the Politics of Identity.* M. Keith and S. Pile, eds. Pp. 1–21. New York: Routledge.

Kinnaird, Vivian, and Janet H. Momsen. 1993. "Geography, Gender and Development." In *Different Places, Different Voices: Gender and Development in Africa, Asia and Latin America.* Janet H. Momsen and Vivian Kinnaird, eds. Pp. 3–8. New York: Routledge.

Kipnis, Laura. 1999. "The Stepdaughter's Story: Scandals National and Transnational." *Social Text* 58, 17(1):59–73.

Kritt, Barbara. 1992. "From Classroom to Class Struggle: Women in the Nicaraguan Student Movement in the 1970s." Paper presented at the Latin American Studies Association conference, Los Angeles, September 24–27.

Kruckewitt, Joan. 1999. *The Death of Ben Linder.* New York: Seven Stories Press.

Kunzle, David. 1995. *The Murals of Revolutionary Nicaragua, 1979–1992.* Berkeley: University of California Press.

Küppers, Gaby. 1994. *Compañeras: Voices from the Latin American Women's Movement.* London: Latin America Bureau.

Laenen, Arie. 1988. *Dinámica y transformación de la pequeña industria en Nicaragua.* Amsterdam: CEDLA.

Lancaster, Roger N. 1988a. "Subject Honor and Object Shame: The Construction of Male Homosexuality and Stigma in Nicaragua." *Ethnology* 27(2): 111–25.

———. 1988b. *Thanks to God and the Revolution: Popular Religion and Class Consciousness in the New Nicaragua.* New York: Columbia University Press.

———. 1992. *Life Is Hard: Machismo, Danger, and the Intimacy of Power in Nicaragua.* Berkeley: University of California Press.

———. 1997. "Guto's Performance: Notes on the Transvestism of Everyday Life." In *Sex and Sexuality in Latin America.* Daniel Balderston and Donna Guy, eds. Pp. 9–32. New York: New York University Press.

Leguizamon, Francisco A. 1990. *The Small Business Sector in Central America: A Diagnosis.* Commission for the Study of International Migration and Cooperative Economic Development, Working Paper no. 46. Washington, D.C.

LeoGrande, William M. 1998. *Our Own Backyard: The United States in Central America, 1977–1992.* Chapel Hill: University of North Carolina Press.

———. 1999. "Central America's Agony." *The Nation,* January 25.

Liebel, Manfred. 1998. "When Children Organize to Work." *Envío* 17(202): 28–33.

Liebl, Justiniano, ed. 1999. *Directorio ONG de Nicaragua 1999–2000.* Managua, Nicaragua: CAPRI (Centro de Apoyo a Programas y Proyectos).

Linkogle, Stephanie. 1996. *Gender, Practice and Faith in Nicaragua: Constructing the Popular and Making "Common Sense."* Aldershot, England: Avebury.

Lock, Margaret, and Nancy Scheper-Hughes. 1990. "A Critical-Interpretive Approach in Medical Anthropology: Rituals and Routines of Discipline and Dissent." In *Medical Anthropology: Contemporary Theory and Method.* Thomas Johnson and Carolyn Sargent, eds. Pp. 47–72. New York: Praeger.

Marchand, Marianne H., and Jane L. Parpart, eds. 1995. *Feminism, Postmodernism, Development.* New York: Routledge.

Marchetti, Peter. 1995. "Palabras del coordinador de los Centros de Investigación de la Universidad Centroamericana." In *Nicaragua en busca de su identidad.* Frances Kinlock Tijerino, ed. Pp. 33–39. Managua, Nicaragua: Instituto de Historia de Nicaragua, Universidad Centroamericana.

Marcus, George E. 1998. "Ethnography in/of the World System: The Emergence of Multi Sited Ethnography." In *Ethnography through Thick and Thin,* by George E. Marcus. Pp. 79–104. Princeton, NJ: Princeton University Press.

Martin, Randy. 1994. *Socialist Assemblies: Theater and State in Cuba and Nicaragua.* Minneapolis: University of Minnesota Press.

Martínez Cuenca, Alejandro. 1992. *Sandinista Economics in Practice: An Insider's Critical Reflections.* Boston: South End Press.

Masiello, Francine. 1997. "Gender, Dress, and Market: The Commerce of Citizenship in Latin America." In *Sex and Sexuality in Latin America.* Daniel Balderston and Donna J. Guy, eds. Pp. 219–33. New York: New York University Press.

Massey, Doreen. 1987. *Nicaragua.* Philadelphia: Open University Press.

———. 1994. *Space, Place, and Gender.* Minneapolis: University of Minnesota Press.

Meiselas, Susan. 1981. *Nicaragua, June 1978–July 1979.* New York: Pantheon Books.

———. 1991. *Pictures from a Revolution: A Memoir of the Nicaraguan Conflict.* GMR Films.

Metoyer, Cynthia Chávez. 1997. "Nicaragua's Transition of State Power: Through Feminist Lenses." In *The Undermining of the Sandinista Revolution.* Gary Prevost and Harry Vanden, eds. Pp. 114–40. New York: St. Martin's Press.

————. 2000. *Women and the State in Post-Sandinista Nicaragua*. Boulder, CO: Lynne Rienner.

Mohanty, Chandra. 1988. "Under Western Eyes: Feminist Scholarship and Colonial Discourses." *Feminist Review* 30: 61–88.

Molyneux, Maxine. 1986. "Mobilization without Emancipation? Women's Interests, State, and Revolution." In *Transition and Development: Problems of Third World Socialism*. Richard R. Fagen, Carmen Diana Deere, and José-Luis Coraggio, eds. Pp. 280–302. New York: Monthly Review Press.

Momsen, Janet H., and Vivian Kinnaird, eds. 1993. *Different Places, Different Voices: Gender and Development in Africa, Asia and Latin America*. New York: Routledge.

Montenegro, Sofía. 1997. "Un movimiento de mujeres en auge." In *Movimiento de mujeres en Centroamérica*, by Ana Leticia Aguilar T. et al. Pp. 339–446. Managua, Nicaragua: Programa Regional La Corriente.

Montoya, Rosario. 1996. "Fractured Solidarities: Utopian Projects and Local Hegemonies among a Sandinista Peasantry, Nicaragua, 1979–1995." Ph.D. dissertation, University of Michigan.

Moore, David B., and Gerald J. Schmitz, eds. 1995. *Debating Development Discourse: Institutional and Popular Perspectives*. New York: St. Martin's Press.

Mujica, María-Elena. 1994. *Meals, Solidarity, and Empowerment: Communal Kitchens in Lima, Peru*. Working Papers on Women and International Development, no. 246. East Lansing: Michigan State University.

Murguialday, Clara. 1990. *Nicaragua, revolución y feminismo (1977–89)*. Madrid, Spain: Editorial Revolución.

Negrón-Muntaner, Frances, and Ramón Grosfoguel, eds. 1997. *Puerto Rican Jam: Rethinking Colonialism and Nationalism*. Minneapolis: University of Minnesota Press.

Nelson, Diane M. 1999. *A Finger in the Wound: Body Politics in Quincentennial Guatemala*. Berkeley: University of California Press.

Nicholson, Scott. 1999. "The IMF and World Bank vs. the Poor of Nicaragua." *Nicaraguan Developments* 7(1): 4–5.

O'Kane, Trish. 1995. "New Autonomy, New Struggle: Labor Unions in Nicaragua." In *The New Politics of Survival: Grassroots Movements in Central America*. Minor Sinclair, ed. Pp. 183–207. New York: Monthly Review Press.

Padilla, Martha Luz, Clara Murguialday, and Ana Criquillon. 1987. "Impact of the Sandinista Agrarian Reform on Rural Women's Subordination." In *Rural Women and State Policy: Feminist Perspectives on Latin American Agricultural Development*. Carmen Diana Deere and Magdalena León, eds. Pp. 124–41. Boulder, CO: Westview Press.

El País. 1992. "Cómo viven los Gays en Nicaragua?" 1(4): 5–10.

PAMIC. 1991. *Diagnóstico de las microempresas de producción y servicios.* Managua, Nicaragua: PAMIC (Programa Nacional de Apoyo a la Microempresa).

Parpart, Jane L. 1993. "Who Is the 'Other'? A Postmodern Feminist Critique of Women and Development Theory and Practice." *Development and Change* 24(3): 439–64.

Pérez Alemán, Paola. 1990. *Organización, identidad y cambio.* Managua, Nicaragua: Editorial Vanguardia.

———. 1992. "Economic Crisis and Women in Nicaragua." In *Unequal Burden: Economic Crises, Persistent Poverty, and Women's Work.* Lourdes Benería and Shelley Feldman, eds. Pp. 239–58. Boulder, CO: Westview Press.

Pérez Alemán, Paola, Diana Martínez, and Christa Widmair. 1989. *Industria, genero y mujer en Nicaragua.* Managua, Nicaragua: INIM (Instituto Nicaragüense de la Mujer).

Pérez Alemán, Paola, et al. 1991. *Diagnóstico sobre la situación de la mujer en la pequeña y micro industria de Nicaragua.* Unpublished report. Managua, Nicaragua: CONAPI.

Pérez Sáinz, J. P., and R. Menjívar Larín. 1994. "Central American Men and Women in the Urban Informal Sector." *Journal of Latin American Studies* 26: 431–47.

Petras, James, and Morris Morley. 1992. *Latin America in the Time of Cholera: Electoral Politics, Market Economics, and Permanent Crisis.* New York: Routledge.

Pigg, Stacy Leigh. 1992. "Inventing Social Categories through Place: Social Representations and Development in Nepal." *Comparative Studies in Society and History* 34(3): 491–513.

Platteau, Stefan. 1992. Interview with author. Managua, Nicaragua, February 24.

———. 1993. Interview with author. Managua, Nicaragua, July 23.

Polakoff, Erica, and Pierre La Ramée. 1997. "Grass-Roots Organizations." In *Nicaragua without Illusions: Regime Transition and Structural Adjustment in the 1990s.* Thomas W. Walker, ed. Pp. 185–201. Wilmington, DE: SR Books.

Prevost, Gary, and Harry E. Vanden, eds. 1997. *The Undermining of the Sandinista Revolution.* New York: St. Martin's Press.

Price, Patricia L. 1999. "Bodies, Faith, and Inner Landscapes: Rethinking Change from the Very Local." *Latin American Perspectives* 26(3): 37–59.

Puig, Salvador Martí I. 2000. "Democracy in the Region? A Decade of Paradoxes." *Envío* 19(228): 30–40.

Quandt, Midge. 1993. "Unbinding the Ties: Popular Movements and the FSLN." *NACLA Report on the Americas* 26(4): 11–14.

———. 1999. "Where Is Nicaraguan Civil Society Going? An Interview with Sofía Montenegro." *Nicaragua Monitor*, no. 85: 5–6.

Quesada, James. 1998. "Suffering Child: An Embodiment of War and Its Aftermath in Post-Sandinista Nicaragua." *Medical Anthropology Quarterly* 12(1): 51–73.

Radcliffe, Sarah, and Sallie Westwood. 1996. *Remaking the Nation: Place, Identity and Politics in Latin America*. London: Routledge.

Radcliffe, Sarah A., and Sallie Westwood, eds. 1993. *Viva: Women and Popular Protest in Latin America*. New York: Routledge.

Ramírez, Sergio. 1999. *Adiós muchachos: Una memoria de la revolución Sandinista*. Mexico City: Aguilar.

Randall, Margaret. 1981. *Sandino's Daughters: Testimonies of Nicaraguan Women in Struggle*. Vancouver, BC: New Star Books.

———. 1992. *Gathering Rage: The Failure of 20th-Century Revolutions to Develop a Feminist Agenda*. New York: Monthly Review Press.

———. 1993. "To Change Our Own Reality and the World: A Conversation with Lesbians in Nicaragua." *Signs* 18(4): 907–24.

———. 1994. *Sandino's Daughters Revisited: Feminism in Nicaragua*. New Brunswick, NJ: Rutgers University Press.

Renzi, María Rosa. 1993. Interview with author. Managua, Nicaragua, July 23.

Renzi, María Rosa, and Sonia Agurto. 1993. *Que hace la mujer nicaragüense ante la crisis económica?* Managua, Nicaragua: FIDEG (Fundación Internacional para el Desafío Económico Global).

Reyes, Fatima. 1991. Interview with author. Managua, Nicaragua, July 18.

Ricciardi, Joseph. 1991. "Economic Policy." In *Revolution and Counterrevolution in Nicaragua*. Thomas W. Walker, ed. Pp. 247–73. Boulder, CO: Westview Press.

Rich, Adrienne. 1986. "Notes toward a Politics of Location." In *Blood, Bread, and Poetry, Selected Prose, 1979–1985*, by Adrienne Rich. Pp. 210–31. New York: W. W. Norton.

Robinson, William I. 1997. "Nicaragua and the World: A Globalization Perspective." In *Nicaragua without Illusions: Regime Transition and Structural Adjustment in the 1990s*. Thomas W. Walker, ed. Pp. 23–42. Wilmington, DE: SR Books.

Rocha, José Luis. 1998. "Wiwilí with or without Mitch: An X-Ray of Underdevelopment." *Envío* 17(209): 44–49.

———. 1999. "Youth Gangs: Armed Rebels without a Cause." *Envío* 18(214): 32–36.

Rodríguez, Ileana. 1990. *Registradas en la historia: 10 años del quehacer feminista en Nicaragua*. Managua, Nicaragua: Editorial Vanguardia.

———. 1994. *House / Garden / Nation: Space, Gender, and Ethnicity in Postcolonial Latin American Literatures by Women*. Durham, NC: Duke University Press.

———. 1996. *Women, Guerrillas, and Love: Understanding War in Central America*. Minneapolis: University of Minnesota Press.

Rosen, Fred, and Deidre McFadyen, eds. 1995. *Free Trade Economic Restructuring in Latin America*. New York: Monthly Review Press.

Rosset, Peter, and John Vandermeer, eds. 1983. *The Nicaragua Reader: Documents of a Revolution under Fire*. New York: Grove Press.

Rushdie, Salman. 1987. *The Jaguar Smile: A Nicaraguan Journey.* London: Pan Books.

Santamaría, Sergio. 1990. *Situación actual de la pequeña industría y artesanía en Nicaragua: Diagnóstico 1990.* Managua, Nicaragua: Fundación Friedrich Ebert.

Sassen, Saskia. 1999. "Whose City Is It? Globalization and the Formation of New Claims." In *Cities and Citizenship.* James Holston, ed. Pp. 177–94. Durham, NC: Duke University Press.

Scheper-Hughes, Nancy. 1992. *Death without Weeping: The Violence of Everyday Life in Brazil.* Berkeley: University of California Press.

Schreiber, Tatiana, and Lynn Stephen. 1989. "AIDS Education — Nicaraguan Style." *Out/Look* (Winter): 78–80.

Solórzano, Carlos José. 1995. *Nosotros los nicaragüenses.* Miami, FL: N.p.

Spain, Daphne. 1992. *Gendered Spaces.* Chapel Hill: University of North Carolina Press.

Spalding, Rose J. 1994. *Capitalists and Revolution in Nicaragua: Opposition and Accommodation, 1979–1993.* Chapel Hill: University of North Carolina Press.

———. 1997. "The Economic Elite." In *Nicaragua without Illusions: Regime Transition and Structural Adjustment in the 1990s.* Thomas W. Walker, ed. Pp. 249–64. Wilmington, DE: SR Books.

Spalding, Rose J., ed. 1987. *The Political Economy of Revolutionary Nicaragua.* Boulder, CO: Westview Press.

Speer, John G. 1997. "The Urban Informal Economic Sector." In *Nicaragua without Illusions: Regime Transition and Structural Adjustment in the 1990s.* Thomas W. Walker, ed. Pp. 265–79. Wilmington, DE: SR Books.

Spoor, Max. 1994. "Issues of State and Market: From Interventionism to Deregulation of Food Markets in Nicaragua." *World Development* 22(4): 567–78.

Stahler-Sholk, Richard. 1997. "Structural Adjustment and Resistance: The Political Economy of Nicaragua under Chamorro." In *The Undermining of the Sandinista Revolution.* Gary Prevost and Harry Vanden, eds. Pp. 74–113. New York: St. Martin's Press.

Stephen, Lynn. 1997. *Women and Social Movements in Latin America: Power from Below.* Austin: University of Texas Press.

Sternbach, Nancy Saporta, Marysa Navarro-Aranguren, Patricia Chuchryk, and Sonia E. Alvarez. 1992. "Feminisms in Latin America: From Bogotá to San Bernardo." In *The Making of Social Movements in Latin America.* Arturo Escobar and Sonia E. Alvarez, eds. Pp. 207–39. Boulder, CO: Westview Press.

Thayer, Millie. 1997. "Identity, Revolution, and Democracy: Lesbian Movements in Central America." *Social Problems* 44(3): 386–407.

Tijerino, Frances Kinlock, ed. 1995. *Nicaragua en busca de su identidad.* Managua, Nicaragua: Instituto de Historia de Nicaragua, Universidad Centroamericana.

Tinker, Irene, ed. 1990. *Persistent Inequalities: Women and World Development.* New York: Oxford University Press.

Traña Galeano, Marcia. 1991. *Breve historia de los cementerios de Managua (1865– 1990).* Colección Managua no. 1. Managua, Nicaragua: Alcaldía de Managua.

Tünnermann Bernheim, Carlos. 1996. "Cultura de Paz: Un nuevo paradigma en Centroamérica." *Cultura de Paz* 2(9): 37–55.

UNICEF. 1989. *The Invisible Adjustment: Poor Women and the Economic Crisis.* Santiago, Chile: UNICEF.

Vanden, Harry E., and Gary Prevost. 1993. *Democracy and Socialism in Sandinista Nicaragua.* Boulder, CO: Lynne Rienner.

Vargas Ruíz, Rafael. 1998. *Managua en mi corazón.* Video. Instituto Nicaragüense de la Cultura, Gobierno de Nicaragua. Distributed by Mantica Waid Co. Ltd.

Villarreal, Magdalena. 1996. "Power and Self-Identity: The Beekeepers of Ayuquila." In *Machos, Mistresses, Madonnas: Contesting the Power of Latin American Gender Imagery.* Marit Melhuus and Kristi Anne Stølen, eds. Pp. 184– 206. London: Verso.

Walker, Thomas W. 1986. *Nicaragua: The Land of Sandino.* Boulder, CO: Westview Press.

Walker, Thomas W., ed. 1991. *Revolution and Counterrevolution in Nicaragua.* Boulder, CO: Westview Press.

———, ed. 1997. *Nicaragua without Illusions: Regime Transition and Structural Adjustment in the 1990s.* Wilmington, DE: SR Books.

Weisskopf, Thomas E. 1992. "Toward a Socialism for the Future, in the Wake of the Demise of the Socialism of the Past." *Review of Radical Political Economics* 24(3–4): 1–28.

Westwood, Sallie, and Sarah A. Radcliffe. 1993. "Gender, Racism and the Politics of Identities in Latin America." In *Viva: Women and Popular Protest in Latin America.* Sarah A. Radcliffe and Sallie Westwood, eds. Pp. 1–29. New York: Routledge.

Whisnant, David E. 1995. *Rascally Signs in Sacred Places: The Politics of Culture in Nicaragua.* Chapel Hill: University of North Carolina Press.

Yúdice, George. 1998. "The Globalization of Culture and the New Civil Society." In *Cultures of Politics, Politics of Cultures: Re-visioning Latin American Social Movements.* Sonia E. Alvarez, Evelina Dagnino, and Arturo Escobar, eds. Pp. 353–79. Boulder, CO: Westview Press.

Zamora, Rubén. 1995. Foreword to *Free Trade and Economic Restructuring in Latin America.* Fred Rosen and Deidre McFadyen, eds. Pp. 7–13. New York: Monthly Review Press.

INDEX

Page numbers in **boldface** denote a photograph or illustration.

enterprises in, 165; modernity of, 3,
19, 47, 56, 67, 191, 243–244, 250;
murals in 53–54, 57; and natural
disasters, 46–47; population of, 52;
and the Sandinistas, 47–48, 49, 52–
55, 269n11; and Santo Domingo,
63–64; security measures within,
67–68, 68, 253, 268n17; shopping
centers in, 61–62, 253–254, 254; and
urban renewal, 53–55, 61–62, 253–
254, 280n9; and utility shortages,
52; youth, 68. *See also* Monseñor
Lezcano
*Managua en mi corazón (Managua in
My Heart)*, 258
Marchand, Marianne H., 177
Marchetti, Peter, 42
María, 91–94, 97, 194, 256
María Elena, 138–145
Marlene, 119–125
Martínez, Denis, 62
Martin Luther King Institute for Re-
search and Social Action, 219, 221
Masiello, Francine, 179
Massey, Doreen, 71, 104
Mayorga, Francisco, 114
McDonald's Restaurant, 60–61, 61, 253,
267n12
MEDA, 157, 166–167, 272n4
Media: attention of, 13, 16, 23, 30, 62–
63, 208–209, 219, 238, 239; and gay
politics, 233, 235–236, 237, 277n19;
and microenterprise fairs, 169
Meiselas, Susan, 13
Mercado Occidental Virgen de la Can-
dalaria. *See* Western Market
Microenterprises, 247, 255, 272n5; establishment of, 33, 58, 144, 161, 163–
171, 182, 185–186, 272n2; marketing
of, 168–169, 168, 170, 189; support
for, 117, 143, 166–167, 272n4; training
for, 165–166, 169, 188
Migration, 48, 52

Ministry of the Economy and Natural
Resources (MARENA), 216, 217
Minorities, 30, 66–67. *See also* Indigenous groups
Modernity, 32, 98, 188, 191
Molyneux, Maxine, 11
Monica, 94–96, 256
Monseñor Lezcano, 70, 71–73, 72,
268n6; activism in, 82–83, 96–97;
businesses within, 81–82, 84, 86,
88, 89–91, 93–94, 147, 191; *cafetín*
in, 94–95, 95; development of, 82,
256; and the FLSN, 209; households
within, 81–86, 193; landmarks
within, 73, 82–83; neighbors within,
84–90; resale opportunities, 98; so-
cial class within, 80–81; and social
issues, 83, 85; workers in, 77, 82
Monseñor Lezcano Church, 93, 94–95
Montenegro, Sofía, 209, 218
Mothers of Heroes and Martyrs, 71,
120–121, 195, 206
Mothers of Plaza de Mayo (Madres), 28
Movement in Solidarity with the
Rights of Street Children, 210
Movement of Child and Adolescent
Workers (NATRAS), 210
Movimiento Comunal. *See* Commu-
nity Movement
Mujer y Cambio (Women and
Change), 207
Murals, 74, 267n7, 268n16
Murillo, Rosario, 238, 278n24

Narvaez, Zoilamérica, 238, 266n6,
278n26
National Chamber of Medium and
Small Industry (CONAPI), 35, 167,
221–229, 243, 255, 271n10, 273n8,
276nn8, 9, 10; and closing industries,
149; and cooperatives, 120, 121, 123–
124, 126–128, 130–133, 137, 140–143,
161–163, 189–190, 193; criticism of,